G000017339

The May Flower

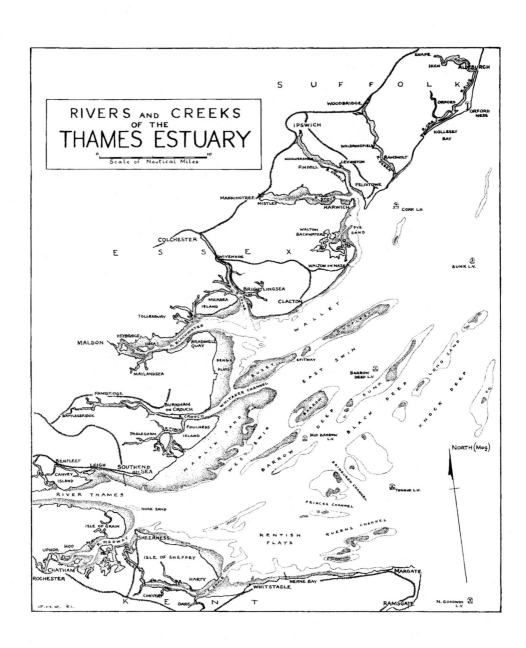

The May Flower

A Barging Childhood

NICK ARDLEY

The
History
Press

For my fellow crewmembers, Andrew, Theresa and Graham:
this is their story too.

Frontispiece: Rivers and Creeks of the Thames Estuary: The area
covered in this book. All charts included in this book were
originally hand drawn by Jack Coote, Editor for many years of
East Coast Rivers, a pilot book published by *Yachting Monthly*. The
charts included are from the 1961 third edition (revised); these are
reproduced with the kind permission of Jack Coote's daughter, Janet
Harber, who is the current Editor of her father's original pilot book
and courtesy of *Yachting Monthly*.

First published in 2007 by Tempus Publishing

Reprinted in 2010 by
The History Press
The Mill, Brimscombe Port,
Stroud, Gloucestershire, GL5 2QG
www.thehistorypress.co.k

Reprinted 2011

© Nick Ardley, 2010

The right of Nick Ardley to be identified as the Author
of this work has been asserted in accordance with the
Copyrights, Designs and Patents Act 1988.

All rights reserved. No part of this book may be reprinted
or reproduced or utilised in any form or by any electronic,
mechanical or other means, now known or hereafter invented,
including photocopying and recording, or in any information
storage or retrieval system, without the permission in writing
from the Publishers.

British Library Cataloguing in Publication Data.
A catalogue record for this book is available from the British Library.

ISBN 978 0 7524 4225 9

Typesetting and origination by Tempus Publishing.
Printed and bound in Great Britain by
Marston Book Services Limited, Didcot

Contents

	Acknowledgements	7
	Introduction	9
	A Brief History	13
1	The *May Flower*, a Trading Barge	19
2	Sold Out of Trade: the *May Flower* Meets the Ardley Family	35
3	The First Passage and a Wedding	43
4	Hoo Marina	53
5	Maldon, Benfleet, St Katharine Docks and Other Places	59
6	Whitewall Creek 1951 to 1966	65
7	Early School Days	83
8	Domestic Life	89
9	The Renewed Stem and other Structural Issues	99
10	The Mainsail, the Sprit and the Mast	105
11	A Spring Refit	113
12	Racing with the Big Boys (Up to 1963)	125
13	Early Summer Sailing Reminiscences	143
14	The New Leeboard	159
15	More Racing (1964 Onwards)	165
16	A Maldon Interlude	175
17	Leaving Whitewall Creek for Twinney Dock (1966 to 1968)	189
18	Callows Wharf, the Early Years	203
19	Our Last Sailing Years	213
20	Callows – Our Last Berth	231
	Epilogue – The *May Flower*'s Final Berth	243
	Bibliography	251
	Glossary	253

Acknowledgements

Words can not express my appreciation to John and Gwen Ardley, my parents, for the extraordinary, exciting and often challenging childhood they gave me, but to them I truly owe this tale. I must further thank my mother for the use of my father's papers, for answering numerous queries and providing a plethora of photographs. To all the people who have replied to my enquiries or given me 'the time of the day' while carrying out research: Professor Richard-Hugh Perks; the ladies in the office of Topsail Charters of Maldon (in 2004); Colin Swindale of Maldon; Richard Scurrey; Bernard Lewis CBE, manager of Green Brothers Mill at Maldon when my parents purchased the *May Flower*; various members of The Thames Sailing Barge Trust, especially Martin Phillips who encouraged me to write this story; Janet Harber for permission to use charts from her father's early editions of *East Coast Rivers*; Tony Winter for some insight about my father; Ian Kemp – a first crewmember; 'Nate' Readdings of Leigh-on-Sea, an old bargeman coasterman and fisherman who remembers the *May Flower* in Leigh during 1950/51; and, particularly, Barry Pearce of Maldon who worked on the barge in 1964. Finally, a special thanks to my wife Christobel and son Alexander, for their patience, fortitude and kind words during many hours of reading through the numerous drafts whilst writing this book (learning many interesting things about my past in the process).

All illustrations, unless otherwise attributed, belong to Mrs G.D. Ardley and Mr N.T. Ardley.

Introduction

There are, as far as I am aware, no personal accounts of the extraordinary plethora of skills that are needed for a life afloat on a Thames sailing barge, or of the sheer hard work involved in maintaining one, as a home and as a living sailing entity.

Connections with the sea abounded in the family. My mother's grandfather had been a fisherman with his own vessel; he was also a lifeboatman at Southend-on-Sea. On my father's side, an uncle had spent a career in the Mercantile Marine, and two direct ancestors had been barge skippers; one was reputedly a barge owner too, during the nineteenth century. So I suppose the sea was in the blood of my parents and it was not as strange as it may seem for them both to have opted for a life afloat, aboard a Thames sailing barge.

During my research, my mother presented me with some box files to look through; these contained many of my father's papers concerning the barge. I was initially looking for details about an incident that took place with another barge. During the sorting of these papers, I came across a mass of correspondence which at the time I was not really interested in. It then dawned on me that this information, which is historical, would in fact make not only interesting reading, but would provide an excellent lead into the story of my childhood on a barge. This information provided the precursor, being the first two chapters, although the germs had already been sprouting in my mind, and provided the impetus to continue the research. Many other people have provided me with some interesting facts. My mother is in possession of the cargo logs dating from 19 July 1927 up to the entry for last cargo carried into Maldon on 12 September 1949. At this time the barge was into her sixty-second year of trading.

Over the years a number of photographs of the *May Flower* in her trading days came into the hands of my parents – some of these were given to them by Fred Cooper, some have been used as illustrations. On the whole the originators are generally unknown. I have been able to attribute some of these old prints to a probable voyage, or voyages, by cross-referencing month and year notations against the cargo records.

My mother said that when they originally viewed the barge, on board were cargo record books covering virtually the complete history of her trading life. During the sale process, one of the record books disappeared from the aft cabin. It is suspected that the missing book covered cargo records of her earlier years, when under the ownership of

Clement Parker of Bradwell – which is a great shame. Some private early accounts were recorded by the first mate of the *May Flower*.

My story starts with some historical details and accounts of the *May Flower* during her trading life, before my parents had even heard of her. I take this period up to the end of her trading days, moving onto the time my parents spent looking for a barge in which they could set up home, after their planned marriage. For this important period I have been able to draw upon documents and letters that have survived.

The story about her sale to my father is adapted from his correspondence, and traces the path which lead to his eventual purchase of the *May Flower*. The barge had been discovered at Maldon through contact with Frank G.G. Carr, the then director of the National Maritime Museum based in Greenwich. She was at the time owned by the Green Brothers, millers of Maldon. They also still had the *Ethel Maud*.

The tale leads on to the early years in which my parents had the *May Flower*, after their marriage and life afloat. At the time this was not quite so unusual, as many people had been using barges as yachts dating back to the 1900s. Arthur Bennett has written about the *June* of Rochester and the *Henry* of London in his books, *June of Rochester*, *Tide Time* and *Us Bargemen*, but these are more about the dying days of barges in trade and not specifically about the life that was lead by the family. Little has been written about living aboard a barge, and the efforts needed to keep up with the maintenance, which had become a regular feature of daily life, especially as the barge aged with its associated problems. These practical needs impinged greatly upon the life that we were to lead.

My intention, and I hope that this has been achieved, is to tell the story of a barge and a family, by looking back to when I was a child growing up, living on an active sailing barge. I take this up to the time that I left home to pursue my own career, marriage and life away from sailing barges.

I have written about the places the barge was berthed and events that happened, before my time, which I have been told about, then moving onto the era after I was born. Reminiscences tell of the life led, as seen through my eyes, of living and growing up aboard a Thames sailing barge with my siblings; of sailing experiences, rig maintenance, tanning and stitching of sails, of painting, tarring, caulking decks, eventually discovering carpentry, shipwrights' tools and developing the skills necessary in their use.

I recount not only the enjoyment gained in this unusual upbringing, but the continual hard work given by all the family to maintain the home and keep this barge sailing over a great number of years, without any form of financial help through chartering or sponsorship. This I believe was a singularly notable achievement, for which I am proud of my little part. I conclude with an epilogue showing what happened to her some years after leaving the care of the Ardley family.

Bob Childs, in his book *Rochester Sailing Barges of the Victorian Era*, said in his chapter '1885-1889 A Slow Recovery' when referring to the *May Flower* on page 98, 'In the event this vessel attained her centenary, albeit being a yacht-barge-cum-houseboat for her last forty years; she was broken up outside Strood Dock in 1989.' This was unique for a Curel-built vessel. You will discover as these pages are turned, how those forty years were spent!

CHARTS

Frontispiece – Thames Estuary from Orford Ness to the North Foreland

chapter six – Upper Reaches of the River Medway to Rochester

chapter seventeen – Lower Reaches of the River Medway

A Brief History

The story of the evolution of the Thames spritsail barge has been told by others in various books, some of which are listed in the bibliography. This is outside the scope of this book, but a brief history is given to acquaint those readers that may not have been previously acquainted with these fascinating and unique cargo carriers.

The Thames spritsail barge evolved gradually through the eighteenth and nineteenth centuries and had reached its developmental peak by the beginning of the twentieth century. They were initially open lighters of a similar hull type still seen on the Thames today, although their own numbers are now greatly reduced due to less need for this type of river transport. These vessels have what is known as a swim head, which is a flat, angled, sloping bow, and a similar stern end which is fitted with a wedge-shaped skeg.

The first sailing barges had a single mast with a sprit or spreet; sometimes they were rigged with a gaff in the fashion of Dutch vessels of the period. It was the sprit which gave these vessels their name, recognisable look and unique ability to be easily sailed and managed by a small crew, often being two in number. Later a mizzen sail was stepped on the rudder head. The mizzen on a barge is used as a useful tool to aid steerage. As with Dutch vessels of the period, that were developed for working in shallow waters, the flat-bottomed spritsail barge used leeboards fitted to each side to counter leeway (sideways drift) when under sail.

By the early 1800s, spritsail barges were beginning to trade out of the River Thames to the other rivers feeding the estuary. The vessels were growing in size to increase cargo capacity and topmasts featuring the familiar lofty topsail appeared. Bowsprits were also added to increase the sail area. By the 1850s some builders began to experiment with round bows similar to more traditional vessels. These bows were very bluff with a rounded fore foot (at the bottom of the stem); the sterns were given small, flat transoms. Most spritsail barges by this time had a mizzen sail; this was a comparatively small sail with a sprit and a boom, initially mounted on the rudder head as all these early barges were steered using a tiller – this was some 15ft in length. The more traditional (as we know it) type of steering utilising a steering wheel and helical screw drive and rods to the rudder head evolved in the late 1870s. This allowed the mizzen to be stepped in board. Developments in this area gave rise to increased sail areas for the very much larger vessels that evolved.

A stimulus for the improvement of hull and rig design was the founding of a series of sailing matches or races in 1863 by a refuse collector and barge owner, one Henry Dodd, a wealthy Victorian benefactor known as the 'Golden Dustman'. The tradition of barge racing continues to this day, being maintained by various committees, stretching from Suffolk to the Solent.

In the eastern quarter of Britain, these vessels had become the lorry of the industrial growth of this period of our history. Throughout the major estuary areas around the British Isles and in Europe, cargo carriers evolved with their own distinctive fashion, dealing with the carriage of goods in a manner much the same as the Thames spritsail barge. However, it is only these vessels that have survived in reasonable numbers into the modern era.

By the end of the nineteenth century, the design of the spritsail barge had reached its peak. This unfortunately coincided with the invention of the combustion engine and all that that entailed. The numbers of barges being built also peaked at this time, with a steady, then more rapid, decline in new builds taking place. After 1932, no new spritsail barges were being built. Many of these latter vessels were built of steel; however, iron, then steel, had been used by builders and preferred by some owners from about 1870. One vessel built of iron, the *Ironsides*, is still operating as a charter vessel today, and she was originally built in 1900. A number of wooden barges, built before this, continue to be active as sailing vessels.

The development of the railway systems had had an adverse affect on transportation of goods by coastal and river craft, but this was not as lethal as what was to come. As road systems developed, along with the ever-improving technology producing bigger and better lorries, they began to take a greater proportion of trade away from the humble barge. Time was moving on and people demanded goods to be delivered sooner rather than later – not at the whim of wind and tide. Generally, the last barge trades were in cereals, ballast (sands and shingles) and coal.

During the early 1900s some sailing barges were fitted with engines; these were more for self-assistance in congested areas than as being the sole means of making the passage. Other barges were built with the fitting of engines in mind at a later date, a small number were built fitted with engines. With further improvements in the reliability of small marine diesel engines, by the 1930s many barges were operating as auxiliaries with a wheelhouse on the aft deck and the mizzen sail having been removed. Further changes were the fitting of larger engines and the removal of the topmast, until finally the spritsail barge became a fully fledged motor vessel. This evolution can be seen in an accompanying photograph.

Changes to Board of Trade load line rules for coastal vessels in about 1962 caused the immediate end to the trading life of many motor barges. Only the larger vessels could be kept in economical service, until the last ceased trading during the late 1980s. The last few trading sailing barges also declined, leaving one serious attempt at maintaining the sail tradition. This was the *Cambria*, owned and operated by Everard's, who ultimately sold her to long-time skipper Bob Roberts. He kept her trading until 1970.

A view looking over the stern of the *May Flower* berthed at Leigh Building Supply (Theobalds) Wharf, Leigh-on-Sea, Essex, in September 1951. Astern can be seen an auxiliary barge with a wheelhouse and no mizzen and inboard of her can be seen a fully fledged motor barge. Unfortunately the names of these barges are unknown. The motor barge does not have a full wheelhouse and is fitted with a timber screen to provide some protection for the crew. These arrangements became popular from the 1920s and '30s. The *Lady Jean,* still sailing today, can be seen fitted with this arrangement.

The changes to the Board of Trade rules released a flood of motor barges, and barges being used as lighters, onto the market. Many of these became house barges, but some were to be re-rigged. A number of these can be seen in the Thames Estuary areas and one, the *Kitty,* is based on the Solent in Hampshire, from where many spritsail barges had operated in past times. By 1964 a growing number of barges were being re-rigged to be used as charter vessels, carrying passengers on weekend and longer sailing trips. This ironically gave the spritsail barge a new lease of life, beyond the principle of merely going 'yachting' with a sailing home.

Before all this was to take place, barges had been sold out of trade to owners who maintained their barges as yachts and sailing homes. This started back towards the end of the Victorian era. One story has been told in *A Floating Home* by Cyril Ionides, first published by Chatto & Windus in 1918 and re-published with additional material by Chaffcutter in 2003. Other people continued to do the same. The well-known marine artists W. Wyllie and John Chancellor had sailing homes, mainly based on the River Medway. Others took barges across to Europe for cruises, but most just sailed locally within the traditional trading areas.

Many of the later sailing homes did not sail for a long period of time; they were either sold on after a period experiencing life afloat, or they became increasingly used as static house barges, to gradually lose their rig. Arthur Bennett wrote about two barges, the *June* of Rochester and the *Henry* of London, both of which he had owned for relatively short periods of time, in three books. The time span that a barge remained in sailing use, in many cases, generally lasted the length of time the sails remained serviceable. My parents purchased the *May Flower* in 1950 and went on to own her for thirty-two years, they kept her sailing for the major part of that time.

Some static barges were later 'rescued' and re-rigged, one such as the *Violet* of Maldon spent a short period as a rigged barge after many years as a static home. Unfortunately, she needed a huge amount of work after years of rudimentary maintenance, and after a very short period of use has since sat in a floating dock for a considerable number of years awaiting a rebuild. In this time she has had three owners. Sadly, she may never sail again.

An increasing number of the remaining active spritsail barges have reached the point where to prolong their lives, a complete rebuild from the bottom up is needed. The costs for this are huge. Reconstruction work is usually carried out in phases during the winter periods to enable the barge to be back in service for the next charter season. One such organisation carrying out this sort of project, at the time of writing, is the Thames Sailing Barge Trust with their barge, the *Pudge*. She was originally built in 1922 and is a relatively young vessel.

The National Lottery has recently stepped in to provide a percentage of the funds for the rebuilding of a few spritsail barges, these being the *Dawn*, built in 1897 as a typical river craft built to carry hay to London for the feeding of the many horses in use there, the *Thalatta*, a large coasting barge originally built in 1906, which has traded for all its life (when she stopped carrying cargoes, she was converted to a school ship and has in fact essentially continued in trade) and lastly the *Cambria*, built in 1906 for William Everard, passing to Bob Roberts in 1966, the last British and North European vessel trading under sail, carrying her last freight in October 1970. From 1971 to 1996 this barge was used by the Maritime Trust as a museum and a shop – this is not the way to preserve sailing vessels. They need to be actively used and repaired as and when needed.

As the years pass, an ever-increasing proportion of those vessels remaining fit for charter work, with the ever-increasing statutory requirements levied, are those that are built of iron or steel. These are eminently far easier to repair and preserve, especially with the modern coatings now available. However, wooden barges continue to be maintained, so their days are not yet over. Both types have their advantages and disadvantages.

What of the future? I sail a wooden clinker- (clench-) planked sloop; she has a bermudan rig and is just twenty-three years old. Generally the first Bermudan sloop yachts appeared during the late 1920s; they became increasingly popular through the 1930s until nearly all yachts built became rigged in this manner. Some old vessels have been rebuilt, maintained and so on. New vessels continue to be built using a rig developed in the early part of the twentieth century, providing people with yachts to treasure and sail as they please.

As with modern Bermudan-rigged yachts, on the whole constructed from modern materials, why not a spritsail barge? It is very laudable to maintain an old vessel, but

I believe that the most important criteria is the rig; how it is operated and used to manoeuvre vessels, in the manner of our forefathers. Thus, it is these skills that need to be preserved to enable the sailing traditions to be handed down to future generations: surely it is this which is of paramount importance. Eventually, if this is to be on new purpose-built steel spritsail barges, then so be it.

chapter one

The May Flower, a Trading Barge

Something that has always struck me as rather strange is the fact that although the spritsail barge *May Flower* spent long periods of her life working out of the River Blackwater in Essex, little mention of her is made in the copious number of books that have appeared over the years covering this maritime trading area. It is true, I know, that hundreds of barges traversed the coastal waters of Kent, Essex and Suffolk (and beyond) over the peak years of spritsail barge trading, but only a few in many respects have ever gained more than a minimal level of historical attention.

Various photographs have surfaced in books showing the *May Flower* rigged with a bowsprit. These are generally from the period 1900 to 1920. They also show her to be a shapely barge; she was built for coasting work and had long chines which made her handy in the shallows. Cargo records show that she went abroad and also spent time trading along the South Coast. A photograph of the *May Flower* has appeared in a recent book *A Conversation with Dick the Dagger*. The barge is in the upper pool above Tower Bridge with St Paul's Cathedral in the background and the photograph is attributed to around 1910. She was then in the ownership of Clement Parker of Bradwell. This is the earliest pictorial reference that I have found in print.

The *May Flower* of Rochester, registration number 94558, was built at Curels Yard in Frindsbury, Kent, in 1888. She had a net registered tonnage of 48 tons (actually 48.22nrt) or 136.46cu.m and her gross tonnage was 61.64 tons or 174.44cu.m. Her particulars are of interest as, even in 1888, against her tonnage entries are the equivalents in metric units! Her net cubic capacity closely relates to her maximum carrying capacity.

George H. Curel had built her in partnership with two other persons. Her registered owners and shares held were: George Henry Curel of Frindsbury, who had thirty-two shares, Captain Crix who had sixteen shares and Mr William Hoare, a relation of Captain Crix, who also had sixteen shares. Damage to the original document makes it hard to discern 'Charles Crix', but 'Master Mariner' is clear. So too is 'Mr (William) Hoare'. Both of these gentlemen are recorded as being from Foulness near Southend and are recorded as joint owners with thirty-two shares. She was operated in general trades. The partnership sold the *May Flower* after a number of years to Parker's of Bradwell.

The *May Flower 6* of 1888 should not be confused with another barge, *Mayflower* of 1882 (84442), built at Milton Creek at Murston, she was also registered at Rochester.

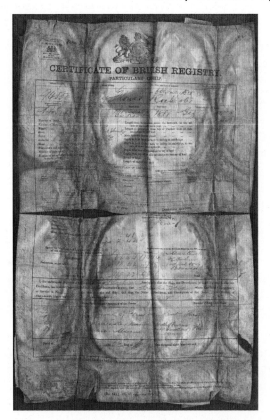

Front page of *May Flower*'s original parchment Certificate of Registration of 1888 – note the capital 'F' in the name *May Flower*. The text for the particulars of her length 'under the bow sprit' had not been deleted, indicating that the vessel was fitted with a bowsprit. Original ownership details are legible.

This barge was smaller than the *May Flower*, being 43nrt, and was owned locally at Teynham by James F. Honeyball. Before regulation came into being, it was not unusual to have duplicate names under the same registry. The 1892 Mercantile List gave twenty-five vessels registered as *May Flower*, only one being a barge, and thirty-two vessels registered *Mayflower*, again only one being a barge. There were many cases of duplicate names registered at the same ports, such as *Marjorie* of Rochester, 1888 and 1900, also the steel *Cambria* built at Southampton in 1898 and Everard's *Cambria* of 1906 built at Greenhithe, both registered in London. Two other Rochester barges were the *Violet* of 1879 and 1884 respectively, both built at Conyer.

The *May Flower*'s cargo capacity was just over 600 quarters of wheat or about 120 tons, but 500 quarters was a typically standard cargo. When she was built, she was considered to be quite a large barge and she was fitted with a bowsprit. My father re-registered the barge in 1977, using her as collateral when purchasing a house; interestingly, the copy of the registration document which is from the original copy held by the Port of Rochester Registrar contains an interesting added entry. In her particulars of length, 'under the bowsprit' has been inserted – this clearly shows her to have been rigged with a bowsprit when built. The re-registering document should not have had this entry, as she was not then fitted with a bowsprit. This is also the case for the document of 1950 registering my father's sixty-four shares!

When sorting through my mother's collection of photographs and papers, my mother remarked that in many publications, *May Flower* is written as a single word. During the late 1950s she had discovered that the starboard rail had a carved dot between the two parts of the name, this was found when burning off the paint one day. The two parts of the name also had a letter spacing gap. On the port bow the dot had not been carved on the rail that had been renewed in the early 1940s.

Barges such as the *Edith May*, *Ethel Ada* and the *Ethel Maud* did not have this trouble, so why the *May Flower*? It is likely that the barge had become known under the single word for ease, and possibly particularly for the written word. The original registration document held clearly gives the name as two words! Log entries also show it as two words, even though there is often no spacing between the parts. Mother reinstated the dot between the two parts and was quite particular that it was maintained as such, during the Ardley family ownership, until the barge was later sold in the 1980s.

A book written by Bob Childs, *Rochester Sailing Barges of the Victorian Era*, is one of only a few references in print which I have come across giving the correct form of her name. Others using the correct form are *Us Bargemen* by Arthur Bennett and *Maldon and the Blackwater Estuary* by John Marriage.

The barge had only four registered owners during her lifetime, including my parents who owned her from 1950 to 1981. During her long life she was maintained as an active sailing vessel for nearly ninety years. For a vessel that traded continuously for sixty-two years, this is, I believe, quite a feat. During the late 1980s she was sold again; this owner had the intention of putting her back into sail, but the venture failed. Much of her fittings and spars were retrieved. She was broken up virtually on the site of her birth.

The mate of the newly built *May Flower* joined the barge on 11 June 1888. His name was James Rippingdale. The skipper was part-owner, Captain Charles Crix. The barge was not launched until 29 June 1888, so the crew will have spent nearly a month assisting in finishing off. This will have been for completion of rigging and outfitting. The barge departed from Strood on 6 July 1888. So began a long life of trading, carrying a great variety of cargoes in the general trades and later being mainly used in the cereal trades. The third hand was Edward Bird, aged sixteen, from Foulness, Essex. Her connection to Essex people was a feature for most of her life.

On 7 July 1888, 110 tons of cement was loaded at the West Kent Cement Works. This was unloaded at the Albert Docks. On 7 August 1888 they unloaded a cargo of flour near Sun Pier. This could have been the old barge wharf in the bight at Chatham, near where the Chatham Yacht Club is sited, or more probably at Hookers Wharf where there was a mill. This mill was demolished in the mid-1970s. A modern hardware store and car park now resides on this site. Ironically, had the mill lasted a further decade, it would most probably have been converted into desirable riverside apartments. The wharf near the Chatham Yacht Club was the base for the *Veronica*, renamed the *Veronica Belle* following her sale by Everard's from around 1964 to the time she went to the Dolphin Barge Museum in the early 1970s.

On 11 February 1889, the crew sailed the *May Flower* out to the sailing barge *Albert*, which was aground on the Maplin Sands and which they towed to the Crouch. I do not suppose many barges have been towed by another under sail, but in those days the availability of a powered tug was not as it is now! From 11–19 June 1889 the barge is recorded as being on the 'Ways'. This will in all probability have been for her guarantee refit, it being the anniversary of her completion.

On 24 January 1890, at an unspecified port, they began loading 100 tons of wheat (this is annotated with 450 quarters). This was discharged at Great Yarmouth. Unloading began on 1 February. On 2 October 1890, they sailed for Calais (France). This was to pick up a cargo of straw; the firm is stated to have gone broke! They then sailed to Dunkerque and loaded 100 tons of rape seed. This was unloaded after arriving at Strood Mills on 24 October. During 1891, various cargoes were carried including elm logs, flour, wheat and stone from Portland. Cargoes for the year 1892 were on the whole wheat, flour and stacks. James Rippingdale left the barge in May 1892.

The Mercantile Navy List for 1892 shows that George Henry Curel was the managing owner. Her net registered tonnage at 53 registered tons could have been an anomaly, or for some reason the barge had been re-measured. The 1895 list records Captain Crix as the registered managing owner. George Curel died on 16 December 1895 aged fifty-five years. He was laid to rest in Frindsbury parish church in a position overlooking the river. The 1897 list again shows that Charles Crix was the managing owner at 48 registered tons. There is, however, no entry on the papers that were carried on board the *May Flower* of any official change of ownership, therefore it is probable that the original partnership still existed, that is, the executors of George Curel's estate owning some shares in the barge. Captain Crix, probably having gradually increased his shares year by year, was accorded managing owner of the vessel on behalf of the other parties.

On 12 September 1898 the *May Flower* locked into Heybridge Basin and discharged 100 tons of iron destined for E.H. Bentall, a local iron works, who on the whole manufactured agricultural machinery. Her captain was G. Hoare. Whether or not he was related to William Hoare, the original part-owner, is not known. The barge was discharged on the 14th, locked out and sailed to Bradwell.

On 15 September 1898 James Rippingdale rejoined the barge, but this time as Master. The mate was John Bowles and Alfred Potton the third hand. They immediately departed for Erith in Kent. The barge loaded 110 tons of stone then departed on the 18th bound for Mayland, having arrived at Brickhouse Dock; she unloaded on 21 September. On 12 November 1898 a huge cargo of 155 tons of stone is recorded (is this a misprint?). This was loaded at Victoria Wharf and unloading began at the Cattawade on the 14th, up above Mistley on the River Stour.

On 15 April 1899, the barge berthed in the West India Dock to load 100 tons of maize, moving up to the Metropolitan Wharf to load 13 tons of coffee bran. This was unloaded on 22 April at Ipswich.

Later the same year, *May Flower* spent several months trading along the South Coast and around the Solent. On 27 July 1899 they began loading 100 quarters of wheat, 280 quarters of oats and 120 quarters of maize in the Milwall Docks. On 3 August they loaded a further 4½ tons of oil cake and sailed for Newport, Isle of Wight, arriving on 9 August. On 21 August they loaded 40,000 bricks at Bouldnar; these were taken to

A barge being loaded with a stack at Bradwell half tide quay, *c.*1934. (Photograph courtesy of Barry T. Pearce)

Portsmouth. The *May Flower* continued to trade on the South Coast for a number of months before returning to the East Coast in the autumn.

On 28 April 1900 the barge was at Bradwell unloading stone. Dressing of sails was also carried out during this period. This provides another clue to the ownership of the *May Flower*, Bradwell being the home port of the Parker fleet. The fleet was always well maintained and each barge would bring a load into Bradwell in turn during the summer, then have a week to refit. In July 1900 the *May Flower* was again in the Solent area taking timber to Portsmouth Dockyard and Cowes. From 8-20 August she was on hire to the War Department at Portsmouth.

On 9 November 1900, a cargo of hay was loaded at Canvey Island. This could have been either Smallgains Creek at the eastern point, or at the crossing to Benfleet, where hay carts were able to go alongside a barge on the hard bed of the creek, which was also the low tide crossing to the island. Several trips were made to the island during that winter.

The agriculture on Canvey Island, in particular hay making, had just about recovered from the floods that had blighted the low-lying parts of Essex on 29 November 1897. The island had been famous for its hay, but subsequently, as time progressed and problems arose over whose responsibility it was to maintain the seawalls, many of the farms were sold off for development.

A photograph of a barge loading hay and one of the *May Flower*, amongst many others, were found at the back of a desk drawer when an office of an old waterside business at Maldon was being stripped out. The barge being loaded with hay is at the Bradwell Half Tide Quay. This print dates from the early 1930s; others, and one of the *May Flower* sailing up past the Hythe at Maldon, clearly indicated this time period – the 'GB' in the topsail of the *May Flower* and the old-looking sails would give credence to this dating – the barge having been only very recently acquired by Green Brothers.

In an accompanying photograph of a barge being loaded with hay, note the 'poles' coming out of the stack. These are stack irons, which were inserted into brackets fastened to the inner side of the rails around the decks of the barge. Their function was to retain the stack in place as it was built up over the decks and hatch tops. A few of these brackets survived on the *May Flower* on sections of rail that were old. The identity of the barge being loaded is not known. However, from the *May Flower's* cargo book covering the 1930s it is apparent that she did not carry a stack after her sale to Green Brothers. An excellent account of how a stack was loaded and sailed (to London) can be found in John Leather's book *The Salty Shore*. There is also a plate showing the *May Flower* at Bradwell Quay dated to around 1912.

During the summer of 1902 the *May Flower* is again at Bradwell, from the 5–21 July, for the dressing of sails and painting. From the 22–30 July the barge is on the ways at Shrubsall's Yard. It is apparent that Clement Parker liked to keep his barges looking good. From this 'wash and brush up' she went away in early August to pick up a cargo of 130 tons of stone from Rainham (Kent). This was discharged at Wilford Bridge, which is situated on the River Deben above Woodbridge in Suffolk.

On 24 December 1902, the barge was at a Victoria Wharf loading 110 tons of stone. This was destined for Burnham. However they stopped over at Foulness, where they berthed on 25 December for Christmas. After two days' rest they departed on the 27th, sailing the short distance to Burnham to start unloading. This was completed on New Year's Eve. Hay and straw was then loaded and the barge sailed on 3 January 1903. The records note that they were held up (by the weather?) until 8 January. I imagine they took shelter either in the entrance to the Roach or near Shore Ends on the Crouch. The skipper, I expect, living locally, got away home during this time to see his family!

On 16 May 1903 James Rippingdale left the *May Flower*. Studying the list of Masters of the *May Flower*, it is interesting that no entries for either Captain Crix or James Rippingdale appear as Master on the registration document; it is possible that they were not recorded though. The entries for who the owner was are decipherable, but the dates are not. The *May Flower* appears on the 1901 Mercantile Register under the ownership of Clement W. Parker of Bradwell. In 1904 the *May Flower* was recorded as still being under the ownership of Clement Parker; this would appear to support my comment regarding ownership during the last years of the nineteenth century. The record of her sale to 'Clement Wright Parker' can be seen, as is some other wording, but not the date. That of her later sale, to 'Green' and 'Green', 'Millers', 'of Essex', is partly visible, as is her transfer to Green Brothers, and finally the entry when sold to my father. What is clearly apparent is that her first change of ownership was to Clement Parker, it being the top entry.

The period from the end of the records maintained by James Rippingdale when he left the barge in 1903 and 1927 is the only gap that I have on the trading history of the *May Flower*. But I have learnt that the *May Flower* locked into Heybridge Basin on 13 April 1906, Captain Appleton being Master, to discharge 116 tons of gas coals for Brown & Sons of Chelmsford. Another event in 1906 is notable too; the Parker fleet was joined by the newly completed *Veronica*, built by Shrubsall at Greenwich. This barge traded for just over forty years, ending her sailing days as a purpose-rigged racing barge with Everard's.

The trading narrative now draws on papers owned by my mother. These start in 1927 while still with Clement Parker's fleet. The barge was now forty years old. During this period the *May Flower* was still fitted with her bowsprit. Various photographs taken of her during the early 1900s show how pretty she looked, with a fine sheer line. In a trading barge, the sheer line was greatly maintained by the heavy cargoes carried in the middle two-thirds of the hull, whilst her buoyant stern and forequarters provided excellent up-thrust, both to keep the vessel afloat and also in good shape.

The Master in 1927 was Mr Clifford French. The cargo log appears to show his initial as a 'G', but on close scrutiny of the registration document I found the entry for his appointment. This is written in pencil in an official stamp. He was to be in charge of the *May Flower* until her sale to Green Brothers of Maldon many years later.

Cargoes carried through this period were a very mixed bag. They included hardcore, tarmac, granite, maize, straw, hay, ragstone (a Kentish stone used for facing seawalls), flints, rubbish, wood and sand. They were traditionally titled 'The General Trades'.

I have picked out a few ports of call which I considered would be of interest to the reader as well as myself. I have also included an example from the cargo log, for added interest. Little notations of amounts of money are entered on some of the earlier abstracts, this is pay received for the voyage, which was split between the skipper and crew in diminishing fractions.

On 15 October 1927, a cargo of manure was carried to Paglesham, arriving on 20 October. There was either no hurry, or the barge had been held up by the elements – the cargo must have been quite high by the time it arrived!

On 27 August 1928, a cargo of sand was taken from Aylesford to Colchester arriving on the 28th. This must have been a fast passage all the way from the upper reaches of the tidal Medway above Rochester Bridge – which would have meant lowering the gear to go beneath. The port should not be confused with Alresford on the River Colne. The cargo log has Rochester, in places, specifically in brackets next to the port name – perhaps to avoid confusion!

On 6 April 1929 a cargo of flints was carried from Hoo to Benfleet, arriving on 8 April. The barge was not to return to this port, until my parents sailed her up to a berth just below the old bridge across to Canvey Island in the summer of 1954.

Later in 1929, between 17–21 August, the barge was at Aylesford for repairs after carrying a cargo of granite. It is quite apparent from the cargo records that during her years under the ownership of Parkers, she was well maintained. Even after her time with Green Brothers, only one of her deck beams (carlines) had end damage. These were susceptible to damage when in bulk trades.

Left: The *May Flower* in April 1932, berthed in Lion Creek (Creeksea), off the River Crouch.

Opposite: Copy of a cargo log page from 1932; note the change of ownership and Master.

On 24 July 1930, a cargo of ragstone was carried from Allington to Maldon (Steeple Creek), arriving on 27 July. On 6 August she sailed from Bradwell to Allington. An annotation above this entry says '10 days' upkeep at Bradwell'.

On 10 November 1931 she carried flints to St Osyths, arriving on the 13th. On 16 November she had an inspection alongside St Osyths Quay.

The 16 April 1932 saw her taking a cargo of flints from Aylesford to Creeksea, arriving on 20 April. This port of call fits a photograph of the *May Flower* was taken laying up a narrow cut. In the background can be seen some higher ground, which I suspect could be the north bank of the River Crouch. Other places that it could be are Foulness Island, when she picked up hay and straw on 4 May 1932, and Great Wakering, where on 22 March 1932 she discharged rubbish; however, these are thought to be less likely due to the background topography. The cargo of hay and straw was the last cargo carried for Clement Parker and, according to the records of the cargoes she carried, was also the last stack carried by the *May Flower*.

On 13 May 1932 she arrived at Bradwell, light from London after delivering a cargo of hay and straw. The next entry is 'Vessel laid up from 13 May 1932 to 3 July 1932'. An annual inspection was also carried out. Then, 'Owner Green Bros Maldon Essex Master J. Bloyce'. The cargo log seems to show the initial as an 'F'. The registration document actually gives the skipper's name as William Jonathan Bloyce.

This period of ownership was to be the final seventeen years of her trading life. From the registration document, ownership of the *May Flower* seems to have been shared

The	of	Master, from _C French_ of
Sailed		Arrived

Shipper	Quantity and Description of	Packages and Goods	Consignee	Delivered
Sailed Jan 6	From Bradwell To	London	With Hay	Arrived Jan 18
" 22	" London	Rochester	Light	" 23
" 28	" Aylesford	Hullbridge	Flints	" 30
" Feb 2	" Hullbridge	Aylesford	Light	" Feb 6
" Feb 9	" Aylesford	Hullbridge	Flints	" Feb 9
" 22	" Hullbridge	Bradwell and Golfall	Light	" 25
" March 6	" Bradwell a Sea	London	Hay	March 10
" 22	" London	Gt Wakering	Rubbish	"
" 30	" Gt Wakering	Rochester	Light	April 5
" April 16	" Aylesford Rochester	Lion Co Cracker	Flints	"
" 26	" Lion Co Cracker	Foulness	Light	" 26
" May 4	" Foulness Island	London	Hay, Straw	May 8
" 11	" London	Bradwell a Sea	Light	" 13

Vessel laid up from 13th ... to 3rd July 193_. Inspected 13th July

Owner Green Bros Maldon · Essex · master J. Blogg

Sailed July 3	from Maldon To	London	Light	Arrived July 4
Sailed July 9	from London To	Maldon with 400 qrs Wheat	Arrived July 11
Sailed July 12	from Maldon To	London	Light	Arrived July 14
Sailed		... with 116...		July

initially by a Mr Green of Lonefield, miller, and a Mr Green of Inglenook, miller, both in the County of Essex. At a later date, another ownership entry is made on the document; this was the transference of ownership to the Green Brothers Company, rather than the brothers themselves.

The *May Flower* was bought by Green Brothers to replace a slightly older and smaller barge, the *Gazelle*. She is thought to have been the Shrubsall-built barge of 1886, registered number 91927, 43 tons net and 55 tons gross. She was built up Milton Creek and initially registered in London. Her early life seems to have been spent with Edward J. Goldsmith of Grays, Essex, before being owned at Queenborough on the Isle of Sheppey for a few years, but by 1923 a Mr William Green of Brantham (Manningtree) was her registered owner. Her registration had been placed on the Maldon registry by 1927, when a George J.J. Watson of Little Wakering was her registered owner, as is the case for 1933, a year after the *May Flower* had been bought by Green Brothers. The Medway barge historian, Bob Childs (Barry Pearce) notes that in 1928 Green of Manningtree (Brantham?) was her owner. It would probably be safe to say that the barge had an owning syndicate, before passing to Mr Watson of Wakering. The *Gazelle* was broken up at Wakering in 1947. Although only slightly bigger, the *May Flower* had the ability to comfortably load a standard cereal cargo of 500 quarters.

Her predominant cargo from then was wheat. Some lightering of timber was carried out on the River Blackwater. Barley and maize appear from time to time, and a few oddities were carried too. The skipper and his mate must have known their way to

London and back by sniffing the breeze: it was completed so many times. I expect even the old girl must have known the way during those seventeen years!

On 3 July 1932 the *May Flower* sailed from Maldon light, to arrive in London the next day. She returned to Maldon sailing on the 9th, arriving on 11 July. This was her first cargo run for Green Brothers and was to be repeated with regular monotony through to 1949, generally carrying 500 quarters of wheat each voyage.

The first deviation from this regular run was in December 1934. After sailing from London on 18 December with 510 quarters of wheat and arriving at Maldon on the 19th, she went lightering timber from Osea Island up to Sadd's timber wharf. This was from 27 December 1934 into the New Year. The next entry on 15 January 1935 shows that the *May Flower* was back on her regular run!

On 4 August 1935 she left London with a mixed cargo of 50 tons of middlings and 200 quarters of barley, arriving at Alresford on the 5th. I have assumed it is this port as an inspection stamp covers most of the entry, however it does start with an 'A' and there is insufficient time for it to have been anywhere else. The next departure is from Colchester to London – back on the wheat run.

May Flower, deep-laden, in September 1936. Note the mate at the bowline, backing the foresail. The two headsail sheets have already been taken up ready for the new tack. The topsail and mainsail are both quivering; the mizzen is still set and, with the backed foresail, is turning her through the wind. The mainsail and foresail had been made for her in about 1935. This photograph was given to my parents by F.S. Cooper. Barry Pearce of Maldon has a similar photograph, which is attributed to a Mr Stimpson, taken off Southend about 1936, titled 'Fair wind for London'. It is possible that both prints originated from the same source. Mr Stimpson was a renowned recorder of all types of vessels traversing the Thames tideway.

She departed from Maldon on 23 May 1936 and arrived in London the same day. This can only have been done with an early departure and with ideal conditions. The barge was light, but even so, this must have been a cracking sail! During June and August 1936 she was lightering timber from Osea Island to Heybridge. The wood was loaded from Scandinavian ships, having anchored in the deeper water of Osea Island. This trade continued well into the last century.

During September 1936, a photograph was taken of the *May Flower* deeply loaded in the throes of tacking. The principle sails appear to be new. She had a new mainsail and foresail made for her in 1935. A new flying jib had been provided in 1932, immediately after her purchase by Green Brothers, and the barge was then immediately engaged on frequent return trips to London.

The information about the sails supports details given on her last annual survey report for Green Brothers. In the photograph the wonderful sheer that the barge still had can be appreciated, especially compared to photographs later in her life when some of it had been lost.

At the beginning of January 1937 a cargo of wheat was taken from London to Felixstowe. The return to London was made on the 13th, arriving on the 14th. This was another fast passage, again probably in ideal conditions.

A couple of interesting cargoes were carried one after the other. On 10 February 1937 a cargo of 80 tons of Egyptian pollards was carried to Maldon, arriving on the 12th. After sailing back to London light, a cargo of 90 tons of nitrate of soda and 18 tons of oil cake was delivered to Chatham, departing and arriving on 20 February.

The cargo carried through the late 1930s continued with pretty mundane entries, with very few departures. A few are recounted. In July 1937 a cargo of 65 tons of middlings was carried from London to Maldon between 28th and the 30th. Whilst all her cargoes of wheat seem to be around 500 quarters each trip, one cargo in 1937 is markedly different. On 5 October, she departed from London with 633 quarters of wheat arriving in Ipswich on the 11th. Another similar quantity of barley was carried to Ipswich later on.

At the end of December 1937 a cargo of 495 quarters of barley was carried from London, leaving on the 17th for Mistley, arriving on the 19th. She then departed light for London again on the 22nd, arriving on Christmas Eve, a busy week indeed! Her next departure was to Fingringhoe, which was on 2 January 1938, with a cargo of 530 quarters of barley, arriving on 4 January. So the crew, or at least the skipper, would probably have been able to get home for the festive season before making this voyage.

In September 1938, following her large cargoes of 1937, another huge cargo of 644 quarters of barley was carried from London to Ipswich, departing on the 11th and arriving on the 15th. A further departure from wheat that year was a cargo of 30 standards of timber was carried from London to Maldon between 24-26 November.

On 25 January 1939 she departed London with 100 tons of cotton cake, arriving in Ipswich on 5 February. Barry Pearce provided me with a list of barge movements at Ipswich from the *Evening Star*, dated 6 February 1939. These listed the barges, captains and cargo. The *May Flower* is reported as one of those arriving on 6 February. As we progress through 1939, it is apparent that the cargoes of wheat from London were being

The *May Flower* bound down past the Hythe at Maldon sometime during the 1930s. Note the two barge boats; one will probably have been that of the local huffler. Hufflers assisted bargemen, often in getting away, but more especially when negotiating narrow cuts and for passing beneath bridges, when the gear had to be lowered – referred to as 'shooting'. Hufflers would generally be retired bargemen or fishermen, or any other waterman. They all performed a very useful function, ensuring that sailormen reached their destination.

taken to differing ports more regularly. This continued into, and throughout, 1940 – was this to spread the holdings of basic food stuffs needed by the country, as a means of protecting them?

On 31 August 1940 a cargo of 110 tons of nitrates was carried to Ipswich arriving on 2 September. In July 1940 a cargo of wheat was picked up from a ship in Buttermans Bay for delivery to Maldon. Buttermans Bay is an area of relatively deep water on the River Orwell, where grain ships anchored and discharged to lighters and barges, for onward transportation.

What was becoming more apparent as I read through these cargo records was that no time was being recorded for routine maintenance since her sale to Green Brothers, as was the case under the Parkers flag. Crews obviously used spare time when awaiting cargoes for rudimentary general upkeep, but by now the barge had been continuously trading for more than half a century and she was being worked very hard.

In 1938 she made forty-two cargo-carrying voyages and in 1939 she made thirty-three. Periods of time 'on the ways' were about to become a feature of her life. After arriving in Maldon on Christmas Day 1939, having waited in London nearly a month for a cargo of wheat, she did not sail again until February 1940. Perhaps this period was used for maintenance.

Following the delivery of a cargo to Maldon on 8 January 1941, her long-time skipper (William) J. Bloyce, who had been with the barge for nearly ten years, departed. This gentleman was universally known as Pincher. The next log entry is for 28 April 1941. It is thought that the barge was undergoing maintenance during this period; it is likely that this could have been when the decks were doubled over or sheathed. This is supported by a tale which was recounted to me by Barry Pearce of Maldon.

Sitting on the hatches of the motor barge *Raybel*, on which Barry was skipper, with cups of tea, on Woolwich buoys awaiting orders, Pincher told me how, one day when skipper of the *May Flower*, he was 'caught out' in a south-west 'blow'. The barge was deep laden with wheat for Maldon. The wind suddenly increased as they came over the Spitway. Staggering up from the Knoll, the *May Flower* was having as much wind and sea as they could cope with.

It was suddenly noticed that the mast deck seams were opening and shutting with the straining of the hull 'about two inches at a time'. (This would appear to be an exaggeration – but the general facts are accepted.) Perhaps it was after that experience that the main deck was sheathed over with another layer of planking laid fore and aft.

Barry Pearce also recounted that the skipper of the *Redoubtable* during the 1930s referred to Pincher Bloyce as 'Stern Light Fred', because he used to tail the slower *Redoubtable* going up the Thames, bound for the Woolwich buoys, to await orders. At the last moment, he would sail the *May Flower* past, and take up the waiting station to claim first on turn to load the next available cargo! I'm told that Pincher was also known as Fred. As previously commented upon, this may be why the cargo log appears to show his initial as an 'F'. Many years later, he worked for J. Sadd's, the Maldon timber merchants and importers, as their tug skipper.

The period above is one of several during the years of the Second World War, when the barge was seemingly out of commission, or nothing was recorded in the cargo log. There were, however, periods when coastal short sea trade was disrupted due to mines and other wartime problems. Others that are recorded are: 'On the Ways at Maldon from July thirteenth to 27 September 1944', then again in 1945, 'On the Ways at Maldon from tenth of August to seventeenth of September'. During these layovers, the barge had her decks and sides up to the wale doubled. The bowsprit and all equipment needed for the fitting of the bowsprit was also removed and not refitted. As told later, the fitting holes for all the additional gear and deck light prisms were still visible on the underside of the decks. The holes were not plugged, and the deck light prisms were not lifted.

A new skipper, Mr J. Mallett, took over the barge after her refit in April 1941. His entry on the registration document is unfortunately completely illegible. He stayed with the barge for only for a short period of time. During the time under J. Mallett, all cargoes from London were to Maldon except one, which was to Colchester, which was quite memorable for him and his mate.

All through the final years of her trading life, the *May Flower* carried wheat, with just a few exceptions. This and the port of delivery varied little; she must have led a charmed life, as she neared her sixtieth year!

An interesting incident that occurred during one of these wartime voyages could have caused the demise of the *May Flower*. I learnt that she had been sailing up the Swin Channel, tack for tack with the *Blue Mermaid*; the *May Flower* was bound for Colchester. The two barges were heading for the Swin Spitway, a swatchway through the sands, when the *Blue Mermaid* struck a mine and was blown clean out of the water. The incident occurred near the West Hook Middle Buoy; several wrecks still lie in this area and one of these will be her remains. She was a steel barge built in 1931 by F.W. Horlock of Mistley. Her skipper was Captain P.J. Bird and her mate Mr G.W. Lucas. Apparently, the force of the blast was felt by the crew of the *May Flower* – they stopped and searched for survivors, but sadly found none.

The originator of the tale was the *May Flower's* skipper, Mr J. Mallett, also known as Felix. His life story has been told in editions of *Topsail* and was compiled by a Mr Rod Minter who visited Mr Mallet before his death. The cargo log of the *May Flower* for that period in 1941 makes no mention about this event, however her cargo logs of the period contain only basic details of cargoes carried with departure and arrival dates only. They were not maintained as sailing logs.

The details for the voyage related are: '8 July sailed from London with 500 quarters of Wheat, arrived Colchester 10 July'. Frank Carr covers this incident in his book *Sailing Barges*. In chapter six, the incident is said to have occurred on 9 July 1941. However, no mention is made to the fact that the *May Flower* attended the area of the stricken vessel! The demise of the *Blue Mermaid* is also covered in Hervey Benham's book, *The Last Stronghold of Sail*.

An interesting account of J. (Felix) Mallett is related in a book by John Leather, *Barges*, however no account of this tale is again mentioned. He first went to sea at fifteen and a half, in 1897, retiring in 1946; he died in 1982, still with an active interest in barges – I wish that I could have met him! Felix Mallett left the barge and Mr Frederick George French took over on 10 January 1942.

On 30 June 1943, a cargo of brick rubble was picked up in London and discharged at Maldon. The rubble came from clearances of the many bomb-damaged buildings that existed around London. Rubble was being moved out to build a runway at a new airfield at Birch, near to Colchester. It was from this airfield that part of the Arnhem glider force departed during the latter stages of the Second World War.

A cargo of 110 tons of clay was taken to Colchester from 23 July 1943, arriving on the 28th. This may well have had something to do with the airfield at Birch too. This was followed by a freight of wood to Colchester from London.

On 12 July 1945 a cargo of timber was again taken to Colchester, arriving on the 13th. These last few cargoes mentioned were about the only deviation from her wheat runs, which predominated during her final few years of trading.

During the refurbishment of some waterside premises in Maldon, which has previously been mentioned, the 1946 records of sails made by a Maldon sail maker showed that the *May Flower* had a new foresail made for her. I discuss more of this in a later chapter.

Records show that on 2 January 1947, Frederick G. French left the barge, to be replaced by George Osbourne. He was in turn relieved by David John Moyes on 5 November 1948; he was the *May Flower's* last trading skipper. These entries are clearly decipherable on the registration document, recorded in the Board of Trade stamp.

During 1947 the barge was 'on the Ways' at Maldon for four months. She had a new keelson fitted during this time. The survey report for September 1947 states that it was new. I learnt from Professor Richard-Hugh Perks and Mr Bernard Lewis, manager of Green Brothers' Maldon Mill in 1947, that an engine, a 44hp Kelvin, was also fitted to the barge during this period, it being removed in 1949. However the survey reports

The *May Flower* off Bradwell during September 1949. Look at that new mainsail on her. Oh, what a picture she looks! Note that the 'GB' has been removed from the topsail. The vertically aligned 'GB' stitchmarks were still visible in 1971. The *Ethel Maud* had her 'GB' stitched into her sail, as written, thus the mill could recognise which barge was approaching!

for September 1947, 1948 and 1949 do not show the *May Flower* to be fitted with any propulsion or auxiliary machinery.

Bernard Lewis also told me that her new keelson was a steel girder. I discussed all of this with him; it transpired that the *Ethel Maud* had had the same engine. To fit it, the aft (skipper's) cabin was dismantled. Some of the removed panelling was rescued and used to make some furniture, of which, incidentally, he still has some pieces. I pointed out that when the *May Flower* was purchased by my father, she had her original cabin and that the arrangements aft, to the aft bulkhead, were standard and no indications existed that an engine had been fitted. There were no shaft bosses on the inner or outer hull, or any signs that removal of such had taken place. Her keelson was most definitely pine. I was left with the impression that with the passage of time, there may have been a mix-up between the firm's two barges. The pine keelson fitted to the *May Flower* is clearly seen in later photographs! Discussing this with a barge historian, no records have surfaced showing that an engine was fitted, and then later, removed.

Of great interest to me is a photograph of my mother's, taken of the barge off Bradwell in 1949. In this she is clearly seen sporting a brand new mainsail; it looks lovely and it would have been an asset had it been passed over with the barge. But, alas, it was not to be. This sail was originally intended for a large gaff cutter. It was made of 18in yacht flax and was apparently very little used. The sail was altered to fit the *May Flower* in 1948.

Her final voyage with a cargo is written no differently to any of the other entries. It is probable that the skipper may not have even been aware that it was going to be the *May Flower*'s last cargo. On 12 September 1949 she sailed from London to Maldon with 500 quarters of wheat, and arrived on 16 September 1949. The *May Flower* had her annual survey on 20 September 1949; this was her last under the ownership of Green Brothers.

Various publications have mentioned the *May Flower* trading to and from Maldon during the late 1940s, when in the ownership of the Millers, Green Brothers, who also still had the *Ethel Maud* under sail. It was a twilight time for barges still trading under sail alone, so vessels that were still active seem to get specifically mentioned. Some comment is made of her stern, which was never really borne out. Yet in time the stern of the barge did slowly loose its fine sheer running aft. So too have many other barges that have not largely been rebuilt. The length of time since carriage of cargoes ultimately catches up with a tired hull and the unsupported aft quarters sag due to the weight of the structure. Wood-built barges that have, or had, a shapely stern end are more prone to this problem than those with a much straighter 'S' curve up from the keel to deck – typically the *George Smeed* is of this latter type – and these also tended to have shorter chines with finer runs. This is a personal view.

The kick up of the sterns of the *Marjorie* of Ipswich, *Edme* and the *George Smeed* are cases in point where major structural rebuilding has returned the barges back to their prime. At the end of 2005, the *Pudge* was having a complete rebuild, from midships to her transom, which had dropped significantly in recent years to almost a reverse sheer situation. Interestingly, some of these barges are only now reaching the age that the *May Flower* was when the Ardley family last sailed her in 1974. The *Pudge* was built in 1922 – thirty-four years after our barge. This, I think for historical interest, puts any adverse comments made into a true and proper perspective.

Another barge, the *Henry* of London, which came out of trade just before the *May Flower*, is recorded visiting Maldon in 1949 in *Us Bargemen* by A.S. Bennett, where an account of seeing various barges coming into and leaving Maldon is given. In this, mention is made to the *May Flower*'s stern. A few years later, these two were berthed at the Hythe for a late summer visit when both out of trade. The *Henry* was berthed outboard and an incident occurred when one of her mooring warps went under the rudder of the *May Flower*. This is recounted later.

As a matter of interest, since the early 1970s, when she was berthed in Twinney Dock (Kent) and owned by a youthful group of individuals, the *Henry* has been undergoing a perpetual refit. After other owners, this eventually culminated in a major rebuild at Faversham in Kent under the ownership of a Justin Ford. Passing her on the water recently was a joy; she looks very well indeed and I applaud the efforts of all involved.

chapter two

Sold Out of Trade: the May Flower Meets the Ardley Family

My mother, Gwendoline (Gwen) *née* Hunt, was brought up in Prittlewell, Essex. Her mother's father was a fisherman with his own vessel. He was also a crewmember for the Southend lifeboat. Her other grandfather worked for a shipping agency, but her father did not have any connection with the sea. During the First World War, mother's father was a member of the Signal Corp, being a bit of a radio buff in his early days.

The sea was very much part of the Hunt family's life; the whole family used to spend most of the summer holidays during the years between the two world wars camped on the beach, often staying overnight! It was not long before Mother began to hanker for a little boat of her own to mess about in. Later she joined the Leigh-on-Sea sailing club in about 1948, where she got to know more people and was able to fulfil her desire to sail. Mother's first boat was a little 9ft 'flatty', a flat-bottomed sailing dinghy with a small lug sail, called *Little Willie*.

The Ardley family on the other hand had had direct connections with the sea and coastal trading in barges. A John William Ardley, born in Paglesham, Essex in 1833, whose parents came from Great Wigborough near Colchester, is known to have been a barge skipper and is thought to have been a barge owner too. At the time of the 1861 census he was Master of the barge *Betsy* and was berthed at Havengore on Foulness Island on census night. His son, a William John Ardley, became a carpenter and after moving to Southend a house builder. He and his wife, Nancy, had quite a few children, of which only my grandfather, Cecil William Ardley, and a sister survived. Another barge connection comes from a Charles Brooks, born in 1831 at Prittlewell, Essex. He was a barge Master too. At the time of the 1871 census he was Master of a barge, the *Emily*. His daughter Nancy married John William Ardley. So barging, or sea faring, was firmly embedded in the family blood.

A sense of belief in what they are doing is a common trait amongst bargemen and it is not surprising to me now that my father eventually hankered for, and bought, a spritsail barge. Most of us Ardleys have this trait to a lesser or greater degree. Family lore has passed down the generations that one member, long ago, paid the ultimate price. A John Ardeley of Great Wigborough, a non-conformist church member, was tried for heresy. He refused to conform to Queen Mary's desire that the population should return to Catholicism, and was burnt at the stake in 1555. This gruesome event is still remembered in Rayleigh, Essex where his name is listed on a martyr's monument. It occurred, almost to the date, 400 years before my own birth.

The Ardley family yacht *Lynette* seen off
Leigh-on-Sea during 1949.

My mother's parents had become acquainted with Mr and Mrs Cecil W. Ardley who
then lived in Westcliff just above the railway line and not far from the water. They had
two boys, John and Robin. They were a sailing family and were members of the Leigh-
on-Sea Sailing Club, Cecil Ardley being a vice-commodore at one time. The Ardley
family for a number of years owned a double-ender, typically an old lifeboat-shaped
hull, called *Goblin*; this was sold just after the end of the Second World War. When my
parents met, the Ardley family had just bought a vessel called *Lynnette*; this was the first
of what became a small class of yacht.

My father eventually had equal shares of this yacht with his father. John (my father) was
a pal of my mother's brother, both being at the same school (Southend High), however it
was with Robin that my mother had her initial friendship! *Lynnette* is written about by
S. Platt in his book *My Three Grey Mistresses*, when he sailed in her with a friend, before
being owned by my grandfather. This yacht was eventually sold to the Blackwater and
Colne area, and was later lost in a North Sea yacht race. For interest it is believed to be
the same *Lynnette* entered on the race trophy boards of the Colne Yacht Club.

My mother obviously got to know both the Ardley boys, and later a romance with
John began. The usual path followed and in 1951 they were married at that well-known
navigational mark for Leigh Creek, St Clement's Church, Leigh-on-Sea, but more of

this later. What was unusual for this couple was the buying of a barge to live on. Their interest in buying a barge stemmed from their combined love of the water and sailing. They could have done the conventional thing and had the conventional mortgage with a conventional house, family etc. But no, this was not to be for them!

My father had met up with Fred Cooper during 1949. On one occasion they had a long yarn sitting on the deck of a barge which was lying off Chalkwell – probably waiting to go into Leigh. It was during his talks with Fred that my father cemented the desire to own a barge. The story that I tell is constructed from the documents held by my mother. I make reference to letters that must have been sent by my father, few of which exist, so the exact content can only be guessed. I paraphrase from letters sent to him by other persons. For me, the content of the correspondence was enlightening. They provide the road map that was to lead to the *May Flower* and, eventually, to be part of the jigsaw that made up the picture of the Ardley barge family for over three decades.

In September 1949, my father wrote to the Port of London Authority (PLA) regarding the legality of sailing a barge on the tideway. His letter itself does not now exist, although the PLA response does. The response from the PLA is interesting, in that it said no special regulations existed for private craft used solely for pleasure. No objections were raised to sailing one's privately owned vessel (sailing barge), providing the usual 'Rules of the Road' are adhered to. This interested me, because much later during the 1960s, a movement was started by a group of young skippers that required all barges to be sailed by professional skippers – in sailing barge matches.

In late December 1949, my father communicated with the Whitewall Barge Company. He was enquiring about vessels and other details. The response in early January 1950 enclosed a booklet on converted barges, referred to in the letter, but now unfortunately not with the rest of the documents, and also a booklet about the Marina Club at Hoo. This contained a map, which was useful for details about entering from the water and for public transport. Father had also asked for the address of Frank Carr, the then director of the National Maritime Museum. On 31 January, Father received another letter from the Whitewall Barge Company referring to the *Atlas*, which they had converted the previous year. They suggested that a better vessel of her type could be purchased.

My father wrote to Frank Carr at the end of January, who responded in a letter of 3 February 1950. This was the first of many letters between them. Frank Carr details various barge books, some of which my father already had in his possession. The address for Arthur Bennett on his barge *Henry* berthed at Hoo, and Mr H.P. Shrubsall, barge owner and surveyor, were given. He also enclosed an application form for membership of the Thames Barge Sailing Club, which had recently been founded. The next letter to my father thanks him for his application and fee for joining the club. Frank Carr says that he had much pleasure in proposing my father for membership. My parents were off-and-on members for a considerable time.

Father then wrote to Mr Shrubsall, who responded with a lengthy letter giving a whole list of answers to the various queries that had been raised. He details some barges that had had works carried out during the immediate period since the end of the Second World War. The *Verona* had had approximately £5,000 spent on her a few

The *May Flower* at the Green Brothers Mill in March 1950. Beyond can be seen a barge and coaster unloading at Greens Mill and Sadd's timber wharf respectively.

years previously. The *Gladys* (of Dover) had had about £2,000 spent on her and there was mention of the *Veravia*, which was rebuilt in 1925 but was assumed to be too big! The final suggestion, which leads onwards, is that only craft that were in use in the dry goods or cement trade would be of any use to him.

Frank Carr wrote to my father on 2 March 1950 enclosing a letter from a Mr Baker, suggesting that the *May Flower* was worth a look at, having just come onto the market. Mr Baker's letter was actually a proposal that the TBSC purchase the *May Flower* – I wonder if that is a previously known fact?! There follows correspondence with Nichol & Ashton (brokers for estuary craft), suggesting a meeting to discuss vessels for sale. Then another letter was received from Mr H.P. Shrubsall asking my father what he was prepared to pay for a barge. From this point, no further correspondence exists.

My father, in the mean time, had written to thank Frank Carr to report that he was planning to look over the *May Flower*, because Frank Carr writes on 7 March 1950 that he is delighted to know that information about the *May Flower* was of use. He was also very interested about the lines that Father had taken off, of the *Emma* of Rochester (1899) berthed up Leigh Creek and another barge, *The Conqueror*, lying on Leigh marshes.

Things were now moving very quickly. My father wrote to Green Brothers of Maldon regarding the availability of the *May Flower*. He had been over to the barge to have a look at her. I understand that his parents at the time were a little flabbergasted by this development, which meant that it was something quite serious!

On one of the visits he took his fiancée, my future mother. This trip must have been with the sanction of Green Brothers as they were on the barge alone. The barge was as it would have been, waiting for its next cargo. She sat alongside the mill wharf, where we were all to visit many years later. During this visit the mainsail was not bent on.

On 21 March, my father received a response from Green Brothers regarding his verbal proposal to purchase the barge, which had been inspected by him and surveyed on his behalf. The survey document does not appear to have survived; however it is likely that this is the September 1949 report. Green Brothers mention repairs my father had asked to be completed to the starboard leeboard, and repairs to, and the bending on, of the barge's mainsail. The barge was being given back an older sail removed when she had a new sail in 1948. They had set in motion the formalities that were required to complete the sale of a registered vessel.

A further letter on 23 March from Green Brothers said that sanction from the Ministry of Transport was required before a transfer of ownership could be completed. Green Brothers said that they were still waiting for the 10 per cent deposit and were holding over other enquiries for the barge for the time being.

On 29 March, Green Brothers had pleasure in receiving a cheque for £60, being 10 per cent as a deposit for the purchase, and the completed MOT form, which had been forwarded to the Registrar (of Shipping and Seaman). Repairs to the leeboard had been completed by Cook's yard and the mainsail was to be bent on early the following week. This meant that the gear needed to be lowered. I do not know if my father attended this process, but I rather think that he would have done. Following this, it is said that the rigging and topsail would be set up ready by the Saturday, as proposed in Father's letter.

On 4 April 1950, Green Brothers received the balance of the purchase sum. The Bill of Sale was completed that week and the Sanction of Transfer of Ownership required by the MOT was in the post. The letter went on to say that Mr (Bernard) Lewis would be dealing with all the outstanding points raised by my father. All the gear would be aboard and the barge would be berthed at the Hythe on the Friday (Good Friday) as agreed. A handwritten note on the reverse of this letter details that the key would be lodged at 10 Butt Lane. So, my father became owner and skipper of a spritsail barge following in the footsteps the footsteps of his maternal and paternal great grandfathers.

My father wrote to Frank Carr on taking over the *May Flower*, after a passage to Leigh-on-Sea. His response refers to his delight at Father's purchase of the barge and that the weather over Easter had not been as kind as one would have wished for a passage round to Leigh, from Maldon. Frank Carr had spent some time on a trading barge, so knew their ways and the waters off the Essex coast. There was also a prompt for the line drawings, which he had mentioned in an earlier letter.

My father later had cause to write to Green Brothers regarding certain items he felt should have been aboard the barge! On 17 April 1950 they responded with answers to his queries. One concerned a second flying jib seen on the vessel when viewed. It was pointed out that this jib belonged to neither the *May Flower* nor the *Ethel Maud*, but was used on either as required. It now belonged to the *Ethel Maud*! (As did the *May Flower's* removed new mainsail.)

The correspondence closed after a letter from Green Brothers dated 25 April 1950, enclosing copies of previous annual survey certificates for September 1947, 1948 and

C O P Y.

MALDON BARGE INSURANCE COMPANY, LIMITED,
6 High Street, Maldon, Essex.

To the Directors:

Gentlemen,—I have surveyed the Barge "MAYFLOWER"

of _Rochester_ whereof _J. Noyes_ is Master

_48_ tons register, and whereof Mr. _Baker_

of _Sudbury_ is Managing Owner.

No.	ANCHORS.	Cwt.	CONDITION.	No.	SAILS, &c.	AGE.	CONDITION AND REMARKS.
1	Best Bower	5	Good	1	Mainsail	New	Exchanged old full (New)
1	Second ditto	3	"	1	Foresail	9	
	Stream Kedge			1	Topsail	7	
1	Kedge	2	"	1	Mizzen	6	All in good repair
	Dogs Leg				Big Jib		Main Brail Winch
					Second ditto		requires re-newing
				2	Flying Jib	3	
					Bridge Sail		
	CABLES, &c.	Fathoms		1	Lead and Line		
				2	Lanthorns (Regulation size)		Good
1	Best Bower	45	New	1	Riding Lamp		"
1	Second ditto	30	Good	1	Stern Lamp		"
1	Warps, forward	25	"	1	Cabin Lamp		"
2	Ditto aft ... 2 ..	20	"	2	Hatch Cloths, forward		"
1	Line	60	"	3	" " main		"
	Tow Rope	-		-	Stack Cloths		
	Wire Rope	-		-	Side Cloths		
	Stack Irons	-		1	Compass		New one on order
				1	Fog Horn		Good
				1	Bell		"
1	Boat		Good	1	Boat Hook		"
2	Boat's Davits		"	2	Booms		"
1	Steering Gear		"	2	Sweeps		"
1	Rudder		Repaired	1	Binnacle		"
2	Leeboard, Port		New	3	Boat's Paddles		"
	" Starboard		Good	2	Coir Fender		"
	Leeboard pendants, falls, preventers		"	2	Life Buoys		"
					Built by		Curels
					At		Rochester
					Year		1888
					Number of hands employed including Captain		2

GENERAL STATE OF HULL.

Outside Chines	Good	Knees	Six fair	
Outside Skin	"	Hatches	Repaired	
Main Keelson	Nearly new	Spars	Good	
Chine Keelsons	Fair	Standing Rigging	"	
Ceiling	"	Running Rigging	"	
Lining	"	Windlass	Good	
Beams	"	Two Sets Pumps and Gear. Condition	Good	

SURVEYED at _Own Wharf_ on _Tuesday_ the _20th_

day of _September_ 19_49_

(Signed) _John Keeble_ Surveyor.

Fee.

May Flower's survey report for September 1949.

1949. Green Brothers hoped that all was well and that the weather had been very rough and disappointing over Easter.

I noted some interesting information in these reports. In 1947 and 1949, the beams were stated as being fair. In 1948, the comment is 'Not too good'. This is a truer reflection, bearing in mind that four were to be replaced in the years up to 1966. Others should have been renewed, especially as the barge continued to sail as late on as she did. None of the documents commented upon any propulsion machinery being fitted. From this evidence, it could safely be assumed that one was not fitted. As said, the barge is reputed to have been fitted with an engine, a 44hp Kelvin in 1947, it being removed in 1949. In correspondence with Barry Pearce of Maldon, he told me that from his knowledge, and that of Cook's workforce, the *May Flower* was not at any time fitted with an auxiliary engine.

The main brail winch and starboard leeboard are mentioned – the leeboard has already been discussed, my mother assures me that the winch was replaced, though I'm not so sure about this. I remember that the barrel and operating spindle were removed during the 1960s for the cogs to be built up and dressed and a spare obtained for future fitting.

Some of the details recorded ring hollow and the dates for ages of the sails are a mixed bag of what I would, as someone who has compiled many reports as a marine engineer during my career, call artistic licence!

The mainsail crops up again. For this I apologise, but it is something that I feel did not seem true. This sail is recorded as being ten years old in both the 1947 and 1948 surveys. If its age for 1947 is broadly correct, then it would fit in with the information found by Mr D. Patient of Maldon whilst carrying out research about Howard's of Maldon, a yacht- and barge-building concern. The 1949 survey report has an annotation against the mainsail 'exchanged with *Ethel Maud*'. My mother was told that the *May Flower* was fitted with her original sail, which was said to be twelve years old when they bought the barge. The foresail was nine years old three years running and, with some fairly minor repairs, lasted up to the barge's last sail in 1974. From accounts found by Mr D. Patient of Maldon, it would appear that the *May Flower* had a new foresail made for her in 1946; however it was quite apparent that this did not come with the barge!

Her topsail is consistent and was seven years old in 1949. This, as you will find out, over the years had much new canvas. By the end of the barge's time in the Ardley family ownership, nearly 50 per cent of new material was all sewn in by hand; the differing shades in this sail can be clearly seen in various later photographs. The mizzen was six years old and was eventually replaced in 1965. The flying jib (staysail) was only three years old. This was a superb sail, probably the best the barge had, and with I would say the topsail, which always set well.

In December 1952, Father received a letter and a form from the Ministry of Transport requesting details of the barge and any other craft that he had in his possession. An appended handwritten note says that it is appreciated that the vessel may no longer be in commission – no, not as a trading barge, but she still had three decades of use to come! My father filled out the form, but he did not appear to send it off, unless it is a copy.

Looking at the registration details of the *May Flower*, she was described as being rigged as a 'Spritsail (Dandy)'. On the original 1888 document the 'spritsail' part is no longer clear, but 'dandy' is written in brackets. Bob Childs, in the front piece of his publication entitled *Rochester Barges of the Victorian Era*, briefly discusses differences and the evolution of the spritsail barge rig during this period; however this designation is not mentioned. He does, though, mention a barge; the *Emily* of 1859 is described as being registered as a 'dandy ketch'. She was built by George Gill and was wrecked off the Norfolk coast in 1867.

It should be appreciated that the spritsail barge is in actual fact a ketch, in that the mizzen is forward of the rudder. The sail areas of main and mizzen in a true ketch would be closer in size and would then have been of the more traditional gaff and boom rig, akin to the big boomsail barges. These big barges have been written about by Hervey Benham and Roger Finch in their book *The Big Barges* published in 1983. These vessels traded far and wide, taking trips to Portugal, Spain and as far away as the West Indies and South America.

chapter three

The First Passage and a Wedding

Upon completion of the sale it was planned to bring the barge to Leigh-on-Sea to commence cleaning out and start conversion work. Tom Scott, a trading skipper, spent some time with my parents explaining sail setting and demonstrating to them the important things that were required. This gentleman was not a trading skipper for the barge; my mother said that he had retired and resided in Benfleet, Essex.

The trip round from Maldon was planned for the spring of 1950, over the Easter weekend, which included the bank holiday. A large crew of family and fellow sailing club members were assembled for this trip. They eventually embarked at The Hythe in Maldon where Green Brothers had put the barge following the sale. It turned out to be a very dirty passage – some vessels were lost in the estuary over that weekend – but after an eventful passage the *May Flower* was brought safely into Leigh.

My uncle, my mother's brother, was at the time my parents purchased the *May Flower* working for Tate and Lyle, the sugar refiners based at Silver Town on the Thames downriver from the East India Docks. He wrote an article about the passage for his works magazine; this was edited somewhat from the original work, a copy of which has not been kept. My mother was given the original at the time – it having more value to her. The written account closely follows a verbal account given to me by an old sea salt from Leigh-on-Sea, Ian Kemp, who crewed during the trip. He has retained an interest in barges, being a member of the Society for Spritsail Sailing Barge Research, and is a qualified Master Mariner who spent many years on the refrigerated fruit ship trade routes.

Ian's father was a photographer based in Leigh-on-Sea and was later commissioned to take the photographs of my parents' wedding at St Clement's church, and of the barge sailing away from Leigh. His account of the voyage is as follows (and you will have to excuse the vernacular):

We all arrived in Maldon after a journey across country on the branch line from Whitham on a Saturday afternoon. After getting our gear aboard, the skipper, a wiry grizzled character, suddenly said, 'Ere the's thirtin bordies on thus 'ere bot Mr Owner'. After some cajoling no more was said! The skipper told us what would need to be done, and when the flood had made towards high-water, we departed from The Hythe at Maldon and dropped

The *May Flower* at anchor under the Buxey Sands, awaiting better weather, Easter 1950.

down to anchor off Heybridge Basin, with the ebb. It was very windy, the weather was not good. Some of the crew departed for home! The barge sat there for two days waiting for things to abate.

When the skipper and my father deemed it time to get moving, the skipper said 'Right, two of you 'eave th's 'ere anchor up short, the rest 'elp me get th's sails a ready.' The topsail was sheeted out and the mainsail block hooked on before being dropped about half out, with sheet block thrashing back and forth.

I was one of the crew on the windlass. The anchor was bloody hard work and when it was time to break it out, it took two each side with another fluking the damn chain over every few turns; it's something I have never forgotten!

We set off into the teeth of the blow, a wind that would have prevented us taking our own little boats out of Leigh. We went out like a train, gybing round Sales Point, and headed in towards the Raysand Channel. It was decided to drop anchor for the night in the hole near the beacon. It was a very windy night and continued into the next day with less force.

Leaving the anchorage, we eventually made it into the wider Thames and with long boards across the Thames, with the tide under us, we gradually made up towards Southend Pier to bring up in the Ray.

The barge was taken up and anchored off Leigh. We all went ashore in the boat to be greeted in the clubhouse to a shout of 'Where have you been?' We were just glad to be safe!

Ian told me that it was all rather basic: the two girls, he seemed to remember, had the fore cabin, my father had the aft cabin and the rest camped out in the main hold on the ceiling. Foul weather gear consisted of army surplus, as did sleeping gear! It was only later that they found out that they had actually sailed through one of the worst late spring blows for quite a long time! They finally completed the voyage on the Tuesday.

In actual fact Ian missed out one surprising bit of information. Going up past Southend Pier, a motor barge was passed which had sunk the previous day. I do not know the name of the stricken vessel, but it was being attended to by the Port of London Authority when they sailed past! My mother said that this was a good recollection of the events during their passage. She did also add that a few of the original volunteers jumped ship while waiting off Heybridge! Also some pretty nasty things happened. A line tangled aloft, the barge boat capsized and the mainsheet block came adrift from the traveller on its horse – a frightening experience!

The barge was kept up Leigh Creek in a berth adjacent to the present station. The berth was just below what was known as the causeway, across to Two Tree Island. Berthed here also was the *Emma*. My father then had to knuckle down and get the barge cleaned up and fit to take a wife away. An uncle has told me that many family members were roped in for the initial cleaning work!

One of the saddest things that I learnt later in my life was the tale of the mainsail, previously mentioned. When initially viewed, the barge was not fitted with a mainsail. A recently made mainsail, that had been fitted, had been removed prior to her being put up for sale and was not included in the inventory. Her original was included, and at the time it was under repair. The new sail went to the *Ethel Maud*! The photograph reproduced in chapter one, taken in the autumn of 1949, shows the barge off Bradwell, on the River Blackwater, sporting a sail to die for. She never again had such a mainsail.

The old mainsail did not last long, due in the main with the use it had. My mother feels that the powers to be in Green Brothers felt it would be wasted on a barge that would in all probability sit out the rest of her days in some quiet backwater. Little did they know! However the sail lasted for nearly a decade, with numerous patch repairs. My mother carried out a lot of these repairs, but some were larger or more difficult and costs for these appear in my father's accounts that he kept during their early years of ownership. Later my mother carried out all the repairs needed until these tasks fell to my brother and me.

In my father's expenses booklet, I found in the entries for August 1950 a note 'Timber from *Arrow*'. Presumably the *Arrow* paid a visit to Leigh and my father bought some timber from her cargo. My father obviously had a lot of work to do before the barge would be fit to live on. I believe it was at this stage they had decided to renew large areas of the linings aft, before doing too much in the way of outfit. This was the start of a long period of staged renewals to keep the barge in a sound condition for sailing and not just as a floating home.

Sundries purchased in the first few months of ownership included large scrapers, a lifter, a putty knife with an annotation of 'lost' against it in pencil! A keep-hot teapot and tar, also drums to presumably put the tar. The large scrapers were fitted with long

Leaving Leigh Building Supply Wharf (Theobald's) on their honeymoon cruise, with 'Just Married' painted on the port leeboard of the *May Flower*! (Wedding photograph by C.G. Kemp)

handles and I remember regularly using these to remove barnacles from under the bow and stern for many years. My mother tells me that Father used to cycle into Southend, going along the sea front, to fetch tar, a drum at a time, from the gasworks!

The page in Father's book for May 1951 shows that a new main sheet block and winch handles were purchased. The cost of the winch handles was a large expense – the originals had been stolen! Various paints and some tar were also purchased. The main block was to replace the one that came adrift from the horse traveller during the delivery sail in 1950, it being damaged. A decent spare was left on board the barge when she was sold years later. It also gives the cost for a new mizzen sheet shackle. This shackle was fitted over the rudder blade, just above the light displacement, to which the lower end of the mizzen sheet tackle is secured. The shackle was designed by Father to replace whatever was previously fitted. From his sketch, using measurement standards of the day, it was 8in wide and 9in in length.

The wedding date, which was in early October of that year, was getting closer. My parents would have been busy both on and off the barge at this time. Purchases of items that come to my notice during September 1950 included a fire front and a chimney.

These will have been for the main saloon fire, which I mention later in my chapter about our domestic arrangements.

Shackles were purchased at frequent intervals; I presume that a large number needed to be renewed. Another other item is quite notable. This is for wharf dues while the barge lay alongside Leigh Timber Supply Wharf (Theobald's) prior to the wedding – a period of feverish activity.

The barge was taken out for some sailing during this period to acquaint themselves with her ways, returning to the mooring by the causeway. On one occasion, after leaving her to the east of the marsh edge, an easterly wind blew up hard, the barge drove up onto her anchor which was picked up on a chine batten, and she fetched up in the marshes! The anchor did not do any damage, but the stock bore its characteristic bend on one side thereafter. Mother has told me that they spent half a night winching her off with the kedge. This had to be rowed out in the barge boat, touching the anchor down at the end of each pull and repeating the process until back in place, all this even before the church bells had rung!

The wedding took place in Saint Clement's church, up on the hill above the old town. The reason for this I am not sure, my mother's parish being Prittlewell and my father's Chalkwell! After the wedding and breakfast, they were escorted to the barge and given a rousing send-off by family and sailing friends. After boarding the *May Flower*, alongside the Leigh Building Supply Wharf along Leigh Creek, a cockle boat that had been engaged towed them clear. They set the sails as they went, casting off the tow when clear of Bell Wharf. They then sailed away to the River Medway on a honeymoon cruise.

Little did they know that family and friends had managed to write 'Just married' on the side of the barge; the message was painted in white on the port leeboard as well as a sign on a piece of sheet pinned to the port bow! The first they actually knew about it was from a picture on the front page of a national tabloid newspaper after going ashore at Upnor! The locals had already nicknamed them the 'honeymoon couple' when they anchored up and went ashore for a drink in the pub above Upnor Hard!

The honeymoon was spent exploring the River Medway and its creeks. On this trip they discovered and sailed into Whitewall Creek, where a berth was found. Here they found a fair collection of barges in various states, either abandoned or being stripped out for useful gear, and some house barges. They were the only rigged barge at that time. Their first berth was astern of the *Emma*, which had previously moved from Leigh. I cover all of this in my chapter about Whitewall Creek later in the book, so will leave further details till then. Suffice to say that with its open aspect to the north and east, it made a most suitable berth for getting away from without the use of an engine.

My father had qualified as an architect and at the time was working in London, as was my mother, as a graphic artist, so access to a railway line was always a necessity. Strood was close by and on the main line to London. So they settled down. Now that could be a question in itself, 'Did they ever settle down?' To all intents and purposes, the answer is yes, but not until they had used the barge for more exploration. They used various berths during the summer periods, returning to Whitewall Creek for the winter. Closeness to a railway line seemingly being the only important criteria.

The cockle boat LO237, *Boy David*, then owned by Arthur 'China' Cotgrove, towing the *May Flower* away from Leigh Timber Supply Wharf after the wedding. My mother is at the helm and father is taking the last gasket turn off the foresail. There were two 'Just Married' signs on the side of the barge; the one on the port bow was on an old bedsheet! The remains of the barge *Eva Annie* can be seen above LO237. Her stern was still intact at the time. To starboard of LO237 is LO334, the *Joy*, and astern of her are LO154 *Victoria* and the *Mabel Evlyn*. This photograph was taken from Victoria Wharf. Information regarding the various cockle boats and shrimpers was obtained from Nate Readdings from Leigh-on-Sea, ex-bargeman, coasterman and fisherman. (Wedding photograph by C.G. Kemp)

During those first few summers, they visited a number of places that are covered in separate chapters. These included trips to Maldon, Benfleet, St Katharine Docks, Leigh and Hoo. They used Hoo for fairly lengthy periods during the early years, generally only as a summer base.

ADDENDUM TO CHAPTER 3 – MY UNCLE'S STORY

The story of *May Flower*'s first voyage as a yacht barge was written for my mother by her brother following their harrowing passage. It is transposed as written.

THE LAST OF THE STALWARTS
THE MAYFLOWER SAILS AGAIN
20th CENTURY *MAY FLOWER*
BARGEES

A short coastal passage in a Thames 'Spritty' barge can be exciting – especially during the Easter gales!

I was a little sceptical as I stood on the quay at Maldon on the River Blackwater in Essex, and gazed down first of all at the spacious decks, the big winches and the enormous wheel of this Thames barge. Gazing upwards in awe at the massive sprit that loomed high above my head, I was struck with the immensity of everything compared with the smaller craft I hade hitherto sailed in.

The Mayflower, an old grain-carrying sailing barge of about 50 tons, with a length of 80ft and a beam of 19ft, is one of the last stalwarts of sail that still frequents the East Coast. But her 'working days' were now over, for John, a friend of mine, had just purchased her with idea of converting it into his future home, and with the party of friends and a local barge skipper to help us, we (had) arrived to sail her round to Leigh-on-Sea on the Thames Estuary.

It was with blissful memories of that lovely sunny Easter weekend of last year that we had accepted John's invitation, but now as we stood there on Easter Saturday 1950, the wind was howling in the rigging and it was not very pleasant at all!

Clambering aboard, we noticed with some concern that their were thirteen of us destined to make the trip; however, putting all superstitions aside, we quickly got to work cleaning the cargo hold and generally making things shipshape, and it was soon 4 p.m. and time to sail.

The weather report at 1 p.m. was not very encouraging – strong westerly winds that hinted of a gale to come – but, undaunted, we cast off from the quay and sped away before the rising wind with only our tops'l set.

Tom (the skipper) looked dubiously at the billowing tops'l as soon as we were out of the lee of the quay, and felt the full force of the wind, and it wasn't very long before John and he decided that it was a little too gusty even with that small amount of canvas up, and so about three miles downriver from Maldon, we rounded up and anchored for the night.

After spending a very enjoyable evening crowded together in the small cabin that constitutes the 'living accommodation' on these ships, we turned in early – the male complement rolling up in blankets down in the hold or 'lower mess deck' as we nautically termed it. Unfortunately, it rained in the night and some of us were awakened by cries of 'Move over a little please, the water's dripping right down my neck!' or words to that effect, for the rear hatch cover was, alas, in dire need of repair.

Sunday morning we awoke to find a westerly gale was blowing, and Mayflower just about to settle her flat bottom on the river bed. We were comforted by the weather forecast, which said that it would veer north-west and moderate later, so we had breakfast and spent the morning exploring the river bed and cleaning topsides.

Tom and Denis, who had waded ashore during the morning in search of cigarettes, found themselves cut off by the incoming tide; a party in the dinghy were soon despatched to pick up the unfortunates, a by no means simple operation under the conditions then prevailing, but, after a hectic row, they arrived back on board just in time for lunch.

After lunch, a get together of the crew resulted in five of them deciding to return home that afternoon, for, as they pointed out, we all had to be back at work on the Tuesday morning, and as we had only covered three miles in a day, it certainly looked as though we should not be home by Monday evening.

An hour later they were valiantly sculled ashore by Tom, for alas one of the dinghy oars broke under the strain just as they cast off.

Soon afterwards the weather seemed to be improving, and bucked up by an encouraging weather forecast – which later proved to be untrue – the now reduced complement of six men and two girls decided to get underway again, and run down to Bradwell to see what the conditions were like. We accomplished this feat quite well, though the winding in of the anchor chain took us a while.

The run down the Blackwater was very enjoyable; under tops'l, stays'l (I believe foresail is meant) and mizzen we went at a fine rate, though the former had to be lowered when Bradwell Quay was abeam, as the wind piped up once more. John swiftly decided to carry on as far as possible that night, so we ran on past Bradwell heading for the mouth of the river.

Gybing off Sales Point, we unbrailed a little mainsail and careered down the Ray Sand Channel against the now ebbing tide. The sun was settling as we picked (our way) by the Buxey beacon, but as the channel is not lit at night, we anchored soon afterwards. Working out our position later, we were pleased to note that we had logged about twenty miles in three hours of sailing, and we were very elated at the fine progress at last being made.

Monday morning dawned and (at) about 10 a.m., although the wind was still gale force, we got underway again, the anchor winch crew now getting the hang of things! Under stays'l and half brailed mains'l we plugged on without leeboards owing to the shallow water, but after only twenty minutes of sailing gave it up as a bad job.

The seas were very spectacular all that afternoon, as can be seen by the photo taken about 3 p.m., but the Mayflower rode her massive anchor quite serenely. We sighted a small coaster battling her way through the seas, and we learnt later that she reported our position when she arrived at Maldon that evening.

As the sun went below the horizon that night, we aboard resigned ourselves to another night on the boards and wondered what our bosses would say on the morrow.

At 6 a.m. the next morning, we hurriedly dressed and, gulping down a very welcome cup of tea brewed by the two girls, we prepared to get underway. The wind had at long last moderated into a fresh north-westerly breeze, and we put 'everything up' in an attempt to get into the estuary of the Thames, where we would have a chance of tacking up against this cursed westerly wind.

In getting underway, however, two incidents happened. The first was when the dinghy fouled our stern and in trying to free it she slewed round and capsized and away floated our one and only sound oar together with floorboards, etc.

The second was when, upon coming about, the heavy mainsheet block (attached to the main horse by a hook which is moused) broke loose, the mousing having parted under the strain, and then, literally took charge of proceedings.

Those of us on deck at the time ran for our dear lives to get out of the way of this swinging horror; it wrapped itself around one of the huge sweeps lying on top of the hatch and flung it overboard as if it had been a matchstick, finally ending its short but deadly career by winding itself around the leeside shrouds, where it was gingerly approached by Tom (who had swiftly brailed up the mainsail) and allowed itself to be led back to its rightful position on the horse.

After this very un-nerving experience, we noticed that we were not making up much against the ebb tide, so at 8.30 a.m. we anchored once more about three miles offshore just east of the Blacktail spit buoy and awaited the turn of the tide.

Luckily, the food was holding out, and, after a hot meal consisting of a stew (the contents of which was rather a mystery) but which tasted excellent, rounded off by pancakes all cooked by the two girls who were sticking it like good un's, we finished our last cigarettes, hauled the dinghy up out of the way into the davits, and got underway on what we hoped was the last lap of our passage.

The wind was considerably lighter but still piped up a little in squalls, which enabled us to hoist all sails. We made good progress tacking across the wide expanse of the estuary with the flood tide under us and by 4.30 p.m. we sighted the Nore forts abeam.

Soon afterwards we sighted Southend Pier looming up out of the haze, and all on board began to feel very thankful at being in home waters again.

About two miles off the pier on the western edge of the Nore sands, we saw the stumpy mast of a motor barge sticking up out of the water with a PLA wreck ship standing by – a grim reminder of the gales which we had battled through!

Coming up past the pier at a fine rate, we were all set on what we thought to be the last tack that would bring us to our destination at Leigh, when a violent squall hit us.

It took us very much by surprise, and the most unkindest cut of all was that in our haste to get the sails down, the tops'l jammed, the mainsheet fouled and all that could be done was to bear away for the shore about a mile distant.

Fortunately, it was over as swiftly as it began, but alas a dead flat calm ensued and we had to anchor just offshore at Westcliff, all of us very peeved at this cruel stroke by mother nature that thwarted us from reaching our anchorage.

As darkness came upon us, we piled into the dinghy and with the aid of the boat hook unceremoniously poled ashore, to be greeted by friends who had seen us anchor. Hiring a couple of taxis, we sallied forth down to the club, to be greeted, to our disgust, by cries of 'Where the devil have you been, across to America and back?'

chapter four

Hoo Marina

Although a berth had been found at Whitewall Creek, my parents used, when not away sailing to other places, a berth, with a number of other barges, at Hoo Marina. This marina had been built on the site of the disused Hoo brickwork's during the late 1940s, using the old wharf with an enclosure formed with concrete lighters sunk to form a breakwater. It is situated on the north bank of the River Medway, opposite the old Chatham Royal Dockyard (Saint Mary's Island). This has since been expanded to include a half tide basin, with a sill to enable yachts to remain afloat.

A number of yacht barges made this their berth for over wintering, or as a permanent base. Some were kept in sail for a number of years, gradually to loose their rigs, down to mainmast only and then to none at all. I remember clearly looking at some of these vessels over the years, when we spent times anchored on the flats. The last of these, the *Alan*, was moved out of the marina and hulked at the edge of the marshes up West Hoo Creek during 2001. Many years later another such vessel was the *Anglia*. She was one of the last barges to work under sail, continuing until about 1960.

For many years the *Anglia* was berthed at Bloors Wharf, Rainham, Kent. She was owned by a schoolmaster, an acquaintance of my parents, and we often sailed in barge matches together during the early 1960s. Eventually she was sold on, and ultimately made Hoo Marina her home, which was her last. The *Anglia* had arrived at Hoo Wharf fitted with spars, and I later watched in horror as these spars were removed by crane and dumped on the wharf. I was berthed in the 'new' yacht basin on my Finesse 24, *Whimbrel*. However, she lives on, for some of her gear went into the *Betula*, a spritsail barge fashioned out of a Dutch barge hull. The *Anglia* lasted only a few more years and in 2001 I found her hulked and breaking up rapidly, sitting in the entrance to Strood Dock, ironically, within hailing distance of the remains of the *May Flower*.

Whilst at Hoo Marina my parents met up with Tubby Blake, one of the active sailing masters still operating barges out of West Hoo with the Brice fleet. Tubby Blake eventually became Master of the Thames Barge Sailing Club barge the *Arrow*; this was his last job before retiring. My mother purchased a binnacle from Tubby Blake, which many years later she presented to the Dolphin Barge Museum at Milton, Kent. Other artefacts from the *May Flower* are also at this museum, including part of her rail. During 2005 the museum had to move from the old barge yard at Milton.

A domestic Hoo Marina: my mother, with apron on, was probably busy doing the chores one morning in 1952. A group of un-rigged barges can be seen through the port shrouds of the *May Flower*. The *Henry* is immediately astern. Note the gap between the two parts of *May Flower*'s name carving. The wharf is the old brickworks' dock wharf.

They also saw a lot of Fred Cooper who, at the time, worked for Lapthorn's on their tugs, amongst other responsibilities. He was often on the *May Flower* for yarns and probably the inevitable cup of tea! Fred Cooper also skippered sailing barges, latterly being best known for sailing the *Saltcote Belle*. During this period he was working on a booklet which became – and probably remains – the bible of the rig and rigging of barges. It is my understanding that some of the sketches are based on what was seen by Fred Cooper on board the *May Flower*, being fresh out of trade and unaltered. He kept in regular contact with the family for many years. (I mention a little story in a later chapter dealing with a short period the barge was berthed at Twinney Dock.) His last visit to the barge came during the 1970s when we were berthed at Callows Wharf – both places are in Upchurch, Kent.

Some of the barges that lay at, or used, Hoo during the time my parents were using the marina include the *Henry*, the *John & Mary* owned by the Clark family, and the *Viper*, owned at the time by John Chancellor, the marine artist. It was this artist who incidentally produced graphics for Fred Cooper when writing his 'little red book'. Others at Hoo were the Thames Barge Sailing Club's barge of the time, *Arrow*, *Violet*, *Swift* and a barge called *Thoma II*. The *Venta* was another visitor, this barge with the *Saltcote Belle* had also used Conyer, off the Swale too.

Collage of barges seen at Hoo in 1951. The white clipper-bowed barge is the *Thoma II*; she is still believed to be afloat as a motor yacht. The hulk is the remains of an old schooner, the *Rhoda Mary*, and parts of her are still standing to this day.

The *Thoma II* of 67nrt was built by Howard of Maldon in 1909. She was purpose built as a yacht barge, having a clipper bow and counter stern. She was cruised extensively around British and European coasts including the Mediterranean. After the Second World War, she had a major refit and was based at Hoo for a period. (Her owner, Mr G.C. Burge, had also owned the *Winifred* of Sandwich up to around 1949.) She took part in the 1950 and 1951 Marina Barge Matches, coming home second in her class on each occasion. She continued to sail for a number of years during the 1950s, eventually being converted to a motor yacht. She is apparently still in existence in this guise and was last heard of based in the Mediterranean.

My mother has a number of pictures of the time they spent at Hoo; some have been included as I believe they have a historical interest. Hoo looks so different now, with the yacht harbour where boats can lay afloat behind the sill. Inside and outside the original line of concrete barges are vessels of an amazing diversity; these include ex-light vessels, retired tugs, Dutch inland trading barges and other interesting types.

A photograph of the *May Flower* alongside at Hoo bares closer scrutiny. At the foot or heel of the sprit it should be noted that there are two spider (ring) bands; the lower is the one that connects with the mast collar (muzzle) and appears to float on the upper, which has the stanlift attached. This is a very strange arrangement indeed. The lower spider band has a too large diameter for the dimensions of the sprit heel. My mother recounted that this was, amongst others, one of the reasons for the sprit being renewed, using another barge's (the *Redoubtable*) cast off. The *Redoubtable's* old spars had lain unused since she had been fitted with steel spars, at the time she was rigged as an auxiliary barge.

Often lying at anchor off the marina was the small sailing barge *Dipper*, owned by Jack Elliott. He would often sail away downriver alone, later returning to his mooring on the

A deep-laden *Cambria* captured through the port wang on *May Flower* while sailing in the Thames Estuary during the early 1950s.

mudflats. He and his wife lived ashore. The barge was sold around 1955, being hulked just a few years later. Jack became one of my godparents. On a number of occasions during the late 1950s, Jack with his wife used to sail aboard the *May Flower* crewing with my parents. As time progressed, they moved to the West Country, but remained in contact. He and my mother met up again during the 1990s, spending a day together on the paddle steamer *Kingswear Castle*. The day would coincide with the Medway Barge Match and they would reminisce. I was saddened to hear of his death in 2002, incidentally just a few days before one of the planned trips with Mother.

Along the beach upriver to the west of the marina is Lower Upnor, where a number of barges were also berthed during the early years the *May Flower* spent 'flitting' around. One such barge was the *Dorothea* and she is still alongside the quay, hulked and partially filled in with rubble, in use as a wharf. This is still an active barge area, with the *Victor* being based here for a number of years, then used by the *Alice*, originally a lighter, radically rebuilt and rigged as a conventional spritsail barge. At the time of writing a

The *Dreadnought* participating in a barge match on the River Medway during the 1950s, the other barge is the *Saltcote belle*. Note the differences in their rigs (mast sail configurations). The *Dreadnought* is rigged purely for racing.

small swim head barge called the *Whippet* is berthed here, and the *Victor* was back for a while, laid up — awaiting new owners. The *Whippet*, by the spring of 2006, had been fitted with a modern barge bow and transom stern. She is topsail and bowsprit rigged. Her overall appearance is balanced — she looks functional and as pretty as a picture.

The *Cambria* was often seen, along with a few other barges, still deep laden with cargoes. I asked my mother why they didn't take many photographs of these last days of sailing trade. Strange as it may seem to us now, she said that it didn't occur to them. By the time they realised what was happening, barges had virtually ceased to trade under sail (this was about 1960), apart from the odd barge sailing as an auxiliary and the famous *Cambria* under Bob Roberts, in which he continued until 1970.

During the summer, usually in June, Mother said that they would often see barges getting ready for the rejuvenated barge matches. These were restarted on the River Medway in 1954, following the Coronation Match on the River Thames the previous summer. She said we were not able to take part as they were for trading barges only. The marina had been running a series of matches for yacht and trading barges, for a number of years, since 1948 — these ended.

My eldest brother, having been born in early 1953, was a toddler during the time that my parents were using the marina for these early summers of their ownership. My mother is pretty certain that by the time that I had appeared on the scene in June 1955, they had stopped going into the marina and were instead using the spacious anchorage out on the mudflats to the west of the marina. The winter of 1954/55 was the last time that they used a berth on the inside. My mother does not know the reason for this; she said that my father always had a good relationship with the marina operators. I expect it to be purely for reasons associated with freedom of movement, independence and, probably, cost! The marina was soon to become well used by smaller vessels and this would have been reason enough! However, they did on occasions use an outside berth.

On the mudflats between the marina west wall and the remains of an old fort lay the hulk of a trading topsail schooner which rests close up to the base of the beach. She was the *Rhoda Mary*. The vessel was burnt virtually down to her waterline many years ago; sometime after this, my father 'rescued' one of her anchors. This was used as a mooring anchor for the *May Flower* at Whitewall Creek and was later transported to Twinney Dock and then on to Callows Wharf, both in Upchurch, Kent. At Callows it was dug into the mudflats as the securing point for one of our two holding-off moorings. It will in all probability still be in use for the lighter that currently uses this berth.

Many other places were visited during the summer periods of these early years, often with a return to Hoo before eventually heading back to Whitewall Creek for the winter. Mother said that they did in fact spend the whole of the winter of 1952 at Hoo.

chapter five

Maldon, Benfleet, St Katharine Docks and Other Places

From information I have been able to glean from Father's notebook of his running costs, I deduced that they sailed the barge to Maldon in the summer of 1952. My mother had recounted that they did in fact take the barge up into Maldon on occasions during the 1950s but could not remember when. I found some entries that jogged her memory.

My mother recounted that they were able to sail right up to the Hythe and berthed under sail. Father's notebook has a cost for towage at Maldon; I have presumed without any other detail that this was following an incident that occurred. During the time they spent alongside the Hythe, the *Henry* was moored outboard of the *May Flower* and one of her mooring warps went under the *May Flower*'s rudder, causing it to be virtually cut in two! This occurred when the *Henry* slid out on the slurry as the tide ebbed.

The barge had to go onto the blocks at Cook's Barge Yard where repairs were carried out. The bottom of the rudder had a strake of timber fitted on each side, through-bolted to reinstate its longitudinal strength; whether or not the long tie bolts were renewed my mother cannot remember, but a new dump must have been driven, as no additional straps were fitted. The repairs proved effective for many more years of sailing. The strakes can be seen in some later photographs.

This repair was the last carried out on the *May Flower* under the care of Walter Cook. My father wrote to Clifford Cook, Walter's son, in the autumn of 1953 after learning of Walter Cook's death. Walter Cook had had care of the *May Flower* over a great number of years while the barge was owned by Green Brothers. Green Brothers themselves wrote to Clifford Cook expressing their sympathy and thanks for the long association they had enjoyed through work carried out to barges they had owned. Other barge owners such as Shrubsall of Greenwich, Josh Francis of Colchester, Sulley of London, Rankins of Rochford and Sadds of Maldon expressed their sympathy. The waterfront at Maldon had lost a gentleman and ambassador for the district.

Some time ago I watched barges coming into the Hythe after a barge match. Most do so under power, which is in many respects a sensible and seaman-like way, but to see it done under sail is a sight to behold. I was lucky to see the *Mirosa* arrive in this way; she, like the *May Flower*, has not been fitted with an engine. Another barge, the *Edme*, not having an engine, has to sail just about everywhere too.

May Flower's rudder after a mooring line from the *Henry* had gone under it! Note the shackle to which the mizzen sheet attaches; this was designed and fitted by father.

The *Mirosa* came up towards the Hythe with the flood tide with a generally easterly breeze behind her, shedding sail as she approached. Just off the Hythe, she rounded up and touched the anchor down; the mainsail was by this time brailed up. The bow came up against the mud edge opposite the Hythe; with the tide under the stern she swung easily, then paid off on the other tack, hoisting the anchor 'up and down'. She came sweetly across to the Hythe to berth alongside another barge. A pure delight! It was this method that was often employed when returning to our berth in Whitewall Creek. A later chapter shows the barge heading in, just before touching the hook down and letting the way and breeze swing the barge into her berth.

In 1954 the barge was berthed at Benfleet, for a period of time, just below the bridge crossing onto Canvey Island. The wharf was located on the Benfleet shore, more or less where the tidal barrier now crosses the creek above the Dauntless Boatyard located on the Canvey side. The creek from Hadleigh Ray in those days had a deeply dished and wider channel. The boatyard was relocated east of the barrier when it was built. My mother recently recounted to me that the voyages were accomplished entirely under sail. On the voyage up to Benfleet, the wind was in the easterly quarter, and the more normal conditions prevailed for the return, with winds from the westerly quarter giving them fair weather sailing; she told me this with much pleasure.

In those days, the old bridge still allowed passage of waterborne traffic – unlike today where authorities appear to do their best to ignore maritime elements in favour of permanently fixed structures! The railway was still in the age of steam: no overhead cables straddled the tracks sitting below the hills of Benfleet Downs. The Dauntless Yard looked very different too, the creek was virtually clear of moorings except for those on the Canvey shore. Another barge later used a berth on part of what is now the site of the Benfleet Yacht Club, along the Canvey shore below the bridge; this was the *Maid of Connaught*. My parents became quite good friends with the old boy who ran the little moorings situated just above the bridge, on the site of the old ferry. It was here that the Ardley family used to lay up their yachts during the winter months, over a number of years.

A view of the *May Flower* berthed below the old bridge onto Canvey Island. Note the strake at the foot of the rudder – part of the 1952 repair carried out by Cook's Yard.

Many years later we came up to this spot in the barge boat, while we were moored off Leigh, during a summer in the early 1960s. The first and original bridge was still in operation, and the Dauntless Yard was immediately to the east of the bridge, on the site of the present tidal barrier. My parents, returning from visiting the *Maid of Connaught*, rescued a couple of lads who had been playing in a dinghy. They had been swept down to the bridge and were pinned by the fast-flowing ebb tide against a buttress and were hollering loudly for help! We, the children, had been left to look after ourselves and eat ice creams, which, as I remember, could be obtained from the hut of the boat yard. Unfortunately, a bee was attracted to my sister's ice cream, which resulted her being stung on the lip – oh what a to-do!

St Katharine Docks were badly bomb damaged during the Second World War but had been re-opened for some commercial traffic; this, however, was quite light, so berths were available and a number of yacht barges and other vessels used the facility during the early 1950s. My parents sailed the *May Flower* up the River Thames to this dock and kept her there for some weeks during the summer of 1955. From this berth, Father had a very short journey into his architect's office for work.

The barge was warped into the lock entrance and through the lock the photograph shows my mother forward. Note the light line to the dock wall and the bridge; the barge was warped in, using the dolly and crab winch drums. The *May Flower* relied upon the wind, tide and sweeps for all her sailing days, with exceptions as talked about through these reminiscences. We occasionally accepted a tow from a friendly coasting barge – these were usually one of Lapthorn's 'Hoo' vessels.

A strange encounter took place in Charlestown in Cornwall a few years back. My wife and I were looking over the harbour, enjoying a glass of beer, when we got talking to a chap about something or other. He seemed to be part of the tall ship organisation that runs the vessels based in this old China Clay dock. As usual it came out what my background was, and to my absolute surprise it turned out that many years earlier he had been the mate of one of the Lapthorn's coasters when they had plucked the *May*

The *May Flower* seen sailing up the River Thames; she is opposite Union Wharf and was photographed by a young Barry Pearce from the *Pretoria* during the summer of 1955. (Photograph from the Barry T. Pearce collection)

The *May Flower* in the entrance to Saint Katharine Dock. Note that the starboard mainmast back stay is still slackened off. The mainsheet still trails back to the main horse, and the foresail is still on deck where it had been rapidly dropped on the way in.

Flower into the entrance of the Medway, probably casting us off by Stangate to fetch up. He said that on another occasion he remembered that the *May Flower* had been towed right up to a position off the Hoo flats, where we were able to make our way over the flats to drop anchor.

My mother recalls that some of the trade coming into St Katharine Docks basin was sugar from Barbados. She said that the dust from this was brown and it got exceedingly sticky with the morning dew; it ended up all over the decks and was traipsed down below onto the polished ceiling! She also recounted that the lock gates did not hold very well – they found this out, rather than being told! On returning from visiting the shops on the first day, they found that the barge was a very long way down. She said that a friendly dockworker loaned them a long ladder for the duration. It was up this ladder that my elder brother, at the tender age of two and three quarters, made a break for freedom!

Barry Pearce of Maldon recounted seeing the *May Flower* during that summer, having taken some photographs of her making progress up the river. Barry was then a lad of about fifteen; he was aboard the *Pretoria*, which was at that time owned by a gentleman in the navy. The barge was berthed at Union Wharf, Greenwich. My mother was particularly delighted to learn of these photographs and others, and for Barry's kindness in allowing my use of the material.

Strangely enough, after many years of stagnation, St Katharine Docks was given a new lease of life by a hotel developer and is now a site of interest as a marina where often a large collection of barges can be found, especially in the winter months. Some of these, although rigged, spend much of their time as static function suites! This is sad in many respects as a barge, like any old vessel, needs to be used in its proper manner to survive properly; lack of use tends to let rot in the door without notice! When in London, I usually make my way into these parts to take a look at what barges are in the basin.

During the passage from St Katharine Docks, Mother said that they tacked away downriver in company with one or two trading barges, swapping tacks with one of them. The barge was one of the last 'ironpots' still trading under sail, and this sight would soon became a memory only. The trip, incidentally, was my first long voyage, at the tender age of two months!

Other places where the barge spent time during the summer would have included Leigh or the Chalkwell foreshore, where they paid respects to respective parents, and visited their Leigh-on-Sea Sailing Club friends. The latter was a regular feature for a few years later on.

Another area in Kent where rigged barges were maintained in sail was Conyer. This little hamlet with its narrow creek had a similar history to Whitewall Creek, in that it had been a hive of industrial activity in cement and brick making. The cement works have long gone and the brickworks had ceased production by 1968. Like Whitewall, barges were built there too, though the Conyer yards were much more productive by far, and turned out some famous craft, such as the *Sara* and the *Westmoreland*.

During the inter-war years, yacht barges started to gather at Conyer for domestic berthing, including the *Waveney*. She had left by the mid-1950s and ended her days, soon after, hulked at Emsworth in Hampshire. Those kept sailing would employ barge

A trading barge, sailing light, is seen on the River Thames during 1955. She and the *May Flower* are swapping tacks on passage downriver. The barge is an 'Ironpot' and is thought to be the *Portlight*.

skippers for summer cruising, something my father, apart from his first sail, did not acquiesce to. By the early 1950s, a veritable fleet had built up, including for a short time, the lovely *Saltcote Belle*, and the *John & Mary*. The *Gold Belt* had also arrived and stayed, but the days of seeing spritsail barges sailing from Conyer Creek were numbered. Arthur Bennett had kept his little barge *June* here when she was laid up during the Second World War. The *Henry & Jabez* had finished her sailing days here by the end of the 1950s. Both the *June* and the *Henry & Jabez* ended their lives here, hulked, and eventually land has been filled over them.

In recent years, the *Mermaid* fell derelict and was cleared out of the dock. On a visit during 2006 I saw the *Persevere* being broken up by her owner after being unable to get insurance cover to move her. Now the only old sailorman left is the *Gold Belt*, her mainmast was still standing with slack stays and she sits with a large deckhouse covering her main hatch, probably awaiting her final hour. My father did not sail to Conyer with the *May Flower*, but I do remember a visit to Conyer by road during the late 1960s and seeing a line of barges, with mainmasts standing, running down the dock. In adulthood, I have often visited since, sailing up the creek on my own little wooden sloop.

During the autumn of 2004, I took my mother to visit Barry Pearce in Maldon. These two had not met since a few days before Christmas 1964, just prior to the *May Flower*'s departure from that port, after having some work carried out. Much reminiscing took place. During one of the conversations, they talked about old barge anchorages. My mother recounted to Barry that during the early 1950s, on a Friday or Saturday evening, they would 'bring up' in Chatham bight, just below the old naval church that sits on a bluff, above the river's edge at this point. She said that on a number of occasions their presence was investigated by HM Customs and Excise – they believing that the *May Flower* was inbound from some port or other! After a while the authorities got used to seeing the barge in this spot. Of course, many motorised barges, auxiliaries and a few sailormen used this port and outwardly the *May Flower* did not look much different from a trading barge.

chapter six

Whitewall Creek
1951 to 1966

In 1951 the *May Flower* had found a permanent berth in Whitewall Creek; she was based here until the summer of 1966. The area was owned by APCM (Associated Portland Cement Manufacturers) who still had works on the land, and chalk pits around Frindsbury.

Whitewall Creek had a very active industrial period during the Victorian and Edwardian eras. Subsequently it turned into a sleepy backwater of the parish of Frindsbury, becoming a depository for various worked-out vessels, mainly spritsail barges.

For a relatively short period of time during the nineteenth century bricks were manufactured within the bounds of the parish, two works being located in Whitewall Creek and three on Manor Farm situated on rising ground to the north-west of the creek. The greater majority of these bricks were destined for the huge housing expansions that were then taking place in London; these would have been shipped out in spritsail barges, many of which were built locally at yards within the parish. These included Currels upper and lower yards, which were later owned by Gill, then London & Rochester Trading Co. (later Crescent Shipping), William Burgess Little at Upnor, then by James Little. Around 1900, the latter was forced to move by the Admiralty, they having requisitioned his site, to a yard located above Rochester bridge, on a site that later became Shorts Yard. By the 1880s the local brickworks were closing because the available brick earth had been worked out.

Cement manufacturing then spread to the area, making use of the huge deposits of chalk that was close to the surface and the availability of mud for which extraction licences were also approved; this was dug from marshland around Whitewall Creek, helping to create the basin it was to become. Local mud had also been used in the brick-making industry.

Several cement works were eventually established on marshland opposite Chatham along Limehouse Reach; of these, the Crown works continued into the early 1960s. Two other works were located within Whitewall Creek, one had been started as early as 1858 by a Faversham company, another works was opened by Charles and James Formby during the 1870s, who also went on to own their own fleet of barges. A barge repair yard existed at Whitewall Creek during this time to expedite repairs that were often needed. During rationalisation of the cement industry into a single local company with the formation of Associated Portland Cement in 1901, many of the sites were closed. The Formby works stayed out of these mergers and continued production until 1911, only closing when it became more and more costly to remove an overlying layer of Thanet Sand from the chalk of Tower Hill, on the northern side of the creek.

The creek then remained clear of industrial development until the late 1960s when marsh reclamation created the Medway City Industrial Estate. Prior to this, it continued as a depository for worn out sailormen and various other vessels. The inner areas, however, remained generally free of hulks and, after the Second World War, yacht barges started to appear on the scene.

May Flower's first berth in the creek was virtually an anchorage and almost alongside the *Emma* of Rochester (1899). The Stubbs family owned her at that time, but she had moved away by the late 1950s. By this time the barge was berthed properly alongside the bank with holding-off posts. In about 1960 Father built a set of blocks to put the barge on for bottom maintenance; we then berthed outboard of these.

The Whitewall Creek berth gave superb access to the River Medway, with its wide expanse of mudflats; this gave manoeuvring room for getting on and off the berth under sail. Depending upon the prevailing conditions, it was sometimes necessary for the kedge to be taken out to haul the barge off, to give more room to manoeuvre. About entering Whitewall Creek, my mother said that when the wind was in the wrong direction, it meant having to tack in as far as possible, and then kedge up to the mooring! Going out generally did not prove to be such a problem, due to the direction of the prevailing winds. My parents got the barge away from the moorings, to a position in which they could set

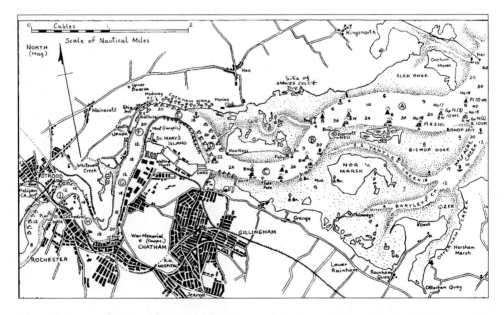

Chart of the upper reaches of the River Medway up to Rochester. (Original by Jack H. Coote and reproduced with courtesy of *Yachting Monthly*)

sail, on numerous occasions using the kedge, and my older brother used to go off in the barge boat with Mother, to lay it, when he was big enough. In later years, Father bought a large Seagull outboard engine; with this flat out, with the barge boat lashed alongside, it gave enough movement to give steerage way to either clear the berth, or get back on.

During the floods that took place at the end of January 1953, my mother recounted that although it had been very windy with north-westerly gales for a period of time leading up to that fateful night, they went to bed unperturbed by the conditions. It was not until the morning that they realised what they had slept through.

She said:

We were at our Whitewall Creek berth for the winter. I do remember it being particularly windy, of which to the day we left the barge, I always was fearful. We were by this time well used to the noises created by the wind moaning and singing through the rigging. But that night the noise was even more intense, with waves slopping against the sides and under the stern. In the morning we woke up to look out upon a scene of utter devastation, with flotsam of all description littering what had been dry land. The low areas to the north of the creek were flooded by the height of the tide. The seawall was breached over on this side of the creek, by the sewage works, the water gushed and roared out through the gap after the tide finally ebbed, the noise was quite distinct.

My eldest brother was just ten days old, and the two of them can have only just escaped from the hospital to be at home on the barge!

I arrived on the scene during the summer of 1955. This period at Whitewall Creek proved to be the *May Flower's* halcyon days in the Ardley family ownership. She was used regularly, often going out on a Friday evening and returning on the Sunday tide. My early memories recall Father arriving home and within a short period of time we would be fetching out of Whitewall Creek, out into the River Medway to drop down stream with the ebb. There were, for a great many years, a long line of rusting grey-painted vessels of various hull types, from old tankers with the old-fashioned low side or well decks, to warships which lay to fore and aft moorings bordering the dockyard. The river provided a feast of interesting things and goings on to keep us youngsters enthralled.

Sailing was not just limited to the summer. Good conditions allowed the sailing home to sail the year round! The rest of the family arrived; my sister in 1956, then another brother in 1961. In time, we all learnt the skills needed to live on and keep a barge alive and sailing. I detail some of these skills, of which I have probably forgotten more than can be remembered, later. A recent sail on the *Centaur*, owned by the Thames Sailing Barge Trust in 2003 brought back to the surface long-displaced skills and knowledge that had lain asleep in my memory banks: this was strangely unnerving!

We learned firstly by watching, and then were taught so many things. If it was the wrong thing, a shout from aft would correct our attentions. We learnt how to haul on ropes to brail the mainsail and mizzen, probably tailing Mother or Father initially. Two of us would be detailed off to hoist the foresail or staysail, getting help towards the nearly up positions; we heaved and sweated in the sheets. We'd watched how the barge was

View from over the *Violet*'s rudder top and steering gear, *c.*1955. Lowering the gear for maintenance was a regular feature of life, my mother out on the sprit end having just bent on the mainsail peak. Note the vessel in the background – she is the steamer *Royal Eagle*. She was later towed away to be broken up.

tacked from our usual aft positions, until eventually, one by one, we got specific areas to tend. My older brother was foredeck hand, often dealing with the foresail bowline.

We learnt how to deal with the topmast backstays, in particular during tacking, when the 'new' windward side needed to be tightened and the leeward slacked away. My parents were proud that, between 1950 and 1974, not a single spar was broken while sailing. I still have a small scar from being in the way of a backstay block. My parents did break a topmast backstay when racing; it parted above the lower eye splice. Fortunately it was while putting it to the lee side; two u-clamps were used to put a temporary eye in the end of the stay. The back stay tackle was re-attached by the time they needed to tack again!

We learnt the art of raising and lowering leeboards using the crab winches on the aft quarterdecks. This for many years was to be my domain, as well as the mainsheet (with Father) and the vangs or wangs, depending upon geographical location. At about the age of eight, I was helping Father aft with the leeboards and vangs. I was asked to ease away the port vang – I unfortunately took one turn too many off the cleat and it ran through my hands. I did not let go until Father shouted to me 'Let it go.' I learnt a lesson and got rope burns! My older brother on one occasion got a crack over the head with a winch handle – it was a rough, hard place to grow up, but we came to no real harm.

We learnt the importance of mousing the hook of the mainsheet traveller block. For those that do not know a lot about barges, these blocks made from wood are about the size of a household bucket. They have two large-diameter sheaves, and an iron band fitted around with a pair of 30mm-diameter pins coming out from both sides of about 180mm length and an ugly curved hook, with an arrowhead-like end. The sheet was sweated in and made off round the pins and locked off, with a single locking turn. During tacking of the barge, the block and traveller would be thrashed back and forth on the horse, by the sail, until with a thud it smacked into one or other of the large bits, which supported the horse as the sail became full on the new tack. It was not wise to get in the way; at times some control was needed by keeping hold of the loose sheet tail and controlling its flicks back and forth! My parents' experience during their first passage in the barge instilled in them the dangers posed by this tamed beast; they in turn duly taught us well.

Scraping, sanding, painting, varnishing and tarring were spring and summer pastimes. Caulking was another feature. This involved raking out a seam, ensuring it was dry before spinning out the oakum from its huge (it seemed) roll, rolling it across the knees, pulling and teasing gently to get the required denseness and thickness. The oakum was then knocked into the seams with caulking irons; of these I seem to remember that we had three sizes. Then we had to run hot bitumen into the remaining fillet to finish off the seam. The bitumen was broken off in lumps from a huge slab stowed in the fo'c'sle to starboard. This was heated up in a big pot on top of a Primus stove. The final job was to prime any bare areas and build up the paint coats to complete the job.

The brail cleats were moved lower down the shrouds to enable us youngsters to reach them. These were paired to the same side of the rigging, and were specifically named. The *May Flower* was fitted with an additional brail, a peak to take out the bag of sail that is often seen on windy days on a stowed mainsail. I have noted when looking at barges today that many of these, especially the larger ones, are fitted with a peak brail – others could do with one! The racing barges such as the *Veronica* and *Dreadnought* were rigged with only four brails during their last racing years. A book by D.F. Davis, *The Thames Sailing Barge (Her Gear and Rigging)*, provides an excellent level of detail about this subject and shows various differences between types and similar-sized vessels.

The brails were called the peak, the uppers, which we termed the upper upper and the lower upper, the main brail (wire and operated by the brail winch), the middles and the lowers. When the shout was made for 'Brail the mainsail', we all had our allotted brails to pull. Probably because I was the smaller of us older boys, I always had the main brail, which, as said, is operated by a winch. My eldest brother had the lowers to deal with, which were to the base of the mast. He also did the uppers as the sail was gathered in; these were arranged to port. The peak was dealt with later; this was on the starboard aft mainmast shroud cleat. The foresail halyard was on the port forward shroud, the staysail on the starboard forward shroud and the topsail clew on the starboard middle shroud.

I remember vividly early summertimes when the sails were tanned. The job was fun and oh how messy we all got! The community in the creek gave us help in carrying the sails. The names of these people escape me, but they are remembered! These are just some of the myriad of skills that were learnt, and many more were to be added to our repertoire as we all grew up.

I recently met the son of one of these couples. He was working on barge repairs at Faversham in Kent. My wife and I were moored on our own boat at Iron Bridge Wharf and I noticed that *Decima*, a barge built of steel, had been given new hard chines in place of

My eldest brother, in 1963, is able to work the foresail bowline. The forward end became my
brother's specialist position over the years. Note the shaping of the foot of the mainmast; the mast
came out of a large coasting barge. Note also the arrangements at the heel of the sprit. Compare
this with the photograph of the barge at Hoo. The topsail hoist is made off on the mast case winch
barrels in 'figure of eight' turns, and coiled down on the deck ready to run free, for immediate
lowering. The mainsail foot tackle can be seen. The sprit yard tackle can also be seen close to the
mast. *May Flower* was also fitted with a sprit head wire and tackle, which came down to the deck via
the mainsail muzzle.

the original rounded ones fitted when built, which were typical of her type. I commented
to a gentleman that her run aft now looked very much like that of the *Mirosa*. My wife
mentioned that I had a habit of commenting and asking questions about barges, because
of my childhood experiences. It turned out that this chap's parents had sailed on the *May
Flower* during the 1961/63 Barge Matches. It's always amazing to be reminded that we all
live in such a small global village!

As we grew up we made friends with other children locally. Some were a little older
than we were, but a couple of other families were of a similar age and over the years
remained in sporadic contact, in the main via our parents meeting up much later in

Three of us at the oars in 1959.

their lives. Mother is still in communication with the then owners of the *Falconet* and the pilot cutter *Mascotte*.

We did a lot of messing in dinghies, sailing and rowing. My eldest brother, from an early age, became quite accomplished at sculling in the barge boat – almost needing a box to stand on. I enjoyed pottering in a dinghy, going round looking at the numerous hulks. I still do a lot of pottering in a sailing tender I tow behind our Finesse 24 *Whimbrel*; my wife is certain that I still haven't actually grown up – she may be right!

I came across a photograph taken by Mother of the three of us rowing – this made me chuckle; it is before the youngest was born. I noted that we were not wearing buoyancy aids, which were not as available then as they are now. We had Kapok buoyancy jackets, and their usefulness compared to today's offerings was low. The choice now, and quite rightly so, is both colourful and eminently wearable! Our four-oared action event took place in about 1960, judging from the age of my sister!

We went on extended country walks, or I should more truthfully say, we were allowed a freedom probably not experienced and enjoyed by many youngsters of today, to go off and explore. We roamed the local woods, chalk cliffs, fields and marshes. We lit bonfires, cooking baked potatoes in the embers and played Cowboys and Indians. We of course had been introduced to, and read, the classic books about the Swallows and Amazons by Arthur Ransome. This was no tale for us — we had it all in real life, around us, happening daily!

To the north of the creek lay high ground with a cliff. In this were caves. They used to provide us kids with a bolthole to while away hot, sunny summer days. I rather think that they were supposed to be out of bounds to us, but hey, that's what kids do! The cliffs were part of the high ground below Tower Hill, which is within the bounds of the Ministry of Defence land used by the Military Engineering School. The cliffs were a remnant from the digging of chalk for the cement industry.

A lot of abandoned buildings had been demolished over this side and it was, looking back, a rather dangerous playground to mess around in. I wrecked a tricycle doing free wheel runs down into this immense pit full of loose rubble and concrete. An area at the end of the seawall, where it ran into higher ground, was covered in brambles and in the late summer we were sent to harvest the abundant juicy blackberries by Mother, who then made pots and pots of luscious jam.

A long line of hulks existed on the north bank alongside the sea wall, the other side of which was the local sewage treatment works. These works are now to the north of the new Medway Tunnel road system, which would indicate that the new road runs thereabouts over the top of these craft! Some of the names I recall are the *Bedford*, *Squark* and *East Anglia*. There were many others, some more intact, others were just a few recognisable timbers. The *Berwick* was stripped out and hulked during the early 1950s.

Also on this north side of the creek lay a house barge, *The Brownie* of Colchester. She came into the creek in about 1960; she lay more or less on the site of Frindsbury Parish Wharf. Close by was a converted wooden lighter, the *Sarah*, on which our friends the McCrumb children lived. My mother is still in touch with the youngest, both living in the same village of Lower Halstow. They had arrived in about 1961 to convert the lighter to a home and, for a time, they lay opposite us on the site of a wharf operated by a scrap and breaking firm.

On top of the hills to the west lay Frindsbury with its landmark, All Saints church, and it was here during my first year of life that the Canon of Rochester christened me. In fact we all were dunked in this church. It sits looking down on the River Medway at the bottom of Parsonage Lane, leading down from the village. The road turns sharply at the edge of what were fields, but are now the edge of chalk excavations, and becomes the road to Upnor. This is now bisected by a new road into the Medway City Industrial Estate. Whitewall Lane came down to a patch of mixed woodland trees and scrub, with a line of poplars running from the east by the sewage works, which are now enlarged. Many years earlier a cottage used to be located at the foot of this lane, and would have been the access to the Parish Wharf. Our access lane then ran through a small patch of woodland before emerging to open ground, upon which an area was maintained as a garden large enough for laying out sails for tanning – its most important feature.

Many years later I returned to this spot, now to the west of the new Medway Tunnel road, and found the remains of *The Brownie*, just prior to her disappearance during further land reclamation for the industrial estate. My young son climbed up and walked about on what remained of her aft decks, treading where I'm sure I had, many years before.

My mother tells me that as a child I visited all the wrecks in the creek and over a period of time made a list of them. Alas, with the passing of the years this has been lost. I suspect that it is doubtful if any complete record exists of all the vessels that were to be dumped here to end their days. We investigated all these old hulks, various types rested peacefully in the mud, their last berths, slowly rotting away. Hatch coamings and decks would eventually collapse, then the sides would fall away leaving a sagging mass of timber, which would in time slowly merge into the environment.

The demise of a hulked wooden vessel often takes many years to complete. Most of our coastal estuaries contain more than a few – remnants from a different, less sophisticated age. The hull can appear to be intact, and then a point is reached when in a very short time very little is left, except for perhaps a stem, stern post and a rudder – if left shipped when hulked. These continue to stand proudly, with a few structural timbers attached or sticking out of the mud. In my young eyes they seemed to last forever.

Barges dumped on mudflats to be covered by most tides disintegrate fairly quickly, often leaving vicious bits of ironwork poking above the general morass for quite a few more years. Some sink beneath the mud, or in some cases become part of the natural regeneration of the marshes, with decks at marsh level, remaining structurally intact. It was later in my life, whilst sailing on my Finesse 24 *Whimbrel* looking at old barge hulks, that I could fully comprehend what I had witnessed when younger; the slow, then rather more rapid nature of this lingering death that a once handsome useful vessel suffers. The hulk of the *Surrey* at Lower Halstow is a typical case: after about fifty years she still had the obvious look of a barge hull, but she has recently gone to pieces leaving her stem, stern post and part of her midsections standing.

During the middle years of the 1950s, the *Gladys* of Dover was berthed near to the *May Flower*, she was owned by a young man who fitted her out for sailing. This barge had two propellers, however I do not know if both were retained following her conversion. She was very soon after, in 1960, wrecked on the Grain sands. She was hulked in Shepherds Creek which runs west from the Swale, forming Deadman's Island. This island lies between Queenborough and Stangate Creek; her hull remained intact for a considerable length of time. Deadman's Island is so named due to it being used during the Napoleonic Wars as a burial site for deceased prisoners, who were kept on old warship hulks moored off the island.

Over a great number of years I have watched her slow disintegration. During the late 1990s, her port bow planking had started to drop away from the stem. Her rails at the time of writing are still visibly white from the last coat of paint that they had received! Deterioration since has been rapid as fastenings at last corrode and fail. By 2003, her port, bow had dropped away completely and her stern areas were disintegrating.

Virtually every year, when I pass this way, I cast a look at the *Gladys* and wonder if perhaps she was hulked before her time! I do not know the full extent of the damage she received, but I expect all her seams were popped when beached. From time to time she did float around in a restricted area, for a number of years, on high tides during the 1960s, until a hole was cut in her port bow.

Later that decade, when berthed elsewhere, I led a raiding party to this barge. I had been renewing some cleats on the *May Flower*. Knowing that many still existed on the *Gladys*, I was given permission to see what was available, armed with cold chisels, levers and a hacksaw! I expect this was in fact strictly illegal, but hey, I was only recycling good solid hardware and did not harm the environment in any way.

Much excitement would buzz through us children when a new barge hull arrived in the creek. I remember being severely scolded by a neighbour when we were found poking around one of these barges. She was, I believe, the *East Anglia*, which arrived in the creek about 1963. In some cases vessels arrived for lay up, most stayed and eventually become hulks.

Continuing with my picture of the creek; it had two shallow forks with an isthmus of land in the centre, this also being at the foot of the lane. In the middle area, the site of an old wharf, a salvage firm was operated by a character known as 'Duchy' Day. The land here contained the detritus of brick making; cinders, broken pottery, molten glass bottles and the remains of overcooked bricks. Many steel barges arrived here for breaking up; the names of those I saw, I do not recall.

Alongside the opposite shore to our berth, which would be the southern side of the isthmus, lay the rotting remains of a barge to which Father ran one of our moorings. Further up lay the *Falconet*, which gradually lost her sailing gear; she can be seen in a photograph looking up this southern fork. For many years she could still set a topsail and foresail, but I do not ever recall seeing her under sail, although before coming into the creek, when berthed on the Thames, she was sailed. Mother still meets the then owners on occasions. At one time, there were four sailing barges in this southern part of the creek.

May Flower's berth was on the southern side of the creek, with an open aspect to the east. At an inner berth lay the *Violet* of Maldon and further in, for a time, another barge, the *Magnet*. Later the *Henry* of London spent some time in this inner berth. When she departed, a concrete lighter fitted out as a houseboat came. This for some years had been berthed on the beach adjacent to the Medway Yacht Club, where remnants of her berth can still be seen immediately below the club slipway. She was replaced or joined by the *Mayor*, which had come out of the motor barge trade in about 1964.

The Bennett family had sold the *Henry* in December 1959 to Mr Hugh St Denis King-Fallow and his wife; they had kept her at Puddle Dock near to the Mermaid Theatre in London. In the autumn of 1962 the *Henry* came into the creek, where she lay until sold to the Young family in the spring of 1963, and so began a fairly lengthy relationship with both the *Henry* and the Young family.

Below us was the Bristol Channel pilot cutter *Mascotte*, beyond which a sprawl of hulked barges lay around the edge of the marshes. A few of these my father had

May Flower sailing into her berth in Whitewall Creek during 1957. The foresail has just been dropped and the mainsail taken in to the sprit; the way will carry her to the berth. The anchor has been lowered to the water, ready to drop up and down, to swing the barge into position.

purchased the right to remove any useful fittings from. My brother and I helped on more than one occasion to remove some sections of iron banding that is fitted along the outside face of the covering board, to replace some sections on the *May Flower*. A length of this was used years later in some work I completed. Any other bits that were useful and needed were recycled from these vessels.

Another arrival to join these hulks was, I believe, the *Squark*. She arrived during the early 1960s, or at least in that period when we were able to go off exploring beyond previous set limits. She still had fairly recently painted decks and rails; the holds were open and decay was setting in. Evidence of her accommodation was still visible – it didn't occur to me at the time that this was once somebody's home! But oh, what a playground they were whilst still in their partially floating condition.

Beyond this area all the way to the River Medway lay a maze of creeks and rivulets that ran southwards with their associated marsh systems – this was another one of our playgrounds. I did not know then that this area, too, had been largely created by man, digging mud for bricks and cement. My eldest brother used to go walking out to the River Medway bank and this caused my mother a little anxiety on more than one occasion – the price of freedom.

There used to be a beach on the river edge opposite the small dry docks where the Historic Naval Collection is now ensconced in Chatham Maritime Museum. On some quiet summer days, we were sometimes taken to this beach in the barge boat with my mother's old dinghy *Little Willie*. Here we would sail, swim and have a picnic. Later, in about 1963, we obtained a brand new Mirror dinghy, sail number 959. This was also used on these jaunts; she gave us modern sailing! I later had the Mirror dinghy from my parents and sailed it from my Yacht Club based in Smallgains Creek on Canvey Island. I also taught my wife to sail in this Mirror and it was a sad day when we eventually, due to too much rot, put it on a bonfire in about 1986.

The beach and marshes are all gone now in the frightening push during the 1960s through to the 1980s to remove the last wilderness areas from the middle of this cosmopolitan conurbation. A ballast quay, receiving thousands of tons of sea-dredged sands and shingles weekly, is now situated in this very spot. Whenever I sail past in my boat, I recall those sunny summer days on the now destroyed beach.

The whole of the western side of Chatham Reach has now been reclaimed and covered in concrete and industrial units with wharves along the river edge. Right on the very tip of Chatham Ness is a small area of original marsh, a lonely little oasis – a sad sight, knowing what has been lost for ever. What a pity our urban planners did not consider the beauty of these marshes, retaining some as a fringe to a riverside park, to provide a home for species such as dunlin, turnstones, curlews, oystercatchers and various other wading birds. Even the little egret, that has in recent times colonised the marshes alongside urban area, such as Canvey Island, could have found a home, but alas!

Round the corner of Chatham Ness was a cement factory, the Crown works. This area was firmly out of bounds to us. However, in our later years at Whitewall Creek, after cement manufacturing operations ceased after 1963, it became part of our playground. When my mother found out that we went exploring to these buildings, the law was very firmly laid down about it being an area strictly out of bounds. It was reached by passing over open rough grassland then through scrub woodland, behind which a railway ran to the chalk pits between Frindsbury village and Manor Farm. Also at the back of these woods was a low cliff, which we would often climb down. Some of our gang very nearly came to grief during one of these forays; my sister and another girl slipped and were only saved by scrub that halted their falls.

During the late 1950s, the Ministry of Defence gained the use of the land on the north side of the creek. They bulldozed the remains of some buildings that went back to the cement works' days. In doing so, the source of fresh water that was used by mooring holders was threatened and disturbed. My father set up an action group together with other residents, to try and sort out the problems that were taking place with the water supplies. The creek itself did not have its own piped supply. Water was obtained from an artesian well, from customary usage, not by right. This did not fit into the way of the post-1940s military system, and entry was forbidden. The community continued to obtain water because it was the only source available. Due to damage done to the well it now needed to be pumped, it being previously 'free flowing'.

My mother has a copy of a Medway Water Board drawing showing the arrangements planned for alternative supplies dated April 1958. This was going to be a standpipe at the top of Whitewall Lane fed from a new pipe laid from near the Parsonage, in Parsonage Lane. The supplies that fed the farm at the top of the lane and the Manor House, which was undergoing renovation at this time, did not have sufficient-sized mains to provide

Barges berthed in Whitewall Creek during the late 1950s. *May Flower, Violet, Magnet* and *Falconet*. This photograph, taken during 1958 when the stem was being renewed. Note the derrick forward.

additional supplies. As far as I am aware, this proposal was not acted upon. Eventually, an agreement was drawn up with the Army Department (Secretary of State) allowing the drawing of water, by certain vessels, from the artesian well via a pipe across the surface of War Department land! I wonder if this agreement was ever terminated. The agreement is dated November 1959. The listed vessels are *May Flower, Violet, Falconet, Magnet, Frolic* and *Lochellis* (these last two were not barges). I found these documents very interesting and for me they answered some queries that I had never previously been able to gain full answers to.

As a matter of interest, the free-flowing water from this artesian well came from the Greensands level, deep under Kent, some 300ft down. The water was pure and soft. This same stratum also serves the free-flowing well located at the top of the hard opposite Harty Ferry on the East Swale. A series of chemists laboratory reports from the period have survived; these were taken to ensure the fitness of the water supply.

The *Magnet* had previously been moored in the bight at Chatham, during the late 1940s and early 1950s. This is told in C.W.R. Winter's book *The Run of the Tide*. The shape of her transom conforms to that of a photograph seen in this book. The owner was the father of Tony Winter who became an acquaintance and friend of my parents later in life. The *Magnet* moved upriver to Allington sometime around 1960, and finally to her last berth immediately below Brambletree Wharf where she was broken up. In this rather tranquil spot, her remains were still visible, poking out of the marsh grasses, with the rotting hull of the *Pimlico* lying outside of her, when I visited during the autumn of 2004. Alongside the wharf was the Howard-built *Violet*, which sat inside a lighter, awaiting a rebuild.

Whitewall Creek barely exists now, just an indent of mud fringed with the detritus of land reclamation with a greatly reduced gully. Perhaps a sensible use would have been to complete the destruction and use the remainder for what I personally believe would be more beneficial to the local environment, that is as a marina development. This could allow removal of some of the moorings that now dominate the river down to Gillingham.

Some of the bonfire nights we had were quite stupendous affairs, mainly for the size of the fires. We would spend weeks scouring the shores and woods for flotsam and fallen branches for the building of the fire. On the night before the day, old clothes were used to build our guy, which was ceremoniously placed up on the top before the match was lit! Hot soup and baked potatoes were eaten towards the end as the embers kept us all warm and cosy. On one occasion we had a communal bonfire near where the *Falconet* was berthed. My memories are a little vague on this event, but I do remember lots of paraffin being used to get it to light up, so it must have been a wet autumn.

Years later I learnt that the *Falconet*, after being sold to others, was buried in land reclamation at a marina which is sited below the Medway Bridge, above Rochester. A rebuild had been started but had faltered and died like so many others did in those days. Her transom, a new piece of timber, was removed and spent some time as an exhibit at a museum dedicated to the River Medway. The museum was a joy and was based at the old dockyard church on a delightful tree-covered bluff overlooking Chatham Bight. Unfortunately, the museum was closed down nearly a decade ago.

A magical photograph taken by a friend for Mother, of the barge leaving Whitewall Creek on an evening tide, is I believe a pure delight! 'The reflections of an evening departure' reach out across the calm surface, ahead of her; it is lightly ruffled from the gentle breeze – enough to lift the bob. The barge has a new sprit and my mother's mainsail. Father is at the aft end hauling in the mainsheet and tending the helm. I can see a figure forward – this will be Mother, who is in position to throw off the last gasket from the foresail to drop it 'half set' to the deck, it only needing a last bit of heaving up to have it fully set and drawing nicely. The staysail head can be seen loose forward with a crewmember who is removing the gasket, ready for hoisting it up.

During the late summer or autumn of 1961, a catamaran capsized in the entrance to Whitewall Creek. My parents, with Eric and Shirley from the *Mascotte,* went out to attempt the rescue. They found a young couple in difficulty and brought them back. My mother took charge of the lady and Shirley the man. Hot baths, dry clothes and stimulating beverages were dispensed. From what I can remember, the catamaran was towed in and placed on the beach between our two vessels. The couple, Arthur and June, spent a while sorting out their yacht in this position, to eventually take her away. They, with Eric and Shirley, went racing with us for a couple of seasons.

The winter of 1962 to 1963 was one of the harshest and most severe experienced in the South East of England for a considerable number of years. The barge was frozen into the sea ice and there was snow several feet deep. My mother said that the grinding

The *May Flower* leaving
Whitewall Creek in 1961
– the reflections of an
evening departure.

of the pack against the sides was eerie and a little disturbing; fortunately no damage
was done.

It started to snow on Boxing Day and seemed to go on for weeks. It was so cold
that Whitewall Creek froze over to a depth of about a metre of pack ice and snow. My
mother recounted to me:'Hearing the wind howling in the rigging, the barge although
afloat and only moving slightly in the ice, was quite strange'. My eldest brother actually
walked out to the edge of the River Medway – the tide was out at the time! Huge icicles
hung from the rigging and we used to have to knock or shake them off regularly.

All through this we did not have any time off from school – you didn't – one was
expected to get in. The huge piles of frozen snow dumped by the snowploughs at the top
of our lane did not clear until April. At school, I can remember the milk being brought into
the classroom, to be put close to a radiator to thaw out! We had old-fashioned radiators,
which rattled and banged, and my class also had a coal stove in the lobby, which worked
the radiators! We had to keep our coats on in the classroom; what luxury is experienced by
pupils of today. A photograph was taken of Father out on the ice. It clearly and graphically

My father out
on the ice,
photographed
by my elder
brother.

illustrates the intensity of the winter experienced. It was fascinating and fun, but very, very cold! I can remember Father having to put water tanks in the back of the Land Rover and accessing the well via a track opened up by the Royal Engineers. Getting this much-needed commodity in the usual way by dinghy was out of the question.

In a photograph of my father out on the pack ice and snow, I noticed that the *May Flower* still has her sailing gear up. The other three barges can be seen. On the far right is the *Falconet*, the other in the centre is the *Henry*, her light blue-painted sprit is reflecting the light; astern of the *May Flower* is the *Violet*.

During the autumn of 1963, after returning from Hoo where a new port leeboard had been made, my father dropped the starboard leeboard off; we floated it to the shore and lashed to the underside of the barge boat. When ashore on the beach, it was jacked up onto a platform for renewal of the lower strake, which was cracked. This was the leeboard that had been repaired prior to my father's purchase of the barge in 1950.

In the summer of 1964, we went off to Maldon for repairs following a collision. This is covered in a later chapter about Maldon. After returning from Maldon, my father built his own steam chest. This was a box some 25ft in length and about 2ft by 18in in section. Steam was provided from a boiler made from a 1ft-diameter tube plugged at the lower end. This came down from the box at an angle of about thirty degrees. A brick fireplace enclosed the tube at the lower end – clear of the plug! This allowed my father to carry out much greater levels of maintenance works. In fact, it was needed to complete the work not accomplished at Maldon.

After a refit in the spring of 1965, when apart from the usual gear requirements, Mother replaced a section of the topsail near the leach and the sheet end. We

A family group, taken during early 1964: my sister, mother, younger brother and I. The eldest is heading ashore! Note the leeboard on a platform ahead of the barge boat. The original barge boat is ashore too.

also completed the work not finished at Maldon. Over the Whitsun Holiday, we went sailing and also took part in the Medway Barge Match. Father also fitted a new mizzen sail.

Our time in the creek was soon to come to a close. Getting a large sailing vessel without power round the bend past Saint Mary's Island was being made difficult as yacht moorings were expanding rapidly. Even outside the entrance to Whitewall Creek, moorings were being laid. On one occasion tacking up past the dockyard, watched by a myriad of workmen, standing about, we picked up an orange mooring, it being trapped between the leeboard and the chine – suffice to say, it came with us!

The area round the point of Saint Mary's Island was always kept clear, however, this was changing rapidly, and it was not long before treble rows to the Hoo side and double rows to the dockyard side were laid. This made sailing to and from Whitewall Creek without fair winds increasingly difficult, especially in negotiating the sharp bend at the junction of Upnor and Cockham reaches. Old copies of the famous *East Coast Rivers* pilot show the differences clearly, as time progressed.

Before the advent of moorings on the St Mary's Island side, we were able to go inside the channel buoy. Anyone who knows this stretch of water will appreciate the set of the tide on the ebb, towards the beach under Cockham Woods. This tidal set was to be our undoing on one occasion; it was the last passage we ever made on the barge along this stretch of water, and I recount this later. Since then I have not seen a barge negotiate this bend under sail alone; her engine is always running, engaged or ready for use.

The *May Flower* at our berth in Whitewall Creek during the late spring of 1965, after our return from Maldon. The gear had been down for overhaul; note the bob with a new fly with its four dots. The relatively high peak to her mainsail can be seen clearly in this view – this was a feature of the barge during her life.

My mother clearly remembers all the times that they had to tack up the reach past the Medway Sailing Club in Cockham Reach, and then often having to do the same up into Upnor Reach, due to the wind tending to follow the run of the river. Regarding one of these occasions she said, 'A tramp steamer's crew doffed their hats to us. The Scandinavian crew appreciating our skill in manoeuvring under sail, to glide under their stern as we tacked against a strong head wind. I'm sure they could see the younger crewmembers doing their stuff!' Yes the comment brought back memories to me as well. Up to about 1958/59, my eldest brother was not even old enough to participate, and this sort of manoeuvring was carried out by just the pair of them, with all the children back on the aft cabin top. However, as we got older, we all had our allotted positions and jobs!

By late 1965, a whiff of the proposed development of the area had reached my parents' ears. This, coupled with the already stated manoeuvring problems out in the river, hastened the search for a new berth.

This chapter is brought to a close at this point to detail events that I have considered as separate entities in their own right, but which are an integral part of the time that the *May Flower* was berthed at Whitewall Creek. These chapters deal with such events as my early school days, the domestic arrangements on the barge, renewal of the stem, the making of a mainsail, renewal of the mainmast and sprit, a spring refit, early racing, a new leeboard, summer sailing and a visit to Maldon for repairs. I return to Whitewall Creek at the beginning of chapter seventeen, where I recount moving to a new berth.

chapter seven

Early School Days

My elder brother, my sister and I all went to primary school in Wainscott, which is now a suburb of Frindsbury, by bus. We had to walk along the lane that skirted the woods alongside the creek, or along the path that fringed the creek-side moorings. These met, at the inner end of the isthmus, Whitewall Lane, a flint-based lane, old and rutted, which lay below deep banks beside the tree-fringed fields. This went up to the Lower Upnor road. Another footpath ran down across the fields from the top of the lane, downhill to the northern side of the creek, to the sea wall by the line of poplar trees, south of the sewage works. Its path is now truncated by a new road. Some of the other children, especially those from the *Brownie*, came this way.

The bus stop was at the junction at the top, opposite Manor Farm, where up to twenty of us would meet in the mornings. At Manor Farm is a unique building, a fourteenth-century Kentish tithe barn; this is some 200ft in length and is one of the largest in the country. By the time I had started at school, the Manor House, which had been virtually derelict for a number of years, had been renovated and was once again occupied.

My first day at school is well remembered by my eldest brother. I had (I understand now, but not then!) been told to wait by the front of the school to be escorted home. Well I had other ideas. I knew the way and so set off, full of confidence. On arriving home to an expectant mother and a smile of 'how did it go?', my brother's absence was spotted and I was frogmarched back the way we had been told to take, eventually meeting a disconsolate, tearful and rather frightened brother who was convinced that I was lost! He lives in Canada now and during a recent conversation I was reminded of this incident.

On another occasion, I had been taken to the dentist and duly deposited back at school by Mother. For some reason I had gotten extremely upset – I think that I'd had a tooth removed! The second year infants' teacher looked after me during the lunch break. Looking back I presume that she missed her lunch because of me. I remember being sat upon her lap; she wore a skirt which was short, and this rode up to reveal the tops of her stockings – little did I appreciate such things then! She spent the time drawing pictures on a piece of paper with incredibly bright red lipstick. I can even remember her name. She was quite a honey too – could this be the reason for my later marriage to a schoolteacher?

Feeding swans after school.

After school, if we were lucky and the tide was in, swans would often be seen paddling around the barge. These birds always look well fed, but will never turn down a free meal! There were always a few scraps of bread with which we were allowed to feed them. Later, other waterborne tasks fell to us after school.

In the summer, we would walk back across pastures full of cows. It was here that I used to tease my sister horribly by daring her to tread on cowpats. These were either dry or had a crust which often gave way, causing the mess to envelope her sandals. This dubious activity is still remembered and my sister and I still laugh about it. A stream ran across the fields, to eventually empty itself into the creek near the sewage works; this was a haven of wild flowers and water creatures, and was used by the teachers at my school for nature work.

The meadow grass was always thick and luscious looking; perhaps we had more rain through those years. In this high-tech age, it isn't so difficult to find these things out, but I'd rather keep my memories as they are. Rain is something one does not generally have memories of, as reminiscences tend to home in on hot, sunny days and after-school picnics, which for my siblings and me were a treat. My birthday, being in June, was often celebrated with a tea spread out on the grass! I remember a treasure hunt organised by my mother to coincide with one birthday in 1964. We spent a happy hour or so with various local friends, roaming the periphery of the creek chasing the clues.

We were occasionally caught 'scrumping' (taking without permission!) strawberries in summer. On one occasion, the local farmer picked my sister and me up along the lane between Upnor and Frindsbury, giving us a lift to Whitewall Lane opposite the farm entrance. Saying a sheepish 'thank you', he passed us a couple of punnets to take home to Mother – he wasn't daft. I expect we had red lips and juice stains on our school shirts!

The old road to Upnor from Frindsbury, now bisected by the Medway Tunnel road from the A228 Grain road into Gillingham, was a very quiet, narrow, leafy lane, but was also the road access to the Royal Engineers' base. We often saw Churchill tanks being transported to the Royal Engineers' grounds that were, and still are, on the hills of Upper Upnor. Other fantastically shaped things included those folding bridge units. Many years later I became familiar with these weird contraptions as an Engineer Officer with the Royal Fleet Auxiliary, transporting military hardware to both calm and troubled parts of our world.

I think it was during the period after our youngest brother was born that Mother had to be rushed into hospital with a medical problem. My sister went off to an aunt and uncle, and our youngest brother was taken in by our paternal grandparents, Father's mother having trained as a nurse. My elder brother and I were looked after by neighbours until Father got back home in the evening. In this way we did not miss school! I have vague memories of Mrs Strong on the *Falconet* looking after us, after school, until Father arrived home. How times have changed: a father can now take compassionate leave. In those days in Whitewall Creek we had quite a close-knit community around us, which at times was a great help.

Whilst staying with my maternal grandparents on another occasion during a school holiday, my sister and I had a mishap in their bathroom. Looking back, I think that it is I who should take the blame. We had left a tap running slowly and somehow or other the washbasin plug 'fell' into place, filled and overflowed the sink (which of course shouldn't have happened) to eventually drip through the ceiling into the kitchen before it was discovered. This was all for the sake of a wash and brush-up prior to being taken off to one of our great-aunts for tea!

As time progressed, school trips began to become a feature of the end-of-year ritual. I went to London to visit the Science Museum; a visit to Bodiam Castle is another trip that I particularly remember and others were made locally. In those days when most of us had school lunches, a school trip meant a packed lunch – these contained sandwiches, crisps with the little packet of salt in blue paper, and a bar of chocolate. Drinks were plain squash – this was before the advent of canned drinks and the multitude of choice now available.

A photo call of the family, gathered after a christening during 1961. We had to wear our school uniform – in those days, this was quite normal for formal occasions.

When I was eight, in the second year of junior school, I, with my classmates, started swimming lessons. This meant a trek to Lower Upnor from the school in Wainscott. The school had an arrangement with the Homeless Children's Society that was located in Lower Upnor and based on the *Arethusa*, ex *Peking* – an old nitrates clipper. They had a lovely pool, and it is in fact still in use today. Boys no longer live on the *Arethusa*; she was sold to America and is now based in New York, I believe, fully rigged, but without sails. The home is now for both boys and girls, based on a collection of small hostel units ashore. In the summer months all children participate in the outward-bound-type curriculum.

On the way to the swimming baths, we would look at a number of house barges which lay in the bight opposite the Ship public house. The moorings were from the boatyard wharf up to beyond where the hulk of the *Dorothea* still rests. One of these was the *Viper*. She eventually sank and went to pieces in a very short space of time during the early 1980s. A Dutch barge had her berth for a while, following the removal of her remains. A floating jetty for the berthing of vessels now sits on the site. The boatyard wharf is built up on numerous buried sailing barges; one of these was the *Emma*, which had used a berth here for a while after leaving Whitewall Creek. The other children, who as far as I knew had not seen our barge, used to think that that was how I lived – it was, in a way, but we also sailed our home away too.

It was about this time that I organised my first strike. My classmates voted for me to lead a strike over something or other – retribution was very swift – we lost our swimming for several weeks.

My mother used to write annual letters requesting time off from school to allow us to go sailing during term time – usually for a barge match. I had the same teacher for my last two years at primary school, and it may have been three years, except for the term in 1964 that I spent at a school in Maldon. She would always ask the class if they thought I could go! The original barge matches were always held in June, during the working week. We needed time to enable the *May Flower* to be sailed to the start area for either the Thames or Medway Barge Matches of 1961, 1962 and 1963. For us, on each occasion, it meant a week off school!

I don't suppose that I, or my brothers and sister, were really interested in the fact that we were missing school. Looking back, I'm sure that what we took part in was an education in itself, as well as being an integral part of British maritime history; the memories of what we witnessed, and took part in, have stayed with us for the duration of our lives.

During the spring of 1964, our teacher took my class to the meadows below the Lower Upnor road to dip for water life and learn about the natural world around us. To reach this we walked across a field on a paved path – the way home from school for us. A new road now cuts through these fields to the Medway Tunnel and Industrial Estate – the path is still there, but now with a footbridge to cross the road.

Following our fieldtrips with this teacher, the class persuaded her to get permission from the Head for us to dig a pond; this took quite a while and a lot of us helped. I expect other unknown persons did their bit too, like the teacher's husband – I say this from experience, being married to a teacher, as I have often found myself hooked into similar jobs. I remember that when we came back from our term away at Maldon the pond was full of life and natural plants. The pond sat just outside of our classroom.

Much excitement spread amongst us when, coming home from school one day, a huge plume of smoke was spotted emanating from the top of our lane. At the spot where we usually waited for the bus to school, we watched what seemed like dozens of fire tenders arriving to attack a fire that had started in a barn next to the old tithe barn! The blaze was straw, which is particularly difficult to extinguish and was threatening the tithe barn. The fire was eventually put out long after we were all dragged off by our mothers for our tea and bed, before respective fathers arrived home – as was the custom in our younger days! The tithe barn escaped with a little damage. We later had a look at the remains of the other barn with the farmer's son, and the still steaming straw that had been spread out.

In 1964 the barge was towed to Maldon for some repairs. My sister and I spent a term at a school there. My older brother stayed at his school in Kent, being boarded out with the family who owned the *Henry*, which was moored in the creek. This was because he was starting at his secondary school and the repairs were originally expected to be completed earlier than they eventually were.

Back in school at Wainscott after the Christmas of 1964, my old pals were really pleased to see me. 'Gaby', my best pal, took me home for tea and I was able to watch television! You have to remember that we did not have electricity onboard, therefore we lived without television. It wasn't until I left home that I had any access to this medium. We watched a Laurel and Hardy film about a pair working on a boat in a boatyard. The men were painting the stern and rudder, one up on deck and the other below, and they had a squabble over which way the rudder was to be pushed. I seem to remember the one up at the top getting tipped out and the one below getting covered in paint! I expect I've got it all very wrong. Gaby sought me out years later when we were both nearing the end of our secondary education. He appeared at the barge and we had a good yarn about what had happened to our old classmates. I must say, some of his tales shocked me; I'd obviously had a sheltered life till then. Lurid tales of drinking parties in the woods by Whitewall Creek, as well as sex and drugs, were all part of Gaby's yarn! One of my ex-girlfriends – she who gave me my first kiss – had gotten herself into trouble!

My classmates and I were taken for a day out to watch the launch of one of the last submarines to be built at Chatham. This was either in 1965, which would have been for HMS *Ocelot*, or it may have been in the late spring of 1966, which would have been the last, the RCN *Okanagan*. I was in my third or last year at junior school. The building docks were almost directly opposite Whitewall Creek and a stand sat on flat ground near the entrance – it was probably a parade ground. It was from here that we witnessed this event. The building sheds now house a collection of old vessels as part of the museum's historic maritime collection. After this, Gaby decided that he was going to join the Royal Navy; whether he did or not, I do not know. I had some information leaflets for a number of years, but I later became an Engineer Officer with the Royal Fleet Auxiliary.

Another notable event happened one summer's day when a huge dark smoke cloud, reaching high into the sky, appeared over the back of the school playing fields. On arriving home, it was obvious that a huge fire was burning in the dockyard. Later we learnt that this was the shed over the basin where Nelson's famous ship *Victory* had been built in 1765. It was completely destroyed. This sad event had been caused by workmen. However, as said, this dock and the others in the group of original docks now houses a historic ships collection.

We had one more season sailing, from Whitewall Creek, during the summer of 1965. This included the Medway Barge Match. My time at junior school was soon to come to a close and all of our lives were about to be turned upside down with a move to pastures new. Before this I remember doing a test, with shapes and such stuff; little did I know at the time that this was the famous 'Eleven Plus'. I did not, unlike my sister and younger brother later, do very well and, like my eldest brother, disappeared into the morass of secondary modern education.

chapter eight

Domestic Life

No drawings have survived of the layout below. The main accommodation lay under the main hatch, where there was an open-plan saloon with a large fire standing at the forward end to port. This part of the saloon had a wide lounge seat, which doubled as a crew berth when needed, and lounging chairs. Aft of this was my parents' room. On the starboard side forward was additional lounging with the dining area further aft, leading through to the galley. My parents' cabin was also port of the galley.

In the galley a storage unit was arranged on top of the keelson, separating the bedroom from the galley. On the starboard side of this compartment was a worktop, with storage to the hull sides and below, with a sink fitted towards its aft end. Aft of this was the cooker, boiler and later a refrigerator. In the galley, after meals and cooking, we all learnt that washing up needed to be done; this was a family chore, not just for mothers, as, when sailing, Mother was the mate and would be up on deck doing other things.

Under the aft waist deck, starboard of the keelson, was the bathroom, with a chemical toilet, a wash basin and a tin bath; to port were storage cupboards, with access through to the aft cabin, which was my sister's domain. This eventually only had one berth to starboard.

Under the fore hatch, to port of the keelson, was a large cabin with three berths, which was for my brothers and me. Built upon the keelson were storage cupboards and a desk. On the starboard side the area was fitted out as a workshop, where I was always to be found tinkering with bits of wood, chisels and perhaps a spokeshave, making little models.

The arrangements in the fo'c'sle were the traditional two bunks and bogey stove, in the 'v' of the bow. The starboard remained available for use and the port side was used to store the staysail; racking aft of this was arranged for the storage of paints and other marine paraphernalia etc. Right forward, the stayfall tackle wire was coiled to starboard and other wires, ropes etc. to port. By the entrance, which was to starboard, lived the paraffin tank and other inflammables! The chain locker was over the keelson, with a ladder to the deck via the fore hatch.

Bottled gas provided the fuel for cooking, heating of water and, later, refrigeration. The coke-fired saloon stove and coke-fired bogey stove in the fo'c'sle, supplemented with paraffin pressure (Tilley) heater and standard wick paraffin stoves, provided all the heating.

Family life at Whitewall Creek around 1958 – on a fully rigged barge the laundry is hung out to dry.

The laundry was carried out by heating water in a calor gas boiler, fitted with a hand-operated agitation paddle. A mangle was fitted to one side. I can remember taking turns with my sister operating these contraptions while Mother would have been doing another job elsewhere.

For baths, we used a galvanised metal bathtub as seen in many 1950s or older films; the water was heated in the boiler. The only running water was to the galley and bathroom sinks, all other domestic hot water had to be heated up in kettles. Running water is something I remember missing at times; especially as I got older and was able to recognise the differences in the way we lived! My wife's parents also had a similar boiler and bath back in the early 1950s before they modernised their Victorian house.

It was very strange indeed, but whilst sitting writing this very section I was listening to a local radio programme; this was back in the autumn of 2003, when a gentleman called in to the presenter and began talking about his early childhood days. He was explaining to the astounded presenter how his mother used to do the weekly washing, and that the same appliance was used to heat water for baths, well it could have been me!

When at the moorings, Mother had a long clothes line from two high points, as is often still seen today, with a pole to lift the middle. I have memories of us attempting to use this as a swing; suffice to say it always ended in failure and, I am sure, probably being severely scolded for our fun! Why we did it I do not know, especially as we were surrounded on one side by woodland, where a swing would have worked! When away on the barge, a line was run from a vang to a forward shroud. With four of us kids,

Having learnt to row, I was then allowed to take my sister for a voyage. The barge in the background is the *Viking*, shortly after coming out of trade and conversion to a house barge. I could now help fetch water with my elder brother!

probably more than one line was needed! Wash day usually meant that water had to be fetched that day or certainly within the next day or so.

When at our moorings in Whitewall Creek, fresh water for all domestic uses had to be collected by dinghy from the artesian well located on the opposite shore of the creek. This, when I was old enough to help my elder brother, was one of the chores we carried out as a normal part of daily life. We sculled or rowed the boat across the creek, where the water was pumped by hand to fill the galvanised steel tanks sitting on the boat's bottom floorboards. It may seem strange, but we did this until moving to a new berth in 1966!

When we went away sailing, these same water tanks came with us, full up and stowed on the aft cabin top and forward on the main hatch aft of the mast case. These tanks can

The water has been collected by dinghy from the well in tanks; it then had to be hauled up in the davit and run down to the main storage tank below. Note the *Violet* astern of the *May Flower*, the owner has also collected water. The other barge beyond is the *Falconet*.

be picked out in many of the photographs taken when sailing. The tanks were hauled up in a davit and gravity ran down to the main storage tank, if it needed filling, if not one was stored on the aft cabin top with another aft of the mainmast.

The main storage tank was the original tank that was on board the barge in 1950, fitted beneath the ladder to the deck from the aft cabin. Father moved it to the galley, where it sat above the keelson with cupboards under, it being aft of the galley storage unit.

We used to take these tanks ashore to many odd little places to fill up. One of the more interesting was on the shore opposite Harty Ferry. At the top of the old ferry causeway on the southern side, now much used again by fishermen, there is a spring of pure sweet water. The water issues freely from a pipe. Incidentally, my wife and I have on occasions used this source when out in our yacht, as do many other sailors.

Our grandmother putting us all to bed; this would be in 1961, as our youngest brother is very small! Note the ends of the deck carlines; these were all, except one, undamaged from all her years' trading.

One of my accidents on the barge was the result of hauling up a water tank. My older brother and I, with our sister tailing the rope, were heaving away when for some reason I moved my hands at the wrong time and, as I re-gripped the rope, which was now going up towards the davit head, I got my hand trapped in the tackle sheaves! This had no lasting effect other than a slightly twisted finger and a scar. Such is life.

The cupboards under the freshwater tank held domestic cleaning consumables, the shoe polishing box and a big floor polish tin. Shoe polishing was one of my chores. Apart from cleaning my own shoes, I also did those of my father and any others that came my way. We all, as kids, also kept the saloon floors polished. The ceiling (the floor) on a barge was of pine, and ours were maintained to a high sheen, showing up the golden colours and graining of the natural wood – this was my mother's pride and joy!

In the saloon, the vast fire gave out a huge amount of heat, as did the other stove, both of which were generally fed with coke. Natural air draughts carried the heat some way, but I do remember that the bedrooms were always chilly in the winter. Coke had to be fetched from a bunker ashore; it became each of our turns in rotation, as we were old enough to fetch this aboard, to ensure that the cauldrons were filled each evening. It was always exciting to see the coal merchant's lorry negotiating our lane at Whitewall to deliver whatever was needed. At our later berths this was always an easier task for the delivery men.

When building a new leeboard at Hoo in 1963, we had to take the barge boat across the Medway to the gasworks at Gillingham to fetch sacks of coke, it being the easiest and shortest possible route. On one of these trips Father stocked up on tar after collecting his drum stock from Whitewall by road!

As we all became old enough, it fell to us to cut and chop kindling for fire lighting. We collected driftwood, which would be left in a stack ashore to dry out. In those days, the river was full of bits of dunnage from ships and it became a natural instinct to collect useful wood. I still can't walk past a piece of hardwood, especially mahogany, iroko or teak that has been thrown aside – to me it is a valuable commodity and a use can be found for most pieces!

The paraffin stoves provided additional heating, especially in the cabins. Paraffin was used for all the lamps, the main lighting being of the pressure type (Tilley). We had a couple of traditional hanging wick lights, which generally were only used on high days and holidays, such as at Christmas, adding to the ambience. In addition, when arriving home in the dark, one of these was the first to be lit to provide sufficient light to deal with the pressure lamps!

Again, as we got older, looking after the lamps became another of the jobs that we had to deal with. First it was just to fill the reservoirs with paraffin and keep the ready-to-use tank full. The lamps were lit with a little methylated spirit burner. The burner was similar to a peg and had two half round-shaped cups stuffed with a non-inflammable wick material, it was clipped round the vaporiser tube of the lamp and was lit to heat the paraffin in the vaporiser. Once hot enough the lamp lit up when the on/off valve was operated; if you were too early semi-vaporised paraffin flooded out! We progressed on to being allowed to light these lamps, initially with supervision, but by the age of eight or nine we all lit the lamps on our own. With this came the responsibility to ensure that the lamps were filled ready for lighting.

I progressed to maintaining the lamps. Pumps sometimes needed a new washer; this was an easy task. The vaporiser tubes needed replacing from time to time, as did the mantles, which were very delicate little tubes of fine material fitted over the vaporiser and touched into shape. When turning on the fuel for the first time, great care was needed to ensure the shape was maintained, thereafter the mantle was the most delicate part of the lamp. Glasses needed to be cleaned regularly. A box of spares was always kept stocked up!

The mellow glow of these lamps, the flickering firelight and the gleam of polished pine gave a special ambience, but it came at a price: I can remember getting chilblains on my feet. I am sure many other youngsters of the period can also remember suffering

Three of us and our friend from the *Falconet* enjoying an afternoon snack. Note that the mainsail stitched by my mother has not been tanned and the mizzen mast is ashore for stripping down and varnishing, Spring 1961.

from them. As said, like the coke, paraffin had to be carried aboard, and then decanted into the ready-use drum located in the fo'c'sle on a bench.

In about 1962, at Whitewall Creek, we had a telephone run to our berth. This required about a mile or so of telegraph poles and I remember the final one being put up and chatting to the workmen, who hadn't been to this place before. The phone was used by a number of neighbours and an honesty pot for payments was kept beside it.

This phone proved its worth in about 1964, when my youngest brother thought that he would go for a swim, not realising that he had not actually learnt how. The alarm was initially raised by a 'girlfriend'; fortunately our eldest brother also spotted his predicament and a family tragedy was averted. My eldest brother, who was not yet

A view of the saloon area on the barge – it must be winter as the fire is going! The only cargo-damaged deck carline is seen in this view, *c.*1976. Note the Tilley lamp as well as the traditional cabin lamp. The upper panelling hides the aft sailing beam with all the registration details. The binnacle that came from Tubby Blake is now with the Trustees of the Milton Barge Museum. Note also the model of a swim head barge.

swimming proficiently himself, leapt in from the side of the *May Flower* and dragged our brother to the floating jetty that was part of the gangway system from the shore. My mother immediately started to give mouth to mouth resuscitation. The little girl's mother, who was a nurse, came rushing to the scene and he was resuscitated. My youngest brother was aware of the world again by the time the ambulance had arrived. We weren't to know it at the time, but he went on to use up more of his 'nine lives' during his early years!

A raised section of the keelson ran some several metres aft of the forward end of the main hold (saloon area), through under the mast waist deck to the forward end of the fore hold, immediately aft of the bulkhead. In the saloon, it acted as a high seat. This was always a prized spot with a comfortable cushion. The keelson, like the floor, was always maintained in a highly polished condition!

After Father had completed the renewal of the inner linings, he did not reinstate the original aft cabin. I later felt this was a shame because it detracted from the appearance of this part of the barge, but it did allow easier access for maintenance requirements under the quarters, as I was to find out later in my early life. On the whole, Father did not believe in totally rigid bulkheads; these were fitted short of the deck head and were held in place by battens. In this way, the structure of the barge could move without causing problems to a rigid inclusion. The bulkheads were constructed from a mix of pine boards and tongue and grooved hardwood which had been acquired from somewhere or other. We lived comfortably enough, but I am sure that the level of conversion fit-out would be considered rudimentary by some, and especially when compared with today's standards.

Looking back, the chemical toilet was horrible! But in many respects at least the effluent was treated to a certain extent. In our time, a pump-out loo was not fitted without a water holding tank; this would not have been very practical when aground. We accepted what we had and did not think greatly about it. Visiting the sailing barge *Wyvenhoe* recently, I was struck by the excellent arrangements and outfitting – ours was basic in comparison!

We grew up without electricity. Things like television, electric cookers and lights at the flick of a switch were a wonder to us when we at last experienced them. Books and the radio provided us with entertainment when we weren't carrying out maintenance or allowed out with friends. Board games were played a lot when we were young.

Electricity would have been a boon though, and I remember telling my parents that it would not have been too difficult to get it organised. I can remember thinking, much later on, how things could have been improved. My elder brother and I made a few of these in our early teens, but as we grew older and moved out into a world that was expanding our horizons, this all stopped, except for general maintenance needs.

The *May Flower* had wide decks which made movement around comfortable. These decks, when we were younger, were our playground for much of our time. My youngest brother used to ride his tricycle around the decks against the instructions of our parents and on one occasion this led to him going overboard! This was in Maldon and I will return to the story later. The wide decks were a boon for my father when he lost his sight due to a detached retina in his one good eye during 1973. He knew his way about the barge, the layout and where the obstructions were, these being imprinted as a map in his mind; we even took the barge out sailing with my eldest brother as skipper during this period.

Over the last decade of my father's life, my wife and I took both him and my mother sailing on our yacht *Whimbrel* on numerous occasions; Father maintained his abilities on the water until his final illness. His last sail was on a blustery day on the River Medway a year before he died, when I took them up past Whitewall Creek, then further up off Strood, to where the remains of the barge sat. My mother wanted one last look at the *May Flower* from the water!

My father, just before he died from complications to his diabetes in 1994, said, 'When we're on the barge, we'll have barge discipline.' We often laugh about this, because the comment epitomised the life we really led. My father had, in a lucid moment, been reminiscing to my wife during a visit we made to him in a nursing home, about his last sail in the barge.

chapter nine

The Renewed Stem and Other Structural Issues

During the autumn of 1957 through to the spring of 1958, my parents undertook a quite extraordinary feat for amateurs. They removed and fitted a new stem and inner apron; this was achieved with the barge afloat during a neap tide period. The stem was removed down to below the normal waterline; the new section was scarphed into the forefoot, which was in good condition. The final cutting away was done during a neap tide when ready to carry out this final fitting. A derrick was rigged over the bow for lifting the immense bulk of these timbers.

The stem band was removed by drawing the bolts with wedges and jacks. It was thought to be relatively new and Father wanted to reuse it. Its condition was still excellent when I visited the remains of the barge in 2001. It is things like this that I still tend to note when looking at barges today; my wife is apt to tell me off, but a new suit of sails etc. is of little use if the fittings holding it all up are in a dubious condition! It was attention to this sort of detail that epitomised much of what my parents did on the barge. Lack of attention was the probable cause for the spectacular collapse of the gear on the *Vigilant* during a Pinmill Barge Match some years ago. Her stem band had failed.

I do not have any memory of this work taking place, but a photograph of my father shaping up the apron reminded me of some of the details that made up our immediate environment, which with time tend to be lost. In the centre, above Father's head, is the hull of the pilot cutter *Mascotte*, which later berthed against a hulked barge beyond our mooring. The *Mascotte*, many years later, came into the ownership of Tony Winter, who had her largely rebuilt and re-rigged at Gloucester Docks.

The remains of a walkway, which was the access to the *Emma's* berth before she went elsewhere, can be seen just above the apron in the top right corner. A gated access to our gangway and a fence along the edge of the ground above the high-water mark marked the boundary within which my siblings and I, when small, were able to roam free.

A vessel in the far distance over the stern of the *May Flower* was the hulk of the *Lively Lady*, an old wooden minesweeper laid up in the early 1950s and eventually sinking. For many people she proved to be a source of quality timber for a number of years. Some of her timber certainly came our way!

The apron was lowered through the fo'c'sle cabin hatch using the derrick in conjunction with slip lines. Then it had to be manhandled forward up into the bow.

The stem has been removed. It was eventually cut back and scarfed into the forefoot. Note the little model boat in the foreground.

They achieved this by easing it down through the hatch on a slider plank, with Father above lowering and my mother down below guiding the passage of the foot as the bulk of timber slid down – which was her usual sort of task. All of us children would have been severely instructed to keep well away!

When researching my father's papers, I came across some sketches he had made when planning this job. The inner plank ends were pieced out and the timber replaced. My mother said that the side planking was held in position with the fitting of a steel plate to both sides.

My mother's clearest memory of this work was the effort needed to keep the cold winds out of the barge, with the stem out. She said that whatever she did, it bore its way in; she added that at times her efforts were almost futile! I was only a toddler of two to three years old at the time and only have a vague memory.

The sheer scale of the size of the timbers can be clearly seen in illustrations. The dangers of it all going wrong were quite high. The experts, at the time they completed

Shaping up the apron, note the rabbit (step) for the plank ends. The *Mascotte* can be seen out on the mud flats, this was shortly after her arrival in Whitewall Creek.

The new outer stem piece is shaped up and ready for fitting. The apron is in; the position of the fastenings can be seen.

My father renewed the hold linings from amidships to the transom around 1952. Both sides were done. Note the old iron bilge pump pipe.

this feat, had assured my father that it was in fact not possible as it would result in sprung plank ends. Mother recounted, 'No yard would consider carrying out the work – so we just got on with it!' Now this work is quite commonplace within the barge world.

The *May Flower* had been fitted with a new pine keelson during the 1940s; this is the reason why, when seen in photographs, it is in such a good condition. This was due in part to the type of cargoes carried during her last trading days, these being, on the whole, only grains, which did not cause damage to the structure.

When the new keelson was fitted, it was not possible to fit such a huge length of timber through the main hatch, so it was assembled in two parts, joined under the mast waist deck over a long scarph. This was in the region of about 5m in length. Above this was a doubling piece, of about 300mm thickness, all through-bolted, sandwiching the bottom planks, floors and keelson in the usual manner.

The keelson doubler ran from the forward bulkhead to about 3m aft of the mast waist deck. My father, and later myself, used to keep an eye on the after end of the doubler piece; an increase in the small gap at this end between the doubler and main keelson would indicate any humping of the berth. If this happened, the barge was then moved out and over a weekend the berth would be levelled; this involved much toil. I suspect that fastenings were in need of attention too.

Later, with my marine engineering training under my belt, I could see possible errors that had been built into the structure of the *May Flower* during the keelson renewals. A steel keelson would have been more appropriate, however the country was probably suffering a shortage of steel due to the Second World War. Wood, being available, was therefore used instead. It could, however, have been strengthened longitudinally by the addition of steel cheek plates through-bolted to the side faces of the keelson.

A consideration that should be remembered is that a barge was built with the intention to carry regular cargoes; this helped the vessels to keep their shape. A steel keelson, whether later fitted as a replacement or fitted in the original construction, made a huge difference to their longitudinal strength and rigidity, but hogging will still occur. Steel barges do not suffer from this problem due to the inherent rigidity of their structure; they can flex, as all steel structures must, but maintain their shape.

I do believe, however, that the connections to the stern frame when the keelson was renewed during a refit in 1947, were not made as well or as effectively as they could have been. They were, I am sure, deemed sufficient for the expected life the owners were probably looking at, which was to continue her probable lucrative (at the time) post-wartime trade and to make use of Government funds which were available to improve the condition of their barges. The aft end became an area that I was to become much acquainted with in my early life, while carrying out repairs with my parents and being responsible for their completion. During later renewal of a number of frames, I remember discussions about why the aft knee had not been renewed when the keelson was dealt with.

I believe that the fitting of a steel knee to the fore and aft ends would have given a greatly enhanced structural integrity in these areas, creating a solid joint between the parts. That said, however, the *May Flower* lasted to her 101st year, and sailed into her eighty-seventh year without any further major rebuilding. Some mention of the poor condition of the *May Flower's* stern frame has been made in various publications. I believe that with the fullness of time this proved not to be the case. This is why I have felt it pertinent to raise these issues.

Another huge job completed to the *May Flower* during the Second World War was the doubling of the sides and decks – that is the fitting of another layer of planking over the original. As the *May Flower* was being employed to carry wheat and other cereals, being maintained as a dry ship was an important consideration. Even later in her life deck leaks were not a major problem. Maintenance of the doubled deck, especially if it was to the original decking, was, however, greatly complicated. We suffered from the usual movement in way of the hatch corners, but did not have the preponderance of tingles as can often be seen on the remaining wooden barges still sailing. As mentioned elsewhere, it was during this doubling that all fittings for the bowsprit were removed.

Father renewed all the linings on both sides from about amidships to the transom during the early time of their ownership. The frames were generally in a superb condition, but I understand that some of these were replaced or doubled up. The inside of the hull was tarred before fitting the new strakes. These were 3in (75mm) thick strakes and through-bolted and spiked.

During 1954, my father fitted a new beam under the aft waist deck in conjunction with re-bolting the main horse chocks. I found a sketch he had made detailing the structure beneath and the method he used to put it all together. The cost of the four new bolts needed for this work to re-bolt the main horse chocks was itemised in March 1954 in his costs book. The chocks were located a little inboard, just a few inches from their original positions. In this position the mainsail sheet traveller block did not cause damage to the raised aft rail quarter boards, outboard of the horse chocks.

During 1961, the inner structure of the transom was renewed or doubled as appropriate and the side planking ends were re-spiked and bolted. Steel knees were fitted to the transom and inner wale, either side, under the deck. These days, of course, this form of repair is not the norm as complete replacement now takes place – which is obviously the best way to go about it, to ensure for a lengthy period before it all has to be done again! Later on, further work to the frames was carried out in this area.

Upon laying a set of blocks in Whitewall Creek in about 1960, my father was able to carry out bottom work. This included some new fastenings to both of the chine keelsons through the bottom and sides and some re-spiking of the bottom. Further spiking of the bottom took place while the barge was at Maldon during 1964.

Other major renewals that were undertaken were the major spars and main sailing beam, during the early 1960s. Following a sailing incident in 1964, major reconstruction of the port bow was needed; this has been treated as a separate issue. The decking across the stern, and beam at the aft end of the aft cabin top, were renewed during the period 1966 to 1968. This and later renewals I cover during the periods they were to take place, as I was with my elder brother, by then very much involved.

chapter ten

The Mainsail, the Sprit and the Mast

The mainsail that came with the barge when she was purchased did not last a long time. If only she'd kept that new one she had made for her in 1949 and seen in chapter one! In about 1958, Father was able to get hold of a small mainsail, this came off an auxiliary barge. They used this sail for a season or two on trips downriver to Hoo and beyond. My mother took many photographs during this period and I am amazed at the sailing they continued to do, rigged in this fashion. The size of the small sail, before enlargement, can be seen in an accompanying illustration.

Mother spent one long summer in 1960, when I was about five, stitching up the new mainsail. This was a feat of epic proportions and it became well known in the barging world at the time. Mother looks back now with awe at what she did during that summer. When talking about it we came across a number of photographs that recorded these events. The Thames Barge Sailing Club, many years later in a letter to my father in 1968, asked for an article about all this, so I hope this at last fulfils that request!

The task was achieved by measuring the old sail and taking off the details when removed. The new (small) sail was similarly measured up before bending on whilst the gear was down. Mother then set about making up a section that fitted the missing area. The new cloths were laid out, cut, and hand stitched at the berth in Whitewall Creek before the summer break. As well as the additional section to create a full-size sail, my mother renewed a large section within the original part; this latter task was done before the summer sailing season. My eldest brother was the only one of us at school at the time and as soon as he broke up we were off.

For part of that summer we took over the berth used by the *Ernest Piper* which had its mooring at Abbots Court Dock, an old farm wharf to the east of Hoo. The gear was lowered for removal of the sail, which was then laid out in the farmer's field after the crop had been harvested. The two parts were then stitched together, and then the new roping with all the associated cringles had to be sewn in. It was this part that my mother remembers most, it being not only hard work but hard on the hands and fingers. Strangely enough, I never saw my father do any sail stitching – it was obviously women's work, or at least that of the crew, as I later learnt!

My mother has told me that during the time it took to stitch the sail together, the farmer had ploughed his field, going carefully round her as she sat sitting amidst the sea of canvas.

My mother is hard at it stitching up a new section for the mainsail.

The two parts of the sail in the farm field, by Abbots Court Dock, during the summer of 1960.

I don't remember that part, only the stubble and beach by the wharf from which we swam and played in Mother's little sailing dinghy *Little Willie*.

During our stay at the wharf, we had a lot of visitors who found their way out to us. These included both sets of grandparents and various work colleagues of my father's; two of these were at the time regular crew members and would arrive with girlfriends. The family album has a number of photographs with much water fun and games taking place.

Once the job was done the gear had to be lowered again to refit the sail. The sail was not tanned until the following season, giving it time to stretch and sort itself out. Mother believes that the stretch would have been better had the sprit not been peaked too high, but could never persuade Father to drop this. Her old sail-making friends from Strood had told her to allow for stretching when working out the material needed!

As I wrote this, I couldn't help but lament for my mother. If only Green Brothers had sold the barge with its new sail in 1950. Mother would not have had to complete this Herculean task and, I am sure, the barge would have sailed an awful lot better than she did, complimenting what we as a family were capable of. My mother has told me that a new sail from, say, Taylor's at Maldon, was at the time not within their budget. I look with envy at the cut of barge sails now: the modern materials compliment the general efficiency of the rig.

This of course was long before the advent of the vogue that developed for companies to buy advertising space on a new sail, which helped with the costs of obtaining new sails. Advertising, of course, was not a new idea as barge owners often used their barge's sails as placards for their own purposes – *May Flower* used to have a huge 'GB' for Green Brothers on her topsail. The stitch marks where the 'GB' had been unpicked could be seen when the sail was laid out on the ground for a coat of tanning.

One of the things, or to more correctly say, group of things my mother always regretted leaving on the barge when eventually sold was her sail-maker's box with all the associated tools! Why, she never really has explained, but I know that certain items such as the special fids for making the large cringles in the sail were dear to her. My mother always said that making these cringles was the hardest part of the task and she suffered from wrist pains for some time afterwards! One of these fids was actually given to her by an old barge sail maker from Strood, knowing that she had been carrying out all the sail repairs that were needed from about 1953, when he retired.

During the early 1950s, my father had discovered some rot in the foot of the mainmast, in way of the steel heel band; this was initially pieced out and repaired. This, coupled with the need for a new sprit, meant that by the early 1960s new spars had become a necessity.

In 1960 Father heard that the wooden mast and sprit from the auxiliary barge *Redoubtable* were available. She had recently been given a new steel mast which had come from the *Xylonite*. The spars were at the old Brice yard downriver at Hoo and were purchased. We had a day trip by barge boat, powered by a Seagull outboard, to Hoo, to tow them up to Whitewall Creek. Can you imagine being able to get away with doing something like that today, in this complicated age that we now live? Incidentally, a few years later, the steel mast from the *Redoubtable* was bought by Barry Pearce and

John Fairbrother and put in the *Emily*, when they purchased her, before selling her on to an owner based at Woolverstone up the River Deben, in about 1964. Incidentally, the *Emily* was originally tiller steered when built.

The sprit was the first spar to be renewed. This was carried out during the autumn of 1960 and spring of 1961. The original sprit was at the end of its useful life; apart from some rot, it was much worn at the pivot point to the mast and the foot arrangements, which have been mentioned previously, needed attention. The new spar was of greater girth so some shape was given to the mast contact point and, due to it being slightly shorter than the original, it was extended with a steel tube. It was lifted aboard using the vangs and a mainmast backstay and rested to starboard of where the original would come to rest when lowered. The old sprit was disconnected and rolled across to port, then overboard. Mother said that Father had removed the steering wheel before lowering the gear to do this.

The original spar was very long indeed and the replacement was finished slightly shorter in length; this suited the new mainsail, which did not have such a high peak as

Mother's new mainsail is aired and stretched at our berth in Whitewall Creek. Note the original sprit is still fitted.

The new sprit is being lifted aboard the barge and positioned on the starboard side. Note the water tank in the davit. Note also that the new mainsail is bent on, but not yet tanned.

the original sail. It also had a distinctive white-painted top, which was a tubular steel extension. The tube was about 2m long, was 'fitted' to the head, effectively increasing the length by about 1m. This shows just how long the sprit on the *May Flower* was, the original spar being 61ft in length! The new sprit was Oregon pine and was a picture when freshly varnished. It was after this work that Mother's mainsail was given its first dressing of tanning.

During the autumn of 1961 work started on renewing the mainmast. The gear was lowered and all sails and running rigging removed. The old mast was stripped of its stays and crosstree ironwork. The old mast was then dispatched overboard. The new mast came aboard up a ramp of timbers using a par buckle system. Easy to say, but a lot of sweat and effort was expended in these operations; power was provided with the use of

The mast coming aboard using a leeboard crab winch and mainsail brail winch.

a leeboard crab winch and the mainsail main brail winch. Two of the regular crew from Father's office gave a great deal of help during these operations. Why the new mast was not lifted aboard before the gear was lowered, my mother cannot remember.

The new mainmast was a beautiful piece of pitch pine — when sanded down and varnished it was a joy to behold. The mast was of a greater section than the original; this had to be reduced to fit the mast case dimensions and was in fact less than the girth of the spar. The shaping can be seen clearly in an illustration in chapter six, in a photograph that shows my elder brother 'doing' the foresail bowline and others.

While work on the new mast progressed, overhauling of the standing rigging eyes was completed. All the shrouds had the serving to the eyes renewed. This is my earliest memory of assisting with these tasks. Although the three oldest from time to time served spliced wire ends, it was, however, to be our elder brother who became the family expert on this task. On many occasions he was to be found dealing with a section that needed

We receive tuition in serving the mainmast stay eyes during rigging of the new mast.

attention, before being asked or directed, doing his last bit in early 1977, days before leaving for Canada.

That spring Father also completed the work on the port quarter rail, eventually fitting the quarter board, which was not finished in the traditional white, but varnished. This had been missing for some two years, since completing renewal of the quarter rail and sections of the covering board.

The new mast raised the rig about a half a metre in height. The difference this made can be seen in the increase in lanyard lengths between the deadeyes of the shrouds, when comparing early and later photographs. After this, the *May Flower* had what we used to call the bonnet fitted to the bottom of the mainsail. This can also be seen in later photographs, and was sewn up over the winter months of 1963 by Mother.

Our old mast eventually found its way to the *Oak* during the late 1960s when the two barges were berthed in the parish of Upchurch. Whether or not it was ultimately used in her re-rigging, I do not know. This barge, built in 1881 by Howard of Maldon, was re-rigged in time to sail in her hundredth year. She did not last long again in sail and has recently been broken up at Milton Creek – a fate that awaits most barges.

The heavy snows of the winter and spring of 1963 did not bite into the planned maintenance programme. Renewal of the mast beam and deck in way of the mast case was put in hand. A support sat under the beam, so stripping away progressed, the gear eventually being lowered to allow completion of this. Later, I wondered why the beam aft of this, under the forward end of the main hatch, was not renewed at the same time. However it saw out her last sailing years! The new beam was constructed of laminated strakes of oak about 50mm in thickness; these were all through-bolted to lock in the curvature of the deck. Father received a measure of ridicule for this procedure, but it worked and never gave us any cause for concern.

Many years later other people used this method of construction. Laminated beams were used on the *Oak*. Her owner at that time lived in Upchurch and borrowed the idea from my father after visiting the *May Flower*, discussing with him the way he had achieved various renewals we completed on the barge. Since then, glued laminated sections have been regularly used in barge repairs, in the rebuilding of the *Dawn* for instance, this being a step further than our through-bolted method. Modern glues are infinitely better than those available to us in the early 1960s.

Once the deck planks had been laid, the mast case wood spreader plates – thick pieces of oak – were fitted. Once this was done the mast case and leeboard ironwork could be refitted. On completion of all the repairs, caulking and preservation, the mast was lowered back into the mast case ready for heaving up. Moving of the mast was accomplished with the use of screw jacks and chocks – it was a case of operate the jack to its full extent, chock up or remove as the case may be, and start again!

The completion of the last project described here was the precursor of the entry of the barge into a major event. My parents had accepted an invitation to enter the last of the series of the original barge matches, which were being discontinued in 1963, the centenary year of the first Thames Match. This would have been preceded by a refit of the gear and completion of general cosmetic maintenance. The mast and sprit, however, had been completed in time for the barge matches of 1961 and 1962.

chapter eleven

A Spring Refit

During the early 1960s, the *May Flower* had not been in better shape for a considerable number of years, including her last years in trade. Renewal of the mainsail and two major spars, plus a lot of fairly major structural work, had been carried out during the preceding few years. In 1961 much effort was put into the barge to ensure that she was looking good for her entry onto the big stage, sailing with the crack racers owned by Everard's and London & Rochester Trading Co. The lack of a full-sized mainsail had prevented entry in 1960.

In 1958 the Thames Barge Match Committee had decided that yacht barges would be allowed to participate in the annual Thames and Medway Sailing Barge Matches. Changes to the rules first allowed private vessels that could conform, that is privately owned yacht barges having a swept hold, still retaining the ability to load a cargo. A further rule change allowed sailing barges used as yachts and fitted out as homes to enter. Years later I learnt that the crack racers of those last few years had not carried cargoes for a number of years, in fact the *Veronica*, due to being damaged in a collision and being laid up for a while during the early 1950s, had not in fact carried a cargo for as long as the *May Flower*! The *Sara* had been kept for racing only, for a considerable length of time, while Eastwood's from about 1957 maintained the *Westmoreland* purely for racing. Were these barges, in fact yachts, being maintained with the express intention to participate in two annual events?

The final rule change provided the impetus and challenge for my parents to participate. I have often wondered if this was a gesture made in order to make up the numbers, or an attempt to say, it's now your time, that is, predominantly for the yacht barge owners to take up the reigns after the planned demise (in 1963) of the original matches. A Victorian benefactor, Mr Henry Dodd, instituted these. This gentleman provided a challenge trophy in 1863 with the express intention to cause barge owners and builders to improve the looks and efficiency of the rig and hull shape, without affecting the cargo-carrying capability of the barge. Frank G.G. Carr covers this in detail in his book *Sailing Barges* and it is worth a read.

Many people have discussed the 'ins and outs' of the ending of the old original barge matches, and the relaxing of the rules just prior to this event, thus allowing amateur craft to participate. I would only add that it is my view that, had it not been for the band of people who took on barges as sailing homes in the late 1940s and continued the impetus into the 1950s, these magnificent and unique vessels would probably have completely disappeared, except for the odd one or two, as has happened in the case of the mighty, practical and picturesque West Country schooners. It is true that a few barges were being maintained as homes for yachting in earlier decades, but these were low in numbers in comparison. The advent of chartering a barge was on the horizon by 1963 too.

The early charter barges were, in all intents and purposes, yachts possibly also used as a home (but not often), with the odd charter providing some income to defray the up-keep costs which were, and still are, quite considerable. I found some of these costs for the years 1950 to 1955 in a notebook maintained by my father; these have proved interesting as they, at times, tied events together when my mother could not solve a puzzle I posed her.

Charter barges became purpose-converted vessels to obtain an income for a living, as well as a means to maintain the hull and rig. They usually accommodated up to twelve passengers who were, and still are, encouraged to help operate the barge. Very few, if any, have been maintained as sailing homes, with a young family aboard!

An early example of an organisation that tried to keep a barge in sail, apart from the old Thames Barge Sailing Club, was the original Thames Sailing Barge Trust; they kept the *Memory* working under sail, carrying cargoes when they could procure them, however this ended around 1960/1. It was then planned to use her as an adventure 'school' ship, taking children on trips, but, due to structural problems following a collision, this venture could not go ahead using the *Memory*. During 1966, the Trust purchased the *Thalatta*, which had the spars, sails and other gear from the *Memory*, which was ultimately sold. *May Flower's* long-time skipper from 1932 to 1941, Pincher Bloyce, was involved in this operation while working for Sadd's as skipper of their tug *Lady Barbara*. The organisation had become the Sailing Barge Preservation Society in 1956. They are still in existence and doing a fine job. In this respect, the *Thalatta* has in fact traded all her life, and recently attracted a National Lottery grant to carry out a complete re-building programme – the establishment's maritime heritage consciousness having woken up to the ever-decreasing numbers of these unique vessels.

My parents had kept the *May Flower* as a home and as a living sailing entity for some fifteen years before this sea change was to become a reality. They did not have the benefit of sponsorship of any sort, as was to become available to charter barge owners during the continued resurgence of barging, which exploded towards the end of the 1960s and early 1970s when a large number of redundant motor barges became available for re-rigging. However, many of these vessels had very short 'new' sailing lives.

Looking at some of the expenditure on the *May Flower*, in December 1951, I noted that the leeboard wires were purchased at a cost of £4 6s, which today is £4.30 multiplied by the inflation index. In September 1953, repairs to 'rudder pin and pintles' (this should have been written as pin and gudgeons) cost £3 1s 6d!

The need for constant maintenance was of paramount importance if the barge was to be maintained in a sailing condition. Looking at April 1952, I saw that a large batch of red and yellow ochre had been purchased. It would appear that two lots were purchased,

Spiking the bottom, the barge is on blocks, which my parents laid in Whitewall Creek. Note tarring of the bottom and sides is also in hand.

after finding that they did not initially order enough, thus finding out how much was needed. This was the first time that they had had the sails off for a coat of dressing since purchasing the barge, although I found that a small amount had been purchased in September 1950.

In April 1954, general stores made up the bulk of the purchases. These will have been required for carrying out the renewals and repairs which were part of the annual, monthly, weekly and daily requirements as they would have been in many respects, when trading. The stores include new rope, repairs to the mainsail, and needles for sail and rope work, shackles and a length of wire, thought to be for the topsail hoist from the sizes.

The greater part of the maintenance work was completed in the middle months of the year due to climatic constraints, as any sailing person will appreciate. On our barge it was quite normal for the winter months to be used for structural repairs, completing these in time for rig work and the plethora of other needs.

Page from Father's expenses notebook for April 1954. Note the mainsail costs – my mother use to 'work with' a sail maker based near the old canal basin in Strood.

Typically, sometime after Easter, the mast would be lowered to the deck and rested upon a purpose-made chock to enable a myriad of maintenance tasks to be completed. Before this, the topmast would need to be lowered. The topmast was held aloft by a 50mm-diameter (2in) pin called a fid, inserted through a hole in the foot of the spar; this rested on the lower topmast hoop at the mainmast hounds and supported the vertical weight of the spar. The upper and lower hoops keep the bottom of the topmast captive.

A permanently rigged wire attached through the base of the topmast led to a purchase block, then down to the base of the mainmast; normally this wire was tied off to a spare link of the stanlift at the heel of the sprit. To lower the topmast, another length of wire was attached and run round the mast case winch barrel with a rope tail to secure it. The weight of the topmast was then taken up. My father would then climb the rigging to remove the fid. As my elder brother and I got older, this job became one of our tasks; I always thought it great to get up on the last ratline before reaching out for the fid.

Winding out the wire lowered the mast. When it was in the lowered position a lashing was placed around the topmast foot to hold it steady to the mainmast. The forestay would then be brought back to one side of the main shrouds and coiled, as were the other standing backstays and running backstays.

Preparations for lowering the mast were completed early in the day, or even the evening before. This entailed hanging the anchor off on its claw (this was a heavy forged steel fitting that is hooked onto the anchor cable links and was normally used when fluking the anchor cable over the windlass barrel during the operation to heave in the anchor). The anchor chain was then slackened away and looped clear of the windlass barrel, over and round the bits, the posts to which the windlass is attached.

When this was done, the stayfall tackle wire was run out from below and the wire was laid out along the starboard side (when not needed it passed through a steel deck fitting right forward and was coiled below). The wire was then carefully laid onto and round the windlass barrel for a number of turns. My mother reminded me that it was in fact three turns. The remainder of the wire still lay down the starboard deck. The wire was secured at the windlass until lowering commenced.

When all preparations were completed, the special stopper knot seizing the stayfall tackle wires together, between the two huge steel blocks, was removed by my mother, who was the person in charge of this! A steel u-clamp was also fitted to the *May Flower*, so this also needed to be removed. A pin, in our case a bolt of approximate 30mm diameter inserted in the base of the mast case, was the last item to be removed. This was essentially fitted to prevent any possible jumping of the mast whilst sailing. If it was forgotten before lowering, the mast would not lower and would stop briefly before trying to ride up over! The pin would not resist a falling weight of spars, rigging and sails. Weight had to be taken back on the stayfall tackle, which meant winding up to allow removal of the pin. I can remember at least one occasion when this happened. I'm sure we are not the only bargemen to have had to do this!

To lower the mast, the stayfall wire was slackened away in a slow controlled fashion, easing the coil round the windlass barrel. One of us used to tail the wire with Father, the others watched for any snagging and kept things in order as a jumble of sails, ropes and rigging descended. On the last occasion that we lowered the gear, my father, who had lost his sight due to a detached retina in his good eye, tailed the wire while my elder brother or I took charge of this operation.

As the sprit came down, the outer end was first brought down towards the Taff rail above the transom, where a system of spreaders from the aft cabin top to the starboard quarter rail, upon which two rollers were arranged, allowed the sprit to 'walk' without causing damage to the spar as the gear came down. The sprit sometimes had to be pulled over to clear the mizzenmast to port or the boat davits to starboard. At the forward end of the main cabin (hatch) top, a chock was placed to take the weight and keep the sprit clear of the cabin top. Further lowering brought the mast down towards the mast prop position; this was placed on some chocks to spread the load and was held in place until the mast rested on the upper shaped end. We could then relax briefly before the real work began; our father would usually, at this point, call loudly for the coffee – wondering why it wasn't ready!

Tanning sails during 1959. Only one of us – the eldest – is actually helping. The rest of us (plus visitor) are too young to help and are obviously up to no good! The old car seen beyond belonged to Dennis Alford, the owner of the *Violet*.

My parents did not always remove the sails and running rigging in the autumn. If this were the case, the sails would be aired regularly on dry sunny days. The sails were removed for large repairs and treating with the special tanning mix that gave the spritsail barge there unique characteristic. If they had been removed, my parents would lay them out on the main cabin top, tented over the top to allow air circulation. Tanning of the sails generally took place every two to four years, depending on the wear of the coating.

Strangely, from an early age I had the job of creating the tanning mix in a huge tub. Various concoctions have been talked about in various books. Generally areas of the coast had their trademark colour mix which was basically a reddish brown, some being redder than others, even tending towards a darker hue, nearer to black. The mix that we used was two parts red to one yellow, codfish oil and water in equal parts by volume. The whole exercise was very messy and must have been a disaster for my mother, who would have had the job of cleaning up clothing afterwards – old clothes were kept for this job.

It was during a refit in about 1960 that I dropped an old half-gallon paint tin full of spikes on my foot. This resulted in a broken bone and a period in hospital. I clearly remember my parents turning up for a visit, looking as if they had virtually 'downed tools' and driven in – they were still wearing old clothing covered with copious amounts of tanning splashes. I have never forgotten feeling mortified!

From an early age we would help Father with the tanning – it was great fun! When the sails had been dressed with the tanning mixture, they needed to be left to dry. This is almost a misnomer as the stuff never really dried and, when it did, it became powdery and rubbed off easily; it was then overdue for a fresh coating. The drying period tended to be from one weekend to the next. They were then carried back aboard and bent on.

1961: a team of helpers carry aboard Mother's mainsail, now freshly tanned.

119

Left: I love this photograph! I am wiping down the crosstrees in readiness for painting.

Opposite: Sanding the spars in preparation for varnishing, I am to the left sanding the sprit; my eldest brother is helping Father. The sheen on the mainmast shows that it has already been varnished. Refit 1963. The sprit mast muzzle can be seen in the bottom of the plate.

For this operation, the often quoted 'many people make light work' cannot be overstated when required to carry a barge's mainsail aboard. An illustration from 1961, showing a team of helpers transporting *May Flower*'s mainsail back aboard after being tanned, demonstrates this admirably. Talking with my sister, she remembered this occasion, saying, 'I brought up the tail, carrying the sprit end eye.' When we were young, we obviously had to keep clear, but as we all grew older, it became a family affair to carry out these tasks.

Blocks had to be cleaned, oiled and painted. Metal blocks were silver and wooden ones were painted a teak brown colour. Sometimes a wooden block would need a new cheek, pin or sheave and would be replaced with a spare from a large stock that had been built up by father. Repairs were generally completed later. As I got older it became apparent that I had the ability and the skills necessary to carry out this type of work and that was that.

From time to time the manila or sisal rope used for all running rigging needed to be renewed. This came in huge rolls. Of course nowadays most barge owners are using synthetic equivalents. These synthetics would of course have been used by trading barges had they been around. A copy of an account with Taylor's of Maldon from 1964 included forty-three yards of 24in number three flax and a significant amount of rope for brails.

All ironwork was inspected, cleaned and painted white as required. In the early 1960s the emergence of a paint product called 'Valspar' proved to be an excellent paint for use

aloft, and it kept its whiteness superbly. It was, I believe, one of the early non-oil-based paints and probably did not contain lead. The *May Flower*, as previously mentioned, had a steel extension to her sprit which was painted white, being a trademark throughout her later years.

All spars were cleaned, sanded and varnished. Provided the weather held, the spars would have been sanded on the Saturday afternoon and, on Sunday before breakfast, wiped and readied for varnishing. This usually took place with the cooking aroma of eggs and bacon wafting out of the galley hatch. Before heaving up commenced, the topmast was given a coat of soft soap. Later I felt sceptical about the usefulness of this exercise, particularly after the initial raising of the topsail.

I loved the wood of these spars; the mainmast had a deep, dark orange-red richness and the sprit glowed yellow-orange, with a deeper, almost vermilion colour of the resin grain. I hold vivid memories of the effort needed to hand prepare and then varnish these spars, but even as a youngster I appreciated the results of our labours.

My youngest brother has gotten hold of the Stockholm tar brush! This was in the spring of 1963. The spars have just been varnished.

My elder brother and I would spend what seemed like hours wire brushing all the wire standing rigging, then having to oil them with a mixture presented to us by Father. Often this was a job that we did after school, between the weekends that the rig was down. This would have meant that we could not go out to play with our friends; I cannot remember how we felt about it at the time. It was something that we just got on with, it being just another job that was needed and had to be done!

My eldest brother became a dab hand at recognising the need for re-making up the serving that covered eye splices and what not. This was carried out in the traditional manner and was taught to us by our parents. An earlier illustration shows some of us receiving tuition at quite a young age – many of these skills continue to be used by myself and other family members.

From time to time various wires were renewed. In September 1953 the mainmast backstay pennants and blocks were renewed at a cost of £1; I expect that these were second-hand and obtained from one of the numerous barges that came into the creek for stripping out and breaking up. The topmast heel wire was also renewed for ten shillings. The last section of standing rigging to be renewed was the sprit yard stay, the central support wire, in about 1968 – this had modern clenched eyes. The *May Flower* was also fitted with a head wire to the head of the sprit, to which the mainsail was seized when rigged, the sail still had the head loop over the sprit end. Family feeling is that Father had this too tight and a slackening of both support sprit stays would have stretched the mainsail properly.

All renewals and good areas of serving were given coats of Stockholm tar; this was a sweet-smelling sticky black varnish-like paint which acted as a preservative to the tarred hemp seizing. A coat of this was also applied to the bolt ropes of the sails when they were tanned. Its smell is very much like the aroma given off by fresh lapsang souchong tea; this tea spent the long journey back from China in the holds of clipper ships like the *Cutty Sark*. The holds of clipper ships were painted with this tar for preservation and hence imparted flavour to the beverage.

The bob would be removed from the top of the topmast and the steel stay cleaned and painted silver. The fly was a deep blue colour and, as more of us arrived on the scene, Mother added another white dot to it. Much later these dots were discontinued. An illustration of the bob can be found in *Racing Sailormen* by F.S. Cooper, though

This photograph shows the arrangements of the windlass for heaving up; note the stay-fall wire tail going under the turns across the proud part of the windlass barrel. The end on the port side is lashed. The anchor cable is laid over the top of the starboard bitt-head; the mast had just been heaved up. The dolly winch has been removed and set aside. Note the shaped holes in the starboard rail; these are a reminder of her many years rigged with a bowsprit.

Photograph taken at Callows Wharf in 1976. The barge to LHS is the *Lady of the Lea*, whilst being worked on by the then owner, additionally, the *Oak* was berthed further round towards Shoregate dock at the time.

the colour depicted is red. Red was the original Ardley fly, with a red star on a light background on the solid part of the bob. From the early 1950s, however, the fly was always blue, with a black 'A' on yellow on the solid part.

To raise the mast, the stayfall wire was put onto the windlass drum with the tail secured beneath the coils and all slack taken up. The first part of heaving up was very hard work! Much care was needed to ensure that the mass of stays, ropes and sails did not become snagged on cleats etc. When just over halfway up, the hoisting of the mast became a little easier; as the sprit went past the forty-five degree point it all became easy enough for one person to wind. When the mast case jump bolt holes were clear, the bolt was fitted. When the mast was fully up, the clamp and rope stopper was fitted again. The topmast was then raised and secured with its pin and the pennant was removed. Sails were set and running rigging checked for clear operation.

The stay-fall wire was then run off from the windlass and run down through the deck into the fo'c'sle, to be coiled up and hung on the starboard side, right forward. Once the wire had been removed the anchor chain was placed back onto the windlass and the dolly winch refitted. All special and spare rigging wires, sheets etc. were stowed in the fo'c'sle from hooks to lie against the port side; the stay-fall tackle wire being to starboard, as stated. When I came across the half-broken-up hull of the *May Flower* in the summer of 1989, these wires and the coils of topmast stays were still in the remains, in a pile up in the fo'c'sle.

It was sometimes necessary to set up the mainmast shrouds. We carried this out using the mainmast backstay as a heaving tackle. A rolling hitch would be put round the first leg of the shroud lanyard and heaved tight, then the second and so on. The other shrouds were each done in turn, finishing off with the special knots and coiling the remainder in the fashion seen on Thames barges. This arrangement can be seen clearly in various illustrations.

From time to time the mizzen spars were cleaned, sanded and painted as required. The mizzen was then set up. This was basically a very manual job. After securing the throat of the sail at the top of the mast, the head of the sail was fitted to the sprit. The foot of the sprit was then heaved and forced towards the mast until the band could be hooked on – I think we used a rope to pull it to the mast. The boom was then set up and all proven in working order.

The next order from my father would have been the painting of decks, rails, covering board and anything else that needed our attention. Lastly, the side of the barge was tarred – oh what fun. The barge was then to all intents and purposes ready for a season of sailing.

It will be seen later that sometimes paintwork was not completed by the time the barge match season came round. In an illustration of the barge finishing the 1962 Medway Barge Match, our rails appear to have been changed to grey; this was an undercoat – still waiting for a period of good weather to apply the finish coats of paint. Mother said, 'Of course I had another young baby at this time and you three older ones were in school. I found domestic needs and collecting you all took a lot of my time. Don't forget it was a long walk into Wainscott – your father did not always appreciate this!'

chapter twelve

Racing with the Big Boys (up to 1963)

After the end of the Second World War it was thought that barge racing had also ended. However, from 1949 to 1953 the Marina Club at Hoo ran a series of barge matches for sailing homes.

An invitation to local commercial craft was extended, but these declined to mix with amateur-owned craft, with one exception – the 1950 Marina Club Match. This had five commercial barges sailing in a restricted staysail class; these were, in finishing order, *Sirdar*, *Gipping*, *Pretoria*, *Westmoreland* and *Ardeer*. The Marina Club had a class for bowsprit-rigged yacht barges in both 1950 and 1951. The *Thoma II* and the *Venta* featured as participants in both of these. A lot of detailed writing exists concerning this era of barge racing and it is well documented in books written by Frank G.G. Carr and Fred Cooper, who wrote *Sailing Barges* and *Racing Sailormen* respectively. The latter is a virtual history of barge racing up to 1962.

My mother said that they took part in the 1952 and 1953 events, but that the 1952 match was abandoned due to a lack of wind. An illustration from my mother's collection, of the group soon after the start of a match, has survived. This match was the fifth Marina Barge Match sailed in 1953, and it is the only match where the *May Flower* finished higher than the last three places!

Of the seven starters, only one other full-size barge was not captured in the view. The barges taking part were *Saltcote Belle*, *Henry*, *Arrow*, *Dipper*, *May Flower*, *Violet* of Maldon, *Viper* and the small yacht barge *Nancy Grey*. Note Darnet Ness Fort in the background and the towing of the barge boats, rather than being carried in davits as was normally customary.

It is ironic that it was the amateur bargeman, though many used professional skippers for racing in the marina events, that 'kick started' trading barge match racing. The first of these was the Coronation Match on the Thames in 1953. This was followed in 1954 with a match on both rivers. The amateurs, however, were now again excluded!

As the old racing rules had been reinstated, my parents could not participate in the rejuvenated racing series. By the end of the 1950s the number of barges continuing to trade under sail was diminishing rapidly, but the rules still required a barge's hold to be clean swept, that is clear and ready to accept a cargo. This meant that converted barges could not participate, unlike 'trading' barges kept purely for these two annual events. As

The start of the 1953 (5th) Hoo Marina Barge Match, photographed from the *May Flower*. This was sailed on 20 June 1953. In the foreground is Jack Elliott's little *Dipper*.

said, this changed gradually from 1958, and by 1960 both rivers allowed amateur owned sailing homes to participate.

After the end of the original matches in 1963, my parents worked with Tony Winter and others during the 1960s on a committee to run an annual match on the River Medway. This resulted in the inaugural match of this new series for private, company and charter barges on the Medway in 1965. A form of continuity was achieved with the presence of a member of the Gill family (London & Rochester), who was an early commodore.

For a number of years my father was a committee member and also went on to do a spell as treasurer, though I believe this was not his forte. My mother produced the artwork for the original programmes, which had an impression of a barge sailing. Later there was a line drawing of a Thames spritsail barge on the front cover. The inside had the course details and barge entrants, skipper/owner details with a sketch chartlet of the course on the back cover.

My mother is still in possession of the original printer's plate of a sailing barge, which she designed for the front cover of the early programmes. It was a white and blue relief. She also holds the originals of the barge line drawing and altered copies for following years, readied for the printers.

Recently, while watching barges during a match leaving the River Medway from the beach near Garrison Point, my mother obtained a copy of a programme. She noticed that a map of the Medway, which had the course marked upon it, was a copy of the original map produced for the early programmes.

What a splendid sight! *Cambria* racing on the River Medway, thought to be in 1955, with Bob Roberts at the helm.

Sara seen during the early 1950s preparing for a Medway Barge Match; note the additional stays to the mainmast to counter the bending forces generated from the increased sail area. This was before she was fitted with a steel mainmast.

The fleet sets off at the start of the 1961 Medway Barge Match. The barges in view are, from left to right: *May Flower, -?-, Ardeer, Arrow, Saltcote Belle* behind, and the *Westmoreland*. (Kent Messenger Group)

My mother has told me that my father fell out with the committee and took no further part from about 1971. I believe this had much to do with the 'professional skipper' saga that had been raging. I read recently about a barge that was disqualified in 1970 for having too many persons acting as race crew. The then current rules allowed for only five and the barge in question admitted to using seven. When challenged, the skipper asked if it would help if it were accepted that they were all well over seventy years old! This problem actually typified the crux of the matter between my father and the barge world of that time. Many of the professionals were getting on in years. He argued that he had as much, if not more, experience than many of the younger skippers that were then around. However, I digress.

My earliest memories of racing go back to the last three original series of matches for the years 1961, 1962 and 1963.

The *May Flower* took part in the 1961 Medway Match; this was sailed on Thursday 8 June. The wind for that day was in the westerly quarter; it later became very fluky, with squalls, dying away to calm.

On the way back up the River Medway, near Stangate Creek, my mother was below feeding my youngest brother, when one particular squall caused the barge to heel rapidly. This gave her a huge fright, and she maintains to this day that it felt as if the barge was going to go over. Things that did not usually move tumbled about down below; I remember this very well – the mess was awful! The wind later became quite light and variable and they did not get back over the finish line until after dark. Mother said that the crew had been very disappointed because they all missed the supper ashore. We came in last.

Barges in the 1961 Medway Barge Match tacking down the river. The view is from the *May Flower*, with the barges passing the BP refinery berths in Saltpan Reach. In the foreground is the *Millie* and to the right is the *Arrow*, then owned by the Thames Barge Sailing Club.

The *May Flower* in the 1961 Medway Barge Match. The crew take up the port mainmast backstay in readiness for the gybe. Note staysail out to starboard. The *Westmoreland* can be seen under the mainsail, immediately ahead is the *Saltcote Belle*, with her distinctive grey and black hull covers.

My mother is hard at it stitching the topsail back together, the day before the 1962 Thames Barge Match.

In 1962, the *May Flower* entered both the Thames and Medway Matches. Father had this year decided to paint the leeboards white. Was he trying to emulate the crack racers or was it a whim? I shall never know, but I believe it was typically the latter. My mother said that they had had a visit from Fred Cooper, and to quote my mother, 'Fred Cooper came on board and said, "What do you bloody well think this is, a bloody butterfly?" I was speechless!' She was instantly recognisable though.

In the Thames Match of 1962, sailed on Tuesday 26 June, the *May Flower* excelled in fairly strong north to north-westerly conditions. But, before this, on the way up to Gravesend, we suffered damage to the tack of the topsail. A cloth had ripped in line with the mainmast cap. After Mother had calculated that sufficient new sail cloth was available on board, Father decided that they would get the sail down onto the deck and repair it. This would allow them a chance to participate.

We had a larger crew aboard for all these matches, the skipper plus three hands being the number actually allowed to crew during the race. They provided the muscle needed. We did in fact have the same crew during all the 1961 to 1963 matches. My mother assures me that for these events the crew had to be male, she therefore, as a passenger, could not touch anything – except of course repair the sails beforehand!

The topsail headstick was unshackled, and the topmast hoop lashings removed. The bulk of the sail was then lowered to the deck by using extra lengths of rope, or wire on the hoist. The sheet end of the sail was not lowered right down.

The tack of the sail was laid out on the main hatch, the sheet, as said, having not been lowered completely, trailed down from the mainmast hounds. My mother spent all the daylight hours prior to the barge match repairing the sail. This was the day before, and the early hours, prior to the start of the race. What is very apparent is that she must have worked exceedingly hard. On completion the crew hoisted the topsail back up to the mast cap, shackled the headstick back onto the hoist, re-made the hoop lashings and shackled on the tack.

An illustration shows a strip of new canvas running across the tack amongst the mass of red ochre-coloured sail. It was normal to allow new material to weather and settle before any application of the preservative tanning. Later a much greater area was renewed before this sail was tanned in the spring of 1963.

I have a vivid recollection of helping one of the crew cook the breakfast on the morning before the match; this was eggs and bacon, with lots of toast and marmalade, which was our usual fare. There were five of us Ardleys plus of course the baby. The others aboard probably amounted to another four adults. During the cooking of breakfast, it was discovered that I had just had a birthday. Later, Eric took the boat ashore with another crewmember, probably his wife Shirley, to do some shopping for provisions. Of course in those days refrigeration in homes ashore was still rare, let alone on a vessel without electricity, so fresh food had to be obtained regularly!

I went along with my sister. Eric disappeared off, telling the pair of us to wait by the pontoon, returning later. Back on the barge, I was presented with a box. It contained a clockwork tin submarine. I kept that tin submarine for a number of years until it finally gave up fighting immersions in salt water! It was powered by an elastic band and had hydroplanes that could be moved; you could make it dive and when the band had untwisted up it came! I have never forgotten this act of kindness.

On the morning of the match, the topsail still needed to be re-rigged. It was Arthur who re-made the mast hoop lashings. My mother told me that as soon as the sail was aloft on completion of these lashings, the sail was hoisted and we set off in pursuit of the rest of the staysail class. This same crewmember later climbed the hoops of the topsail and lashed himself onto the mast to remake a hoop lashing that was coming adrift.

I do not know how long after the start that we eventually crossed over the start line, but Mother said that it was before the champion barges started. It was a cracking run out, catching up with the staysail class tail end and eventually finishing ahead of the *Anglia* and behind the *Arrow*!

The champion class bowsprit barge *Veronica* surging along behind the *May Flower* during the 1962 Thames Barge Match – she soon overtook us! These two barges were once 'sisters' in the fleet of Clement Parker for a large number of years.

Left: The repair to the topsail can be seen in this shot taken of my father by my mother during the match. Note also the little patch below the headstick; this caused complications and the demand for more repairs later in the year.

Opposite: 1962 Medway Barge Match programme. This details the restricted staysail class entries. Note that the *Ardeer's* build date should be 1895.

During the return, going past Shell Haven, beating back upriver, we were lifting the chine out of the water. This has often been described as a memorable barge match. For us it certainly was, and especially so for my mother, it only being possible due to her efforts with the topsail. This was the most exhilarating barge match in which we were to participate.

My mother said that she did not go ashore for the supper, but had to stay on board with another crewmember. Apart from the fact that four children were aboard, some attention to the pump was needed due to a leak along the starboard chine. This was caused by the hard beat back upriver. My mother recounted to me that ladies were allowed to attend the evening prize-giving supper for the first time. She had had a special frock for the occasion – but keeping leakage at bay had to come first. They later dealt with the leak using the blocks that had been laid in Whitewall Creek.

RESTRICTED STAYSAIL CLASS

High Water at Rochester — 10.37 a.m.

10.20 a.m. Preparatory —First Gun and Flag B hoisted
10.25 a.m. Five Minute —Second Gun and Blue Peter hoisted
10.30 a.m. START   —Third Gun and Flags lowered

Barge	Built at	Year	Reg. Tons	Owners	Master	Sailing Colours
ANGLIA	Ipswich	1898	53.75	Mr. & Mrs. M. P: Burger	M. P. Burger	Flag T—Red, White & Blue vertical stripes
ARDEER	Rochester	1885	45	W. C. W. Brice	A. Josh	Flag P—White square on Blue
ARROW	Rochester	1897	54	Thames Barge Sailing Club	Capt. W. Wickenden	Flag M—White Cross on Blue
MAID OF CONNAUGHT ...	Greenwich	1899	45	D. P. L. Antill	Mr. D. Ling	Flag E—Blue over Red horizontal halves
MARJORIE	Ipswich	1902	56	Alan W. Pipe	Peter Light	Flag U—Red & White quarters
MAY FLOWER ...	Frindsbury	1888	48	J. G. Ardley	J. G. Ardley	Flag S—Blue Square on White
MILLIE	Brightlingsea	1892	49.65	R. D. Duke & D. T. Allen	M. J. Lungley	Flag F—Red Diamond on White
SALTCOTE BELLE	Maldon	1895	49	R. Hopewell-Smith	Fred Cooper	Flag V—Red Cross on White
VENTA	Maldon	1893	69	J. Lukins & N. Hardinge	F. Wilson	Flag X--Blue Cross on White
WESTMORELAND ...	Conyer	1900	43.31	Eastwoods Ltd.	E. Harknett	Flag H—White & Red vertical halves

First Prize - SILVER CUP—presented by *The Shipowners Protection & Indemnity Association Ltd.*
CHAMPION FLAG—presented by the *Associated Portland Cement Manufacturers Limited.*
Master and Crew £30 0s. d.

Second Prize - SILVER CUP—presented by *Medway Barge Sailing Match Committee.*
Master and Crew £24 0s. d.

Third Prize - SILVER CUP—presented by *Lenton Transport Limited.*
Master and Crew £20 0s. 0d.

The Master and Crew of each barge (other than prize winners) finishing the course will receive £16 0s. 0d.
(The crew of each barge consists of the Master and three Hands).

The *May Flower* coming up to the finishing line in the 1962 Medway Barge Match. Print courtesy of Barry T. Pearce. Original by Alf Pyner, lately of Burnham-on-Crouch, Essex, now residing in Canada.

For the 1962 Medway Match, sailed on Thursday 28 June, the wind was in the westerly quarter. I remember vividly the championship class coming down astern of us with their huge staysails billowing out in a blaze of colour, more reminiscent of yachting than barging. We came in last, but at least stayed in touch with the tail. I have included a part copy of the programme for this event, which details some of the competitors.

The only barge which continues active sailing that appears in the programme is the *Marjorie*. She has had an immense amount of work done to her in recent years and should continue sailing for many more seasons. Incidentally, she is the same age as the *Sara* was then. This puts into sad perspective what was to eventually happen to the champion class barges. All the others have gone, except the *Westmoreland*, still languishing at Faversham in Kent, awaiting major work.

Note that, in the list of Barge Masters, my father is listed as Master. This, as previously mentioned, became an issue with the younger 'professional' skippers. However, amongst these seasoned professionals, he was accepted as the master. Another section showed details of the champion class bowsprit barges. It was interesting to note that the *Dreadnought* sailed under the ownership of Cattedown Wharves Ltd of Plymouth, although was generally known as an Everard's barge.

The *May Flower* actually outlived most of the barges listed, remaining active for a further twelve years. The amount of prize money is quite interesting; this would have been no mean sum in those days and must have provided some incentive to the crews to beat their rivals.

A photograph was passed to me of the *May Flower* participating in the Medway Match, showing her sailing past Hoo Island, about to cross the finish line at Gillingham Pier. My mother can be seen aft with all us children; the youngest is in his pram carry cot, which was always secured at the foot of the mizzen when sailing. Other crew can be made out by the shrouds. It looked as if the staysail had just been stowed. It struck me that she could have benefited from a larger mainsail; this would have improved her sailing ability. The two repairs carried out before the Thames Match had held out – though both areas were to receive extensive sections of new material during the winter. She does, however, look as pretty as a picture with her sails setting well.

The 1963 Thames Match was sailed on Friday 14 June. For this occasion the champion class was joined by the *Venta*, which was also fitted with a bowsprit. The previous year

On the Medway, my eldest brother is contemplating the scene before the 1963 Medway match. The other barge is Eastwood's *Westmoreland*.

135

she had sailed in the staysail class – remember this barge was sailed a decade earlier as a yacht barge sporting a bowsprit, in the Hoo Marina Club Matches.

The restricted staysail class had some new entrants not seen in the original series of barge matches for a number of years, or at all: these included the *Memory*, *Edith May*, *Henry* and the *Joanna Kate*. The *Joanna Kate* had been rigged out by Fred Cooper for her owner and was a small barge similar in size to the *Lady of the Lea* presently based in Faversham.

The race was completed in the most favourable conditions, with a 'soldiers' NNE force 4 wind that generally allowed a reach out and a reach back. It not being as spectacular as the previous year, I can't actually remember much about it, but reading the account in Frank Carr's book, *Sailing Barges*, it was as I remember – a simple affair. The entrants and the order in which they all finished were: the champion class *Veronica*, *Sirdar*, *Sara*, *Dreadnought* then the *Venta*, and in the staysail class *Spinaway C*, *Memory*, *Westmoreland*, *Marjorie*, *Millie*, *Edith May*, *Maid of Connaught*, *Saltcote Belle*, *Arrow*, *Ardeer*, *Ethel Ada (Ipswich)*, *Henry*, *May Flower*, *Anglia* and *Joanna Kate*.

For some reason, on this occasion we did not receive the food pack provided by the committee for the crews of participating barges, given out before the start. I remember a motor vessel, probably one of the Everard's coasters, chasing us down the Thames. The coaster eventually caught up with us when we were going down past Mucking: she came up on our starboard quarter and the pack was thrown across into our little dinghy carried in the single davit then fitted. I can't remember what the exact contents were, but chicken quarters springs to mind. My mother cannot remember this incident, but it is something that I have – probably due to being aft in our spot, taking in all that was going on around us. A family photograph shows the coaster on our starboard quarter with some crew at the ready.

After the match, the same barges made the passage to the River Medway for the finale. The previous year there were ten sailing in the restricted staysail class, for this there were fifteen – a grand end and a compliment to the last trading barges, and these later formed the nucleus for a number of barge matches on the Rivers Medway, Blackwater, Orwell and off Southend.

For the 1963 Medway Barge Match, sailed on Monday 17 June, we had a team of BBC cameramen and reporters on board. The BBC produced two programmes, one for radio and the other for television news. My parents were offered a copy of the film, but did not accept due to not having electrical power. In hindsight this was a huge mistake. The radio programme with an interview with my father went out on the home service during August of that summer. I tried, unsuccessfully, to locate the film, but a recording of the radio programme is still held by the National Sound Archives.

I vividly remember warning a cameraman about the position he had insisted on taking up. He was leaning out holding the port shrouds with one hand, camera in the other, and his legs astride the foresail horse. We were in the throes of tacking and my father sent me forward to tell the gentleman to move. He failed to do so, so when the foresail banged across, he was struck on the back and only just avoided going overboard with his expensive gear.

The *Spinaway C* during the pre-start manoeuvres before the 1963 Medway Barge Match as seen from the aft deck of the *May Flower*. Look at the cut of her sails.

We would sometimes lay over on the edge of the Hoo flats prior to a match on the Medway, getting underway early to meet up with all the others doing the same. It was a grand sight to see, feel and hear the barges making preparations – the clank, clank of the windlass pawls during the weighing of anchors, the click clack of patent blocks, the shivering, shaking and slapping of heavy flax canvass caressing back and forth as it moved to the breeze. Finally, barge after barge got away and clear, to allow their sisters to do likewise. Then there developed a melee of barges, jockeying for position as the start time approached. A prize for the first barge over the line was always awarded; this was not always the eventual winner by any means. Engines were not allowed in those days during this pre-match period.

The champion class barges would be making their preparations during this time too. The start for these was anything up to thirty minutes after the staysail class. From a photograph of the *Veronica*, a champion-class barge, taken before the start of the 1963 Medway Barge Match, let me draw a picture: she is seen manoeuvring along the

Doing a pirouette: the *Veronica* preparing for the start of the 1963 Medway Barge Match. She is seen with the low-lying Hoo Island behind. The proportions of her oversized rig can be visualised from the crewman midway along the bowsprit. (Kent Messenger Group)

southern shore of Hoo Island in the throes of a complete turn, or pirouette. The foresail is being held to windward to complete the tack, her mainsail and topsail are about to pull, her leeward leeboard would be down too, allowing her to pivot round on these. Crewmen are busy about her decks preparing for the pre-start jostling that will start once the staysail fleet has cleared away.

The extreme proportions of her rig are stark; the height of the mainmast, which by now was of steel tube, the position of the crosstrees sited well above the shrouds and throat of the mainsail – all alien to her more humble sisters. The topmast foot housings are located above and below the crosstrees, an arrangement that allowed the carrying of these over-length spars, giving additional support to withstand the forces of equally oversized sails. She carried a huge foresail on the forestay which was lodged just below the mainmast cap. A bowsprit of an enormous length which must have put untold stresses on the forward hull is already bowsed down. These barges rigged in this manner were a sight to behold – the barging equivalent to the huge J-class yachts of an earlier era.

The wind was in the south-westerly quarter, which allowed for a run downriver. My mother had a number of photographs capturing the sight of all the champion class barges under sail, but sadly they appear to have been lost. Just prior to my parents selling and leaving the barge, they were burgled and various articles were stolen. It is thought that

The aft guard on the *May Flower* during one of the 1963 barge matches. Note the old fashioned kapok lifejackets!

these were part of the haul; my mother always regrets the loss of these photographs.

This was, for me, the third occasion on this river that I was privileged to see and be able to take part with these championship class barges. The memory has stayed with me. Mother said to me that my father held back at the start, to allow the cameramen to make the most of the spectacle with a clear view.

I have never forgotten the glorious sight of a froth of billowing creamy canvas bearing down on us from astern soon after the champion class started. They raced up behind us, with the huge red and white striped bowsprit jibs of the Everard barges and the russet with a huge white crescent of the London & Rochester *Sirdar* billowing out and pulling hard, they bore down on us as if we were standing still, passing us with foaming bow waves. I was not to realise until many years later that this was a historic sight, a moment in time which was being consigned to history.

The class was lead by the *Sirdar* with the *Dreadnought* and *Veronica* close behind her. I'm sure that the great *Sara*, in my view probably one of the finest barges that sailed in barge matches up to 1963, would not have been far away, with the *Venta* taking up the rear.

Later in the day we were able to see the head of the fleet coming towards us, the *Sirdar* having held the lead until after the turn for home in front. Soon the *Sirdar* and *Veronica* passed the *May Flower*, fighting it out in a duel, homeward bound on their return passages followed by the other two. We were still to reach the outer mark, out in the estuary. Most of the barges were round and on their way home before our rounding happened, as was nearly always the case. The *Veronica*, during the tacking duel up the River Medway to the finish off Gillingham Pier, eventually took the lead, holding the *Sirdar* off to win this last race. She was followed home by the *Sirdar*, *Sara*, *Dreadnought* then the *Venta*. The *Veronica* became the undisputed champion of the last bowsprit barge championship.

The staysail class came home in the following order: *Memory*, *Westmoreland*, *Spinaway C*, *Ardeer*, *Arrow*, *Maid of Connaught*, *Millie*, *Saltcote Belle*, *Henry*, *Edith May*, *Anglia*, *Marjorie*, *May Flower* and *Joanna Kate*. Our position near the rear in thirteenth place was the result of this endeavour, but hopefully the BBC team were able to obtain the views they wanted! Looking back did it really matter? No it did not, because we were there, taking part, mixing with professionally crewed barges and showing that we too could sail our family barge, with her not so well fitting sails and at a fraction of the cost.

This really was the end of an era. Everard's and London & Rochester Trading Co. had made the decision to call a halt to their participation in these barge matches and this was the last of the original series brought about by Henry Dodd, one hundred years before.

Not wanting their barges to fall into the hands of amateurs, Everard's decided to break up the *Dreadnought*, and later the *Sara* too, but the *Veronica* was spared this degrading treatment. It is my opinion that all of these vessels should have been sold, if no longer wanted, to be allowed to have had further useful life. By today's standards the destruction of these two barges was a heinous act of maritime vandalism. The *Dreadnought* was a young barge, being just fifty-six years of age, while the *Sara* was a little older at sixty-one years; by contrast the *May Flower* was seventy-six at the time. She sailed on into her eighty-seventh year and lived into her one hundred and first year. This puts the action of the owners into perspective. It's ironic: ultimately it was these very same amateurs that were instrumental in the continued survival of the spritsail barge. Many have, over the past two decades, been partially or completely rebuilt – a continuing tribute to the sailormen who worked these vessels in a bygone era.

London & Rochester Trading Co. (later becoming Crescent Shipping) decided to keep the *Sirdar* as a charter and promotional vessel. She was maintained in sail until about 1971, when her rig was transferred to the much younger *Cabby*. In that time she gave many people an awful lot of pleasure. I for one thoroughly enjoyed my sails on this barge during a barge match or two. Eastwoods, on the other hand, presented, as a gift, the *Westmoreland* to the Thames Barge Sailing Club, who continued with her care until an unfortunate incident at Hoo in 1973 ended her sailing life. At present this barge rests in the mud at Faversham.

Years later, the hull of the *Sirdar* lay for a while on the west bank of Otterham Creek, near the entrance, up against the seawall. I visited her during this period: she was waterlogged and her hull planking was already coming away from her transom; she looked forlorn and sad. I obtained a section of her rail; this was later fitted to the *May Flower*. Eventually, she was towed up into Funton Creek and hulked in the area known as Bedlam's Bottom, where her hull disintegrated quite rapidly. Ironically her remains are laying near to her racing rival the *Veronica*, which was hulked here too, near the remains of some other vessels.

I viewed the hulk of the *Veronica* in 2001, her stem stood proudly upright, her bow pointing out across the flats; the stem and windlass bitts still had the remains of white paint visible. The rising tide seemed to float her, ghost like. I mused on memories of long before. Her forward section back to aft of the mast waist deck was also in a remarkable condition. It is apparent that she was fitted with new wales, covering boards and rails during her 1950s refits. Beneath the three mast waist deck beams she was fitted with three substantial steel support posts sandwiching a thick oak longitudinal spreader of a girth equal to a beam. These beams had been renewed in steel, as had the keelson, which looked quite substantial. Huge fabricated steel plates were bolted in way of the rigging chocks; these also supported the leeboard pivots, with a number of position notches available. These changes would have allowed her to carry the oversized sail area and withstand the forces involved.

By the summer of 2004 it was quite noticeable that deterioration had been more rapid. Her aft quarters had dropped away leaving the stern post and parts of her transom standing. The starboard bow and fore deck had all but gone and the windlass bitts had toppled. White paint was still in evidence, clinging on tenaciously.

At the same time, I visited the remains of the *Sirdar*. Sadly, she had all but disintegrated, with only a section of her port side standing; this still had a trace of her famous russet brown paint on sections of the sheaving (doubled planking). Her starboard side had completely gone; here the marsh had encroached over her bottom floors and keelson. Soon, she will merge with the environment and be but a memory for the few who can still remember the glorious sight of these crack racers in full flight.

These two barges were companions and competitors of the river for many years, their remains peacefully linger on, slowly decaying, within hailing distance of each other, with the same waters lapping gently around them in their sleep.

It was thought that the ending of this era would see the end of bowsprit barges, but with the *Venta* rigged with one, other people like John Fairbrother, skipper of *My Kitty*, ultimately followed; he had in about 1964 purchased the *Kitty* with others, including Barry Pearce of Maldon, and they set about re-rigging her. She had been used as a lighter on the Blackwater for some years and had fallen off the register. When re-registering the barge it was found that another vessel held the name and a change was required. So as Barry Pearce had the smack *My Alice*, it was decided to call her *My Kitty*. The '*My*' was only carved on to the transom as required by yacht rules, and not on the bows. Some years later John Fairbrother painted out the added part.

My Kitty was brought round to the River Medway in 1970 sporting a bowsprit. She created a stir sailing alongside the other staysail barges, but did not race. This led to other owners fitting out in a similar fashion, and from 1972 barges again sailed in two classes. After a few more years, this was extended by splitting the staysails into two classes, one for slower and another for faster performers.

chapter thirteen

Early Summer Sailing Reminiscences

My earliest memories of summer sailing date back to about 1959, when I was four. In that year I ended up in hospital with a broken foot. Messing about with a tin of spikes, which I dropped on my foot, was the cause of this. I have already mentioned the visit I had from my mother and father covered in tanning.

That summer we were not to be limited to the River Medway, as was the case for the previous summer. My mother said that by the second season with the little mainsail, they were confident in the manoeuvrability of the barge. During one trip, stopping off at Hoo, they also sailed without the mizzen; my mother cannot remember why this was, but Father had renewed the port quarter rail and the quarter board was not fitted.

Tarring the sides of the barge was a summer activity. This was sometimes done on the Hoo flats as seen in an illustration. I can't remember when we started to help, but it was from quite a young age. By 1959, my older brother would have had a brush given to him, that is for sure. In later years we would, on numerous occasions, be tasked with this job. It could be a messy activity, firstly one is walking about in the mud, an amount of knee bending to get low down is needed, and the tar itself, if one is not careful, can get everywhere.

The tar was heated on a primus stove to reduce its viscosity; this eased its application and improved penetration of shakes in the side planking. It is amazing, but I do not remember any of us getting burnt while heating tar. I still have the scar from molten bitumen though!

During the summer of 1959 we visited the River Crouch and the River Roach. We were there at anchor on some of the days during Burnham week; this in those days was attended by a large party from the Leigh-on-Sea Sailing Club and other Southend foreshore clubs. During the voyage up from the Medway, we spent an afternoon having a picnic, swimming and playing on the Buxey Sands, while waiting for the tide to turn, to enable the flood to assist us in calm conditions.

While at anchor in the River Roach, we went on voyages of exploration in the barge boat, which Father rigged with a sail. My mother said that we went right up into Rochford, probably to fetch stores. The summer periods often allowed time while at anchor for completion of some of the smaller jobs that needed to be dealt with. On this occasion Father re-wooded the windlass while we were at anchor. The strakes were of oak, these on our windlass were clad alternately with a softer pine wood, which allowed the anchor chain to bite or grip the barrel. The softwood strakes needed to be renewed fairly frequently. I have since been on other barges and chain slippage is something I noticed. These windlass barrels did not have the alternate softwood strakes.

When I was about five, which would have been 1960, we did a lot of sailing in and around the River Medway, often taking some of my father's work colleagues and family friends on day trips. This was, as will have been read about, the year my mother sewed up her mainsail while we borrowed a berth at Abbots Court Dock.

On one occasion, two of the characters that were aboard a lot during the early 1960s crewing, Norman and George, came out for a weekend with us for a sail down the River Medway. We had slipped out of Whitewall Creek on the Friday evening tide, to drop anchor in the entrance to Stangate Creek for the first night. The Saturday was spent on

Tarring the sides, it looks like we may have been helping. Note that the port quarter board is not fitted.

Above: The *May Flower* at anchor in the outer reaches of the River Crouch in 1959. Note the small mainsail.

Below: The dinghy rigged for sailing on voyages of exploration.

Father is busy
re-wooding the
windlass barrel. This
had to be carried
out from time to
time.

I get a lesson,
learning to row
a barge with
George, a weekend
crewman. My older
brother is dealing
with the mainsail
upper brails.

May Flower at anchor on the mud flats to the west of Hoo marina concrete barge perimeter in 1962.
Note the sweet sheer line and relatively high bow.

a trip out into the estuary, then back into Stangate. The wind died on us that day and, without any form of power, the sweeps had to be used. These were very long bulky oars which were worked in crutches, which dropped into sockets in the rail at the aft end of the bow curve.

We did manage to reach the entrance of Stangate, but not before having to fetch up along the edge of the shallows inside the oil tanker moorings. These lay along the northern side of Deadman's Island. The port authorities came rushing alongside in a launch to enquire from my father what his intentions were. I remember the banter afterwards; as a pluck up into a safer area seemed out of the question, we therefore stayed where we had fetched up. The evening brought a breeze, which enabled us to sail sedately into Stangate Creek to anchor for the night.

In 1961 my mother's old school chum Faye came for a trip downriver from Hoo. They had both been at Saint Bernard's School in Westcliff, then later on at Southend Art College. Faye had married a military policeman and subsequently spent a fair amount of time abroad. On this occasion they had recently returned from Nigeria for a period of

Above: We watch dinghies racing from the rivers best vantage point, during a visit to the River Crouch, during Burnham Week in 1959. We came back in 1962.

Opposite: The *May Flower*, sailing in company with the *Arrow* on the River Medway during the 1962 season.

leave. They arrived for the weekend sailing on the barge with their children. I remember this occasion for its spell of settled sunny weather with light breezes. We had a very lazy sail down to Long Reach, to anchor off the Slede Ooze. From this anchorage, which was a favourite for powder barges and yachts, an excellent beach was available for swimming. There was an old jetty on the north shore of the reach, where the Kingsnorth Power Station with its associated coaling jetty now dominates the environment. When built in the early 1960s, it removed a huge chunk of navigable water from the river. A bit of a beach still exists on the edge of a piece of marsh to the eastern side of this flat shallow area, and often it is in use by families in the summer months. Looking back, these weekends – and there were many of them during a lengthy period – were idyllic.

Just upriver from the power station was Abbots Court Dock, the old farm wharf at which the *Ernest Piper* was then berthed. During our stays at Hoo, which was a regular anchorage for a week or two, Mother would take us for a walk along the seawall to visit the lady of the barge, who always gave us some tea. It was reached from the marina via a track through the Lapthorn's Wharf area, now a small industrial business centre.

This came out by a track at the base of the seawall. Lapthorn's shipping offices are now located at this junction. It was a fair walk along the wall or track. Over the top of the wall, up against its base, rested a number of old barge hulks: the remains of some are still visible.

When the power station was being built, the owners of the *Ernest Piper* had to vacate their berth. Where they went I do not know, and Mother lost contact with them. The remains of the wharf at Abbots Court Dock are still visible to the west of the power station, roughly due north of the Hoo Beacon, and can be seen across the mudflats.

The *Ernest Piper* was eventually sold to other owners and restored to full sailing condition again. In about 1970 she came to grief while in the Swale during a bout of high winds, her windlass bits sheared off at the deck – they had dry rot. She fetched up against the old Bowater's jetty, near the entrance to Milton Creek, suffering quite a lot of damage. She was eventually hulked in Shepherds Creek east of the *Gladys* of Dover, often floating around on high spring tides. She finally sat up on the marshes with her bow protruding over the edge; this resulted in her bow dropping off into the gutway below.

A fine view of the *May Flower*, airing her topsail, alongside in Lower Halstow Dock framing the ancient church of St Margaret beyond, during our stay in 1963.

I pottered up this creek in a dinghy some years ago with my young son to visit the hulks of the *Glenbury*, *Ernest Piper* and *Gladys* of Dover. We climbed up onto the *Ernest Piper* to look around. We saw a mass of smashed up outfitting panelling, children's toys and detritus of a home, abandoned to the elements; it was a sad sight. The other thing I noted at the time was the preponderance of rot in the inside of the hull – still fitted were the pipes for a central heating system and the probable cause of her relatively early demise. The barge had been stripped of virtually everything that could be considered useful. However, I digress. Other remains exist up this creek, but landing is not encouraged due to it being a wildlife preserve.

These early trips are but a faint memory, they did not have the excitement that entering a barge match engendered. By the time I was six, going on seven, the experiences that I was to enjoy left a lasting impression on me, resulting in a greater clarity of recall. I did not have the forethought in my early years to keep a diary, neither was I, from memory, ever encouraged to. Unfortunately, my parents were also not great log keepers, unless something important needed to be noted down. It's all so different in today's world, when every voyage, however short, is required to be recorded.

I had had vague memories of a voyage we had taken up the coast, beyond our previously known areas, to visit the waters around Harwich. It was not until I came across an old photograph and questioned my mother about it, that I was to learn, or be reminded, about the summer of 1961. She said that we went into the Walton Backwaters and the River Stour. Whether we went up the River Orwell to Pinmill, my mother is not sure, but thought that it would have been unlikely that they would not have done so, however there is no record.

In 1962, we sailed up the coast again after school had broken up. I especially remember being at anchor in the River Roach, below Wallasea Ness. We took the barge boat into Burnham for stores, water and paraffin. My elder brother and I were left to tend the boat while my parents went shopping for the stores, with the younger two in tow.

We took it in turns to go ashore, where we found that a lot was going on and this was all very exciting for us. The army was in town that day doing a recruitment drive, probably as part of the town regatta attractions. What I do remember to this day, and have felt aggrieved about since, is a conversation I had with a corporal or sergeant, who with some of his men was showing off a big gun. They talked about typical reasons for joining the army and proceeded to ask the group of kids, of which I was a part, where

Dangerously high up – my little trick on Mother at the age of just eight in 1963. The areas of the sail that my mother renewed during the winter following the 1962 season can be seen clearly. They are below the headstick and in the tack.

we were from. I piped up that I was from the barge over there in the distance, to be responded to with 'Don't tell fibs sonny'. It hurt then, and still rankles a little now, even with the passing of time.

An old family acquaintance who had many years earlier attended my parents' wedding and helped get the barge ready to leave the Leigh Building Supply Wharf afterwards, recently recounted a little tale to me while my wife and I were attending his seventieth birthday celebrations, held at the Leigh-on-Sea Sailing Club.

The gentleman, Ian, with a posse of other LSC members, was attending the annual regatta at Burnham on the River Crouch. He remembers vividly the appearance in the distance of a barge, coming in from the Whitaker under full sail. He said, 'This barge continued into the river, romping through the fleet of yachts and dinghies as if they weren't there!' Well, provided the rule of the road and an acknowledgement of what others are doing, the river is not just for the racing fraternity is it? This bit of information was quite interesting in that it confirmed that my memory was proving to be in good order! During this sailing holiday we also went up into the River Colne, but I do not have any memories of it. My mother has told me that on this occasion the river authorities did not charge them light dues, as had been the case a decade earlier.

In 1963 my parents took the barge into Lower Halstow. We berthed opposite the church, up above the berths still being used by Eastwood's mud barge, the *Lastholme* – then a purpose-built motor vessel with a grab crane mounted on the deck. She brought clay in from the digging grounds in Bedlam's Bottom. This somewhat oddly named place is off Funton Creek, which runs east, then south at the foot of Stangate Creek, and was then a source of quality brick-making clay.

The *Durham* was still occasionally being used as a dumb barge, bringing blue clay in from the marshes for the manufacture of bricks. She lay just below the end of the wharves. In not so many more years she ended up on the beach, known as glass bottle beach, at the east side of the entrance to the creek. Here she lay in a half-floating condition for a number of years, attracting a certain amount of vandalism. She was ultimately burnt in the late 1960s.

The *Henry*, under the ownership of the Young family, was using a berth here; this was at a private wharf situated on the south side of the dock. The wharf has since then fallen into total disrepair. After purchasing the barge early in 1963, during the cold winter, at Whitehall Creek where she was berthed, Mr Young took the *Henry* to Lower Halstow.

It was while at Lower Halstow that my parents became acquainted with the Young family. Twinney Dock, where both families' barges were berthed later on, was just round the corner at the head of the middle creek that fed into the bottom of Stangate Creek. The *Henry* came back into Whitewall Creek for a period of time prior to this event taking place, during 1964 – she left sometime in 1965.

We had anchored off the dock on the flats outside. The barge was sailed up towards the entrance and then warped into the dock using the dolly winch. I expect that some of the Eastwood's staff gave a hand in the dock area; people were always very obliging when they saw that manoeuvres were being carried out by people using long-tested equipment and skill. I have often said to my mother that had the barge had an engine,

The *May Flower*, sailing slowly into the East Swale, during the summer of 1963. Note the mizzen jib set and the huge tanned staysail is in use, this had a yellow tanning mix applied. Several little heads can be seen up by the windlass bitts.

life would have been simpler at times. The *Westmoreland* had departed, having been handed to the Thames Barge Sailing Club, and was very quickly put into use by the members. Eastwood's had carried out this unique and generous deed after the last of the original matches on the River Medway of that year.

My father travelled up to London on the train from Newington daily for a couple of weeks to preserve holiday leave. It was while we were here that I experienced my first taste of hoodlums. Father had us – I say 'us' because we were by now being taught by the action of 'doing' – airing the sails at the weekend. A group of local kids thought it a great idea to try and pepper the topsail with holes using a catapult. This ceased when my father erupted with loud furious bellowing and gave chase. They never returned to do it again. I don't know if they had been caught up with, to receive my father's wrath, or, knowing the terrain, made their escape! Strangely enough, later on I ended up going to Rainham Secondary School (Kent) with some of these boys – none of whom ever admitted being part of the gang of perpetrators!

One event, which nearly caused my mother to die of fright, took place in this dock. We had hoisted the topsail for an airing; I remember using the mast case winch with my brother to get it all the way up. I then decided, for some strange reason, that it would be a grand idea to climb up the mast. Off I went up the ratlines, however I did not stop at the last one, I decided to go on up to the crosstrees, on up above the sprit yard stay, to eventually stand on the mainmast cap. My mother was aghast, but once she had got over the shock of seeing me up on high, she managed to take a picture as I was making my way down. For me it was a moment in time, as a boy of just eight!

During the late 1950s and into the early 1960s the barge would be sailed across to the Leigh-on-Sea shore, where we would often spend up to two weeks or more of the summer laying off the Leigh-on-Sea Sailing Club. I do not know why we did not use one of the wharves, but at that time these were still in use for the ballast and timber trades by motor barges and small coasters. Of course, sitting at anchor on the flats cost nothing. The London, Tilbury and Southend line still had steam locomotives pulling the trains. My eldest brother spent many an hour watching these and he almost became a member of that band of people who record the movement of trains. The sound and sight of these steam engines was splendid and has remained imprinted on my mind since.

During a visit in 1963, my mother's old friend Faye and her children were back at their house in Leigh for the summer; the children would come out to the barge and we would go up to their house. On one of those days, we were invited to have lunch with them; we had a huge dish of delicious braised lamb and vegetables. We all used to

The *May Flower* leaving Stangate Creek in 1965. We were on our way up river the day before the start of the Medway Barge Match.

spend as much time as possible out on the sands, often going out to the banks of the Ray at low water and coming back as the tide turned. It was during this stay that I learnt to swim.

My maternal grandparents, who lived in Prittlewell, visited often. They would be picked up by Mother in the boat on a day when the tides were suitable, at about eight in the morning, and be dropped off on the afternoon tide about five. Ice creams were always a bit of a treat and we had lots of those when they visited. Toffee apples were something else that I would be allowed to choose on these occasions. These treats were bought at the little café which is still in existence today. Ironically, this café is called the 'Mayflower', however this is named after the Pilgrim Fathers' ship which reputedly visited here in the sixteenth century before departing for Plymouth, then finally to the East Coast of North America.

At the weekends when Father was home during the daytime, a visit to the clubhouse for drinks was another treat which came our way. An old barman with a very correct manner used to spoil us quite badly. I don't recall the gentleman's name but can picture his face, with heavy jowls, very short cropped grey hair and a correct military manner. He would keep us supplied with lemonade. It was on the return voyage back up the River Medway that we broke our port leeboard.

One of the jobs that my mother had spent the spring of 1963 doing was to sew together a bonnet to fit beneath the foot of the mainsail. This was to increase the working area and restore the sail to its proper size in relation to the height of the mast. A new mainsail would have been better. The bonnet got its first official airing for the 1963 Thames and Medway Barge Matches. The bonnet did improve the sailing ability of the barge and we were better able to keep pace with other barges when we came across them. This was borne out when, during the start of the 1964 Southend Barge Match, we were in the fore when an incident with another barge took place and we had to retire.

The summer of 1963 must have been quiet wind wise; most family photographs show a distinct lack of wind and lots of sunshine. A plate showing the barge slowly sailing into the East Swale exemplifies this! It is also the first time that I can remember sailing in these waters. Years earlier, Mother said that they used to visit regularly.

The flats of Leigh and Chalkwell have long been used by barges for a scrub and side paint. We did just this before the 1964 Southend Barge Match. During the start period the *May Flower* was struck on the port bow by the *Venture*. This episode curtailed sailing of the *May Flower* for the rest of 1964. Later in the year we went off to Maldon for repairs. The story about this and our subsequent visit to Maldon is covered separately.

Over the spring bank holiday of 1965, we took our pals from Whitewall Creek, Bob and Jim, sailing. It was a memorable occasion because a gentleman took a delightful photograph of the barge sailing out of Whitewall Creek on the Friday evening, with the sun setting in the west behind us. My mother was presented with an enlarged copy of this picture, which she has treasured for many years. Very few people ever gave us a copy of a photograph they had taken of us; this is why it is so special to her.

We dropped down to Stangate to anchor up in the entrance overnight. The next day was spent sailing out into the estuary before returning to the Medway in the afternoon.

We brought up, on this occasion, in the Swale, outside the entrance to Shepherds Creek, down from the hard at Queenborough. This part of the Swale is another place that became increasingly busy with small craft moorings during the mid-1960s; however it was still possible to anchor a barge on this western shore. We were taken ashore to a sandy beach that used to be located on the eastern end of Deadman's Island. There is still a bit of sand today, but much smaller than I remember it. On the Sunday we departed early to make our way upriver again, to sail back into Whitewall Creek on the evening tide. This is one of many sails that fill my memory.

In the summer of 1965, however, we anchored off Chalkwell because the moorings off the Leigh Sailing Club were creeping out somewhat and this would have meant anchoring some way off. We had not tarred the sides and Father decided on this bright sunny summer's day to have us all over the side for this annual event. We had just finished when some shouting and laughing was heard from the other side of the barge; we were by the dinghy which was lying alongside for access to and from the sandy mud.

Father went to investigate; a small group of louts were busy covering the freshly tarred side with dollops of muddy sand! His loud, angry shouting erupted and the boys, seeing and hearing my father, turned and fled for the shore, little realising that that would not be the end of it. My father went away after them; unfortunately he still had a long-handled tar brush (used for getting to the underside of the stern). Later a policeman came wading out over the mud to take a statement. I believe my father got a verbal warning – the kids, I assume, having got away, had then made a complaint – or a parent. After leaving Leigh, before a return to Whitewall Creek was made, we stopped over at Hoo to lie on the flats for the rest of the school holidays.

This obviated having to sail up into Whitewall Creek with the increasing problems of negotiating the proliferation of yacht moorings if the wind conditions were not favourable. These were being laid on both sides of the river close to the main channel buoys from opposite Whitewall Creek in Upnor Reach and along Cockham Reach, and was an invidious problem. By staying at Hoo, we were able to leave and return on the weekends with consummate ease. We would catch a bus to our school from a bus stop at the entrance to the Marina Caravan Park.

During the summer of 1965, while at Hoo, Father took the barge down into Pinup Reach to help a couple who had stranded their Dutch Botter yacht on the shoal at the entrance to Hoo Middle Creek. We anchored close by and they joined a team on board the Botter getting her dry at low water. We were all left aboard. During the afternoon the Medway Conservancy vessel appeared and ranged alongside the *May Flower*; I remember the look of consternation when they learnt that we were alone. This was normal life for us. The ultimate fate of the Botter yacht is not known.

My parents did not limit sailing to the summer periods; if the weather was fine and the tides were right, a weekend was used for a run down to Stangate Creek or some other anchorage for a night or two. My mother has told me that these were some of her most memorable sails, being due in part in not having to worry about stores, and water especially, over a short period.

Richard Scurrey, one of our regular crew members, stands at the lee bowline ready for the next tack.

During the summer of 1965, we took the barge round to the Swale again. I particularly remember this as we went in the barge boat up to Faversham for stores. One of the problems my parents had was finding a garage or supplier of paraffin, which could fill two five-gallon drums. The Swale and Faversham still remains one of my, and now also my wife's, favourite sailing bolt holes – the basis of this affection is now over forty years old.

While in the Swale we put the barge up onto the Horse Sands for a scrub and a coat of tar. We also visited the *Oxygen*, then berthed along the wall opposite Hollow Shore, on the west bank of Faversham Creek. A hulk of a wooden lighter can be seen here today. My parents knew the couple and they took the opportunity for catching up on gossip and things to do with trying to keep a barge in operation. The *Oxygen* was not at the time rigged, but they had plans. Many years later she was placed alongside the hull of the *Scotia*, a steel barge built in 1899, in the marshes opposite Maldon Hythe; initially this was to await a planned rebuild, however she is now hulked and rapidly going to pieces.

Later that summer we took delivery of a new mizzen sail. Amazingly, the drawing produced by my mother for the sail has survived. Looking at it, I noticed that it had been attacked and given a 'bob' by one of us children. It was at about this time that I was becoming more aware of a number of newly re-rigged barges appearing on the scene. Many of these had new sails, which were left un-tanned for a season to allow the sail to stretch. My earliest recollection of new sails was the *Spinaway C* in the 1963 barge matches; the cut of her sails was a sight to behold. These in many respects do not compare with those cut from the modern materials now available. At the time we would exclaim, 'Look she has a white topsail' or 'Look she has a new white mainsail' etc.

One weekend during 1965, a couple of guys, Alan and Patrick, from Father's office came away sailing – they had not been for a while and Patrick was due to go off to New Zealand. The plan was for us to stay during the week down at Hoo, at the end of the weekend's sailing. It was agreed that Alan and Patrick would be dropped off near the beach at the entrance to Whitewall Creek. Why, looking back, I do not know, but it transpired that it took him an age to walk a long way round the marshes to get back to our berth. My mother said that it probably had something to do with a car waiting to be used for their journey back to London. This is all part of the spice that goes to make up the trials and tribulations of sailing and this was especially so for anyone who sailed with my parents!

Numerous weekends were spent out sailing, taking with us family friends, or just ourselves. These short voyages fell into a fairly pedestrian category. Lesley Proctor, a guy called Neil Power, now deceased, and Richard Scurrey would often enjoy a sail in the summer. I treasure these years with much affection: what I remember most is that we went out often.

After about 1962, one of the major changes to the river that I especially remember was the disappearance of the laid-up naval vessels, the destroyers and small tankers with their raised central tanks and low side decks. In their place, yacht moorings were laid. These gradually crept round the corner of Saint Mary's Island. My father was not pleased with this development and would scold us for waving at the crews – having made his objections known to the river authorities. It was years later that I was to realise the difficulty the loss of the availability to slide round the corner, sailing an engineless barge, had created for us.

During the spring of 1966, my father started a large project on the aft end of the barge and, apart from an occasional weekend and a move, no sailing was had. I was by now eleven and my older brother thirteen years old. For me this was the time when I became much more involved in the running, up-keep and maintenance of the *May Flower*. I was by then, as my older brother had been since the 1964 barge matches, now considered a fully-fledged crewmember, in all that that entailed. We would regularly vie with each other to climb the ratlines to ready the topsail for hoisting, or stow it!

chapter fourteen

The New Leeboard

After the last of the original barge matches of 1963, we had had an active summer of sailing. While on our way back during the latter part of the school summer break, from our visit into Lower Halstow Dock, the Nor Marsh mudflats in Pinup Reach on the River Medway added another barge leeboard to its tally of breakages. We had been tacking up the river, with my mother up forward, swinging the lead and singing out the depths. Father, with me helping to work the leeboard winches and my eldest brother doing the foresail bowline, was tacking from edge to edge and making ground over the mudflats out of the channel.

Over on the Gillingham side in the shallows we did not come round quickly enough or just pinched too much. The result was that the barge pivoted round the port leeboard, the crack was clear and audible as it gave. The tide was still making and fortunately we were virtually clear of Folly Point and could fetch into Gillingham Reach. We got up to Hoo using only a small amount of board on the port side and anchored in our usual spot to the west of the marina concrete barge perimeter. Father considered it inadvisable to attempt tacking up the higher reaches up to Whitewall Creek. Of course my father could have chosen to take a tow, or used a temporary berth at the marina, but did not do so, for reasons that are unknown.

It was apparent that the leeboard was beyond repair, so it was decided to drop the leeboard off and remove it to the shore. A beach, which still exists beside where the concrete barge jetty system meets the shore, was the chosen location for the building work.

The sequence of events to get the leeboard to the beach was as follows: after taking the weight off the forward end with the use of the mainmast backstay tackle, the special securing 'J' toggle was removed from the pivot linkage. The aft end was lifted on its wire and a plank of wood slid beneath. The board was then lowered away, using the tackles, onto other planks of wood that were laid on the mud. The bottom edge was levered away by the use of angled planks to the side of the barge to the forward end of the board, until by force of gravity the board slid out as it was lowered. The leeboard wire was then unshackled. Lines were made fast and as soon as the rising tide reached the board, the barge boat was floated above and lines quickly secured. Once this was accomplished the boat with board beneath was floated to the beach. The old barge boat having been collected from Whitewall Creek was used for this task.

Shaping of the aft end of the leeboard, Father is wielding the two-handed saw. Final shaping was carried by hand planes.

Wood was ordered to make a replacement; this was 3in-thick oak planks, roughly 2ft wide. There used to be a timber firm on the lower Chatham road near to Rochester station from where seasoned oak could be obtained. My father had his sources for most things. Attempts to burn out the wood from the two huge steel plates at the forward end of the leeboard failed, so new plates were ordered also. We were able to reuse the straps and other fittings by burning the wood to free them successfully.

The wood arrived on a huge lorry, after it had negotiated the roads round the mobile homes which were part of the marina development. It trundled along what was then a pretty rudimentary roadway leading to the western end of the marina; this fell away to generally marshy ground and a stream came out across the beach just to the west of the old wharf. The timbers were then levered off the back of the lorry as close as possible to where Father wanted them. We had to move them the final 100 yards or so on rollers, towing them with the Land Rover.

The leeboard arriving along side, hooked on, and dinghy ties are released!

The barge was moored close inshore to the beach. To achieve this, a stern line had been taken ashore to keep her in a more or less constant position. An illustration of my father at work on the leeboard shows the barge moored on the beach. A hulk lay ahead of the *May Flower;* this was *GCB*, one of the last Brice barges. She lay on the flats for a number of years in a derelict, partly waterlogged state, sometimes not floating. Much of her gear was gradually stripped off by hunters of what even today in the barge world are valuable items. A team of men would regularly be seen visiting the *GCB* from a dinghy and feverish activity would take place, removing winches and what not. I hasten to add my mother put the *GCB* firmly out of bounds for us kids.

Eventually the *GCB* was finally put along the edge of the beach, to the west of the old wharf, to gradually disintegrate, finally being broken up many years later during foreshore work by the marina operators while developing this old wharf area. During the summer of 2001 the scattered remains of the *GCB* could still be seen on the beach at Hoo and I photographed some of these remains. It was amazing to see the sharpness of stepped joins on plank edges as good as the day they were crafted. The area now hosts a berth for a large vessel and much redevelopment has taken place, with land reclamation covering the *GCB*'s final resting place.

The new timbers for the leeboard, when shaped, were arranged on top of a set of trestles and the steelwork put in place. An arrangement of straps to tie the assembly down failed on one occasion during a southerly blow, which brought rollers tumbling onto the beach; my mother had a nightmare time preventing the whole assembly from breaking up. However, once the steelwork fitting commenced, the assembly had the ability to stay in one piece.

I was too young to get too involved with the woodwork, but my eldest brother did. I did help with the drilling of the holes, with either an auger or brace and bit, and helped

The leeboard is in place – fitting the securing 'J' toggle to the pivot linkage.

fit the bolts. Everything was assembled and liberally coated with coal tar. The bolts were counter sunk on the inner face of the leeboard to avoid chafe on the chine.

For the period of time whilst the leeboard was being built, school was reached by bus into Wainscott. A couple of my classmates actually lived in Hoo village, so this was a bonus. Often we would come back along the Lower Upnor road, along past the *Arethusa*, then along the shingle beach to Hoo Marina. Getting ashore to a large extent was controlled by the tides. When the tide was making and around the barge, we used the boat to get ashore. When the tide was on the ebb, we often had to wait until it had receded sufficiently to wade out to the barge and home. Our boots were left at the top of the beach under a clay bank; during the whole of the time they were never interfered with or stolen. My mother said that on fair days with afternoon tides, she would potter down towards Upnor in the dinghy with the little one, to meet us.

By the beginning of October, the job was completed. To return the leeboard back to the barge, it was necessary to reverse the removal procedure. The leeboard was placed upon the beach and the barge boat floated over as the tide made. Lashings were secured and, as the tide rose higher, the leeboard was raised from the beach, to be towed back to the barge and positioned alongside.

The new leeboard was hooked onto hoisting tackles ready for lifting into position. The young seaman in the dinghy in the picture is my elder brother. The sprit port vang can be seen attached at the aft end of the leeboard, onto the bowsing in eye. The hoisting tackles used to lower the leeboard when it was removed were again used to raise it up into position, with the additional use of the topmast backstay tackle. The after end had the crab winch-operated raising wire shackled on as soon as it surfaced from the water. The forward end was jiggled into place and the 'J' toggle, placed through the end of the pivot assembly to secure the board to the pivot assembly. Following completion, we sailed the barge back to Whitewall Creek.

The new leeboard was not painted white until the next season. It had to be given several coats of a fluid called 'Killtar', which stopped the tar leaching through the white paint.

Later that autumn we dropped the starboard leeboard off and put it on the beach adjacent to the berth. The lower strake that runs for the full length of the leeboard was renewed. At the same time the two steel plates were renewed. This obviated any difficulty in trying to remove the wood sandwiched between them. This leeboard had had a repair carried out following her 1949 survey. What was done is not stated, but I can always remember that this board had a weakened bottom strake, which by the time of our repair was a complete crack.

My sister, through her career as a deputy headteacher of a school in Wiltshire, came into contact with a fellow headteacher who was a member of the Thames Barge Sailing Club during the 1950s and 1960s. He asked her if she was of the same family that lived on a barge, by the name of Ardley. On gaining the knowledge that he had at last met a member of 'the family', he recounted a story about a 'mad man' that towed a leeboard across from the gasworks at Gillingham! Well, as you will have read, and can see from the photographic evidence, it was only a short distance across West Hoo mudflats, but it just goes to show how oral history can be misleading.

On a recent visit to Hoo to look at where we carried out this work, I found the beach had been excavated for a houseboat berth; with new pontoons being built westwards, the wharf remains have now completely disappeared and a large vessel is now berthed along the line of this.

chapter fifteen

More Racing (1964 Onwards)

On 20 June 1964 we took part in the Southend Barge Match. This match proved to be very eventful; there was a good sailing breeze, generally west or north-west. Some detail is given in Frank Carr's 1989 edition of *Sailing Barges*. What is not mentioned is the fact that the *May Flower* was hit by the *Venture* and forced out of the match. This took place as we were on our way up to the line. The only point made is that two barges lost topmasts; one of these was the *Westmoreland* belonging to the Thames Barge Sailing Club.

As the start time approached, we were on the starboard tack heading for the line; the *Venture* was seen to be heading our way, on the port tack towards our port side. Other barges were away on our starboard side, and under the stern. It soon became apparent that our position, if the *Venture* did not tack, was becoming tenuous with nowhere to go. The crew had been told to prepare for a tack, or any other evasive action that Father had in mind. To have bore away to port would have made the situation worse as we would have picked up speed rapidly.

As the *Venture* got closer, members of the crew up forward shouted to her to tack, but she did not do so. Then, Father spun the wheel and called 'coming about' bringing the barge up into the wind. We were now on the new tack with the foresail being held to windward to force the barge round faster. The *Venture* continued towards us and came onto our port bow.

At the moment of impact everything shuddered and shook. There were several grinding bumps before the *May Flower* went off on the new tack and we cleared each other. What the barges to our starboard did, I do not remember clearly, except that they passed very close, with shouts and flogging sails, as they made way for us. We did in fact very nearly clear the *Venture*, however if we had succeeded we would have been on the wrong tack for the barges on our starboard and astern of us.

My mother was quite traumatised by the event and grimaced when I asked her for more details – she reminded me that the barge was after all our home.

The point of contact on the *May Flower* was on the curve of the port bow. On the *Venture* it was in way of the starboard leeboard chock. No damage was reported as far as I can determine from the documents held by my mother, who later went and inspected the *Venture* on the hard at Pinmill. Her hulked remains, downriver from the hard at Pinmill, show that no lasting damage was incurred in this region, which is still intact.

The 1964 Southend Barge Match, a melee of tightly packed barges all jostling for position at the start of the race. This is thought to have been taken by a crewmember immediately following the collision with the *Venture*. The barge in the foreground is the *May*. Note the 'silver'-painted forward end of her leeboard. She and the barge to her starboard are on the port tack, the barge beyond is on the starboard tack, the former are standing into danger and will probably need to tack – having got out of our way!

To this day I do not understand why the *Venture* did not tack as she should have done, or why the barges to our starboard side did not give water earlier to assist in prevention of the situation. Probably each had navigational reasons, to do with the domino effect that would have resulted in the attempt to clear the way. The whole incident is now confined to history, but my father always felt aggrieved by the experience. I believe that the other barge skippers thought that the *Venture* would tack as required by the rules.

My mother and a member of the crew went to inspect for damage. Water was seen to be squirting in from some of the bow seams and other damage was evident; this was duly reported to my father. Later, it turned out that rather a lot of damage had been sustained. So far as I understand, the *Venture* got off very lightly, but for us it meant a period of time at Cook's Yard in Maldon for repairs and the loss of all further sailing for the year. After the incident we retired and went to anchor.

Studying the reports and correspondence relating to this incident, these imply that the *Venture* was trying to squeeze past the pin, and ignored the rule of the road in trying to make this manoeuvre. Their defence in the main revolved around the fact that Father was not a 'professional skipper', something he never denied. The documentation goes on to support Father's position. I quote: 'The other side accepts that your (my father) not being a professional skipper had no bearing, or was not a contributory factor leading to the incident.'

Other papers from this time include a duplicate of a note that was sent off to the insurers. It states: 'Amongst my claims is the acceptance of my status as a skipper in the Thames Barge Race. The last of which was in 1963. The races were open to barges skippered by professional skippers and I was the only amateur skipper in the race.' Unfortunately the document referred to was not copied before being sent off to the insurers. The correspondence for this episode went on into June 1966.

In July 1964 the *May Flower* was towed to Maldon for repairs. We did not sail, for reasons that were probably an insurance company requirement, and because of the leakage caused by the collision. This is related in a separate chapter.

From 1964 onwards, our crew, when taking part in matches, was apart from the family, supplemented by members of the Leigh-on-Sea Sailing Club. These would have included regulars such as Lesley Proctor, Richard Scurrey and others, all of whom were experienced sailors.

In 1965 we took part in the first of the new series of barge matches on the River Medway. We had been downriver to Stangate Creek, where a number of other barges had collected prior to sailing up to Gillingham on the day before the start date. Out in the River Medway a mass of barges that had come across from Southend were making their way upriver. The wind direction, a light southerly, allowed for some reaches to be just that. The south-west – north-east reaches needed a tack to be put in to weather the corners.

In Pinup Reach, between the old forts which are situated on Darnet Ness and Folly Point, barges seemed to be everywhere. The wind was, as said, light, and the tide was still making. Some barges ahead of us were across on the Nor Marsh side of the river. We were sailing up on the starboard tack standing across to the Nor mudflats, with the tide under us to put us to weather off Folly Point, and some yachts were immediately alongside us to starboard. The barges ahead of us seemed to stop and now lay right in our path. These were the *Edith May* and the *Lord Roberts*. A tack was made. The barge slowly started to come round, with the tide taking us towards the other two barges. Unfortunately, our anchor caught the side of the *Lord Roberts* immediately abaft the starboard leeboard. In a vessel the size of a Thames Sailing Barge, the space needed to tack is quite large, and the distance covered over the ground during a tack can be quite phenomenal with a tide under you, so if another vessel for some reason stops in your path without power, little can be done.

Apart from a gouge and some splitting to the planking, no lasting damage was done and it was all quickly sorted out. The outcome of this incident was punctuated by a terse letter from our insurers instructing my father to write to the other party pointing out that the *May Flower* had right of way and could not initially tack without causing an incident with the yachts. Father was supported on this occasion by another barge skipper. From the correspondence, it was apparent that the *Lord Roberts* also forced the *Edith May* onto the flats, where she grounded. Talking with Tony Winter about this incident, he remarked, 'The *Lord Roberts* got winded as she made a tack and stalled, and therefore lay in the path of the *May Flower*.' He went on to say, 'I had forgotten about the *Edith May* being to the other side of us.' He did say that quite a lot of work was needed – though I suspect it already did, looking at the reports.

The Nor mudflats have caused many a barge problem over the years, including, as you will have read, the *May Flower*. It was along this reach that the *May* shattered a leeboard coming up towards Gillingham; I believe this was in 1969. She lay alongside the wharf upriver from Gillingham Pier and of course could not race. I recall looking over her with some family friends before the match.

At the time of the incident, the *Lord Roberts* was owned by Tony Winter and his father. The family had, as previously mentioned in an earlier chapter, owned and lived on a barge as a floating home during the late 1940s and early 1950s. This barge, the *Magnet*,

The *May Flower* prior to the start of the 1965 Medway Barge Match. Note the *Sirdar* away to starboard, the barge ahead is unknown. (Kent Messenger Group)

ended her days hulked, like many others before her, in the marshes fringing the River Medway. Tony Winter and his father had bought the *Lord Roberts* as a motor barge and converted her back into sail. They kept her for a few short years, in comparison, and the barge finally had an ignominious end alongside a Thames-side wharf, where she had become derelict, sank and was broken up during 1992.

The *Lord Roberts* used Lower Halstow Dock for a while, berthing at a little wharf on the same side as the church. The dock was still just about in use by Eastwood's, the brick manufacturing company, who owned the dock and wharves opposite to the church. The manufacture of bricks ceased and the works were closed down during the late 1960s. The *Henry* also used this berth during the early 1960s. Before the *Henry*, a barge called the *Maura*, which was a house barge, used the wharf. The wharf is privately owned, but now lies derelict and has disintegrated.

Tony and his wife later became friends of my parents. As has previously been said, they, with others, were involved with the new Medway Barge Committee. This had been set up with some senior members of the barge fraternity, and my father was asked to join them. My father was a member of this committee for a number of years.

On the evening before the match, I can remember my father being very angry after returning from another barge on which the pre-match discussions took place, some of which revolved around use of 'professional' skippers. During this period a movement led by the younger barge skippers wished for the original status quo of only professional skippers being allowed to race a barge. This was all very well, but it did not take into account the acceptance by the original match committees of my father being a skipper in his own right. The concept was ultimately accepted as most of the barges being operated were in the infant charter market. In 1965, 70 per cent of the match starters were company-owned charter or function barges. The result of this was that if a barge owner wished to sail his 'home' in a match, a professional skipper was needed. My father objected to this principle and after 1965 the *May Flower* did not take part in any further racing. Incidentally, we sailed the only barge also being used as a family home.

The 1965 Medway Match was sailed on 7 June. The day dawned with a very light breeze in the westerly quarter. There were eleven starters; the *Lord Roberts* did not start. The course was shortened to a buoy inside the river. The participants and order in which they finished were: *Edith May, May, Westmoreland, My Kitty (Kitty), Venture, Centaur, Memory, Millie, Ardeer, CIV, May Flower.*

An illustration of the *May Flower* before the start shows sufficient breeze to set the sails properly, but manoeuvring in these conditions is cumbersome and slow. In these light winds, the *May Flower* did not perform well; she liked a much stiffer breeze. The *Sirdar* followed the match with a 'cargo' of spectators; this was a role she performed for some eight years after the end of her racing days. The *Edith May* took line honours in all the barge matches of that year, these being the Southend, Medway, Blackwater and Pinmill.

In 1966 we did not take part in any of the barge matches as work was being done on the barge. We also moved to a new berth at Twinney. The *May Flower* did not sail during the 1967 season either. We had the stern deck up with the aft main deck beam

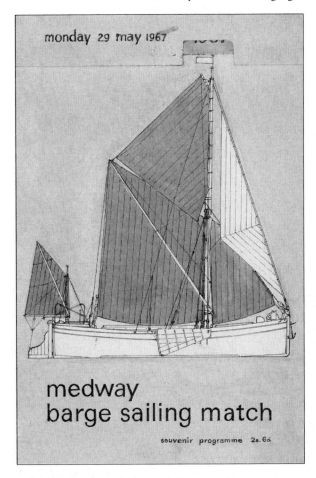

medway
barge sailing match

souvenir programme 2s. 6d.

monday 29 may 1967

Pre-print copy of the Medway Barge Match programme front cover for 1967. Note that in those days, before the advent of computers, it was still done by using the old cut and paste method.

out for renewal. Little did I know, but our racing had come to an abrupt end. About this time, other interests outside the barging world took priority over the barge and in many respects, looking back, my parents should have sold-up then.

Back in the spring of 1968 a gentleman in Lower Halstow, who was also on the Medway Barge Committee, tried to persuade my father to take a professional skipper – the late Jim Diddhams – aboard. My father refused to do this on the grounds that he had, at the time, over a decade and a half of experience as skipper. I discussed this with Tony Winter. He said that my father was proud of what he (and my mother) had achieved with the barge and their ability to sail her. Tony also alluded to a point that I myself much later came to realise, that towards the end of the 1960s, my father's eyesight was not as good as it used to be. This apparently was the main reason why the committee wanted him to take a skipper in the barge match, where much closer sailing was the order of the day. He did in fact have good sight in only one eye from his late teenage years.

For each successive year we prepared the *May Flower* in time for the Medway Matches. This involved a lot of hard work, but my parents seemed to have lost the spark and desire to go. This, combined with my father standing by his principles on the issue of the 'professional

The *Mirosa* and *Westmoreland* in Pinup Reach, running before the wind towards Gillingham Reach, a gybe is imminent. The *Westmoreland* had the key position at the gybe round Folly Point and went on to win in 1968.

skipper' in barge matches, meant the end of our racing days. I have many regrets about not participating. My elder brother and I were hungry for action, but were deprived of the experience and the expertise that we would have gained. I can vividly recall the sadness I felt as the barge was readied. I deeply regret that my father didn't feel able to follow the matches. It would have made all of the hard work more palatable. From our moorings at Callows we could look north across the marshes, into Kethole Reach, and see all the barges in action; this was bitter indeed.

Talking recently to two barge masters, while sailing on the *Centaur*, about my early years sailing and racing on the *May Flower*, I was told how the system fell into disrepute with arguing and infighting by the early 1970s. The outcome, finally, was that all barge masters now have to complete a course of training and certification, which is administered by an association on behalf of the Maritime and Coastguard Agency. I may not be entirely correct on this point, but it lies outside my story and there it will remain. (This will, I'm sure, be correct for both chartering and racing.)

In the summer of 1965 we took part in the annual Nore Race as a yacht. During a conversation with Brian Dawson, the present Chairman of the Thames Sailing Barge Trust, he recounted to me about seeing the *May Flower*; he himself was crewing on another yacht. Goodness knows how the handicap was worked out. The race is an annual event run by the Benfleet Yacht Club and we sailed under the burgee of the Leigh-on-Sea Sailing Club, to which both my parents were longstanding members. Neither my mother nor I can recall much about it, except the huge number of vessels under sail in a fairly small area of water. I do believe we completed the course though. Many years later I followed, participating in my Finesse 24, *Whimbrel*. My son and I, in three starts to this event during the last decade, have finished a credible fourteenth, seventh and second overall, on corrected time, and in the last being robbed by just a few miserly seconds!

For a number of years after we had stopped racing, my father went on the committee boat, which generally was the Medway Conservancy vessel, to monitor the race.

medway barge sailing match 1969

Commodore   M. O. Gill, Esq.
Vice-Commodore   W. C. W. Brice, Esq., O.B.E.

Committee
Chairman   W. F. A. Davis
Treasurer   J. G. Ardley
Secretary   A. R. Winter
     H. Eagles
     M. J. Clarke

Race Committee
M. O. Gill, Esq.   W. C. W. Brice, Esq., O.B.E.
W. F. A. Davis   A. R Winter   J G. Ardley
H. Eagles   M. J. Clarke

introduction

A golden age, it is for most of us an era passed and forgotten. Gone is the common sight of the sturdy working barge, which in vast numbers sailed our estuaries and creeks carrying the products of the land and the refuse of the town, crewed only by man and boy.

Our race is supported by the enthusiastic owners of the few barges still sailing, and by persons interested in protracting the vanishing days of sail, which alone should be enough to preserve and maintain the Thames Sailing Barge.

This year entries include barges recently rerigged, having completed their useful commercial life as motor barges or lighters, and it is hoped that their new owners will enjoy this annual event.

As before, a supper dance will be held at the Corn Exchange as an additional attraction, tickets being available to members of the public.

The long stretches of the Medway, often close to the road, permit the match to be seen from many vantage points.

entries

10.20 Preparatory — First Gun, and Flag B hoisted
10.25 Five minute — Second Gun, and Blue Peter hoisted
10.30 START — Third Gun, and Flags lowered

Barge	Built at	Year	Reg ton	Owner	Master	Sailing Colours
CENTAUR	Harwich	1895	60	Centaur Barge Chartering Co. Ltd.	T. Baker	Flag E
C.I.V.	Sittingbourne	1901	45	D. Heaton	W. T. Webster	Flag D
DAWN	Maldon	1897	54	Gordon Swift	C. Horlock	Flag F
EDITH MAY	Harwich	1906	64	V. S. Harvey	J. Spitty	Flag G
MARJORIE	Ipswich	1902	56	A. Pipe	J. Lawrence	Flag A
MAY	Ipswich	1891	57	Silvertown Services Lighterage Limited	F. R. Wells	Flag M
MAYFLOWER	Rochester	1888	48	J. G. Ardley		Flag 7
MILLIE	Brightlingsea	1892	49	E. W. D. Rodwell	M. Lungley	Flag R
MIROSA	Maldon	1892	49	Alan J. Walker	H. Farrington	Flag S
MY KITTY	Harwich	1895	65	Maldon Yacht & Barge Charter Co. Ltd.	J. Fairbrother	Flag K
SPINAWAY C	Ipswich	1899	57	W. C. W. Brice	J. A. Lapthorn	Flag Y
VENTURE	Ipswich	1900	58	John Bassett		Flag U
VICUNIA	Greenwich	1912	76	G. W. G. Swift	R. Springet	Flag B
WESTMORELAND	Conyer	1900	43	Thames Barge Sailing Club	V. Wadhams	Flag V

The inside pages of the 1969 Medway Barge Match programme. Note that the *Kitty* is entered under her re-registered name, *My Kitty*.

My elder brother and I often found a place with a family friend on a spectator vessel, and on at least one occasion we were on the *Sirdar* following the race as part of the party on board. A couple of our regular crew and family friends, Lesley Proctor and Rick Scurrey, were with us on this trip, as they would have been had we been sailing. Mother had to keep the other two with her; they followed the barges from various vantage points. One of these occasions was 1968, when we witnessed a very close finish between the *Mirosa* and the *Westmoreland*. This resulted in the latter winning by a very short distance.

On a number of occasions, my eldest brother and I were taken to the prize-giving suppers held at the old Corn Exchange building in Rochester. These were my first forays into public life and boy did I have a ball. I was allowed to drink beer and be grown up, though I'm sure that Les and Rick kept a very beady eye on me. Father did in fact enter the *May Flower* for the 1969 Medway Barge Match. The programme does not show an entry in the space for skipper; interestingly, neither is there one for the *Venture*! We did not take part, for reasons previously given, and this was the last time the barge was entered. Our regular crew still came over for the weekend and attended the supper, as crew of an entrant.

In 1969 Mr and Mrs Walker, owners of the *Mirosa*, offered my eldest brother a berth for the Medway Match. He helped sail the barge away from Lower Halstow, where she was berthed at a jetty which is now the site of the Lower Halstow Sailing Club. This barge did not, and still does not, have any auxiliary power – he was used to this. They berthed alongside a wharf in Gillingham and apparently discharged a mass of gear and articles, which were in the main hold – her conversion was not yet completed at the time. This was to reduce weight. I don't know how well she fared, but she was at this time up against the crack racing barges *May* and the *Edith May*, as well as the fleet-footed *Westmoreland*.

At the end of the supper in 1969, I spent all my pocket money on purchasing raffle tickets for a huge basket of fruit for my mother. I redoubled my efforts by bumming a bob here and there for more tickets from whosoever was willing. Many of the skippers of that time knew that Mother did a lot of the organisational work behind the scenes. Amongst some of the older ones, her feat of stitching a mainsail together was well remembered and many of them were very generous indeed, even giving me tickets. Amazingly, I won the prize. My eldest brother, having crewed on the *Mirosa*, was not party to my antics and I expect he was rather glad. It was my first raffle win and my mother was given a huge cheer when the basket of fruit was handed over.

It was after one of these barge match trips on the *Sirdar* that the skipper, Tom Cook, went off home for his supper, sat down in a chair and passed away. This I am sure was a very sad event for his family and friends, but the romance of such an event is memorable in itself.

I still take a passing interest when I see a group of barges collecting for a match, be it off Southend, the Swale, and the River Medway, or up the coast. Strangely enough, I have not been on the River Medway during a barge match since 1983. In that year I was sailing with my wife and young son, who was then barely a year old, on our Yachting

World Peoples Boat, *Blue Tail*. We had anchored up on the edge of the mudflats near Cockleshell Beach, inside the North Kent channel buoy, under the shadow of the huge imposing structure of the Grain Power Station; here we watched the parade of sail. The log entry for that day, 4 June, says that this was a glorious day and my wife wrote of the 'spectacular sight' as we lunched and lazed in the cockpit.

Although my wife and I had met during my parents' later tenure of the barge, she never actually had the chance to sail on the *May Flower*, and had only experienced being afloat on the barge with her bare masts. When we saw the mass barges on the River Medway in 1983, my parents had only recently sold the barge. My wife, after witnessing this sight, was able to visualise how the *May Flower* would have looked in all her rigged glory.

Forty years after sailing in my last barge match, I took part in the Blackwater Barge Match of 2005, sailing aboard the *Wyvenhoe*. I was part of the aft guard, working the leeboards and generally assisting with main sheet and wangs. It was an enjoyable occasion and brought back numerous memories. The skipper for the day was Mick Lungley, who recounted seeing the *May Flower* with her menagerie of youngsters aft, and then later helping as the 1960s progressed. He was skipper of the *Millie* during the last of the original barge matches and again skippered her, under a different owner, in 1969.

chapter sixteen

A Maldon Interlude

Following the incident that took place when the *May Flower* was in collision with the *Venture*, we sailed to Hoo. We berthed on the outside of the marina perimeter near the TSBC mooring. For a couple of weeks we went to school on the bus to Wainscott, often walking home via the Lower Upnor road and the beach beneath Cockham Woods. Things moved quite rapidly, I only know this now after researching the records.

A survey of the damage was arranged. This took place between 30 June and 3 July 1964 at Brice's Wharf. It became apparent that the damage was quite considerable. I have wondered since whether or not, against the actual value of the barge at the time and the costs to repair, it would have been more preferable to sue for a constructive loss. However, insurers move in mysterious ways. The *May Flower* was also our home. No local yard would quote for the work, or were not able to complete the extent of renewals needed. In this respect, the barge repair industry is probably in better shape forty years later than it was then. Only Cook's Yard of Maldon said that they could do the repairs.

The barge was towed by a Lapthorn's tug to Maldon on the 16 July 1964 for the repairs. I still remember the farewells from my classmates at school; they could not understand why I was going away before the end of term! If the truth were known, perhaps I didn't either. It is only now, scouring the reports and digesting details of the extent of works required to put right the structural integrity of the barge, that I can appreciate why things needed to be done sooner rather than later.

My eldest brother was due to start at his secondary school. He was boarded with the Young family on their barge *Henry* for the term from September to when the barge was repaired, and could be brought back to her home berth. This for various reasons was later than expected and eventually turned out to be in December 1964. The *Henry* at that time was using a berth at the head of the Whitewall Creek up from our berth; my mother said that they did also use our berth. Before that, there were the six weeks of school holidays and the anticipation of pastures new. Mother had already been on a visit to Maldon to arrange for my younger sister and me to attend the local junior school as it had become apparent looking at letters from Mr Clifford Cook that the works would take longer than previously estimated.

On the day of the tow, the tug arrived early in the morning. The tug seemed such a huge thing to my eyes, and took up position alongside to port, just forward of the leeboard. For the trip, my eldest brother and I crewed with my father, Mother having been dropped ashore with the two youngest to take our Land Rover round to Maldon.

The day of the tow was hot and sultry; the sea was like a mill pond all the way up the coast. The quietness was probably a godsend, as an alongside tow in any seaway would not have been advisable. We were allowed on the tug for some of the passage. It had a crew of only two men. Sometime during the early afternoon, we anchored for a while to wait for the tide to rise before the final passage up to the Hythe at Maldon. From records the following may be of interest: towage from the marina berth to Brice's Wharf, then back to the Hoo flats, came to the princely sum of £6 and subsequent towage from Hoo to Maldon came to £58.

During our stay in Maldon, a local artist produced a pen and ink sketch of the *May Flower* sitting on Cook's half blocks. This was later used by the Maldon Salt Company on their packaging label for packets of Maldon Sea Salt. The label shows one other recognisable barge, the *Saltcote Belle*. Our Land Rover is shown parked by Cook's shed, now demolished, which was on the site of the present boat shed and Barge Charter offices. Also featured is the steaming shed, now demolished.

The barge was not put onto the blocks straightaway; this took place a little later. We berthed at the Hythe with a number of other barges. Maldon, at the time, had quite a collection of barges, some rigged as sailing homes, as in our case, others maintained as yachts and some in the process of being rigged. One, the *Ida*, was just out of trade. She was fitted with a short stump mast with a derrick, and these spars had come out of the *Ethel Maud*. The *Ida* was owned by Barry Pearce and John Fairbrother, and was being used as a store for barge fittings that they were obtaining and selling on for reuse. The *Ida* later became a house barge at Heybridge, then a shop for second-hand boat gear and was ultimately broken up on this site.

The *Ethel Maud* had only recently been sold by Green Brothers and she was being re-rigged by her owners, a Mr and Mrs Jackson. Her gear came from the *William Cleverly* following the death of her owner, John Otter. His old barge was hulked where she lay along the seawall at Heybridge.

Some other names that come to mind are the *Saltcote Belle, Marjorie, Edith May, Gipping* and the *Olive May*. Incidentally, the *Ida* and the *Gipping* were tiller-steered barges when originally built. The *Olive May* was in Maldon having a new engine fitted. An old Crossley was removed and a big Kelvin took its place. This barge continued to trade as a motor barge for a further few years.

We missed by only a year the *Black Eagle* built by Curels in 1880. She was purchased by the Maldon Little Ship Club in 1939 and used as their base until 1963, when she was broken up.

There were other visitors I am sure, but names do not spring to mind, as this is, after all, primarily about my memories as I saw things – though Barry Pearce has been very helpful in this respect. Smacks lay along the steeply banked shoreline downstream, on the other side of which we soon found the park and lake. This was a whole new experience for us.

Eventually the *May Flower* went onto the half-blocks at the bottom of a ramp that lead out of the steaming shed. There was another berth, but this was not, as I remember, in

My father contemplating the work on the port bow, new frames have been fitted. Frame fastening is in progress.

use at the time, though the *Remercie* berthed astern of us for some while. The half-block berth later became the upper berth and a new set of blocks has since been laid adjacent to this. The *Edme*, and later the *George Smeed*, both sat on this upper berth during their lengthy restorations. A gangplank bridged the gap to the shore.

My mother fortunately took a number of photographs of the work in progress during the repairs at Cook's Yard. This was, as far as I know, one of the last jobs undertaken by the firm as it was then constituted, becoming known as Cook's Yard and operated by a team of barge enthusiasts.

The work progressed slowly: the outer wale and next row of planking was removed, as was the in-wale and other areas of internal planking. New frames were fashioned and fitted in position before removal of further outer planking, thus maintaining the hull shape. As this progressed, it again became apparent that the full extent of the work

A view out of Cook's old steaming shed looking at the *May Flower*. The shed has since been demolished and the site is used for wood storage.

One of Mr Cook's team of shipwrights busy marking out a plank ready for cutting out. Note the child beyond the yard worker; it is my sister.

required was expanding. The planking was ultimately renewed down to the water line, along a plank line back from the stem to about the forward hold hatch. An illustration of the barge after she was hulked clearly shows the extent of these plank renewals and can be seen in the epilogue.

The extensive nature of the work needed to put right the damage brought home the fact that had she not been doubled, following the collision – foundering would have not been inconceivable. We did leak a little, so I'm sure both my parents were very well aware of this at the time. My mother would not be drawn on this issue greatly.

Many of the frames were renewed in their entirety to the curved bow floors, others half length and doubled. At least the stem was in superb condition, it having been renewed not so many years earlier. The beam in front of the windlass bitts was removed completely and renewed as it was shattered.

The inner wale was renewed back to the forward bulkhead. Forward of the bitts, that is forward of the original fo'c'sle bunks, was not lined; this area was almost completely taken up with frames. A later illustration shows all the new structure, taken when I visited the remains of the barge in 1989.

All knees were renewed but some of the side infill chocks were not fitted as my father decided that circulation of air was a more sensible option, though I do remember that they were provided for fitting. In 1963 Father did not fit replacement chocks between the beams when renewing the sailing beam beneath the mainmast waist deck. Visiting the *Cabby* recently, I noticed that these chocks had not been fitted above her lining in the saloon (main hold), allowing air circulation to take place.

The covering board was not removed; I suspect that this was due to the complexity built in when the decks were doubled some twenty years or so earlier. It was cut back to good wood and a new outer piece let in, this proved to be satisfactory and was still intact, even after many years sitting as a hulk.

When making up the new frames, a pattern of the shape was first made, then Mr Cook would walk to Sadd's, by the Fullbridge, to match the shape and to obtain the best piece of wood with correct grain run. On a number of these occasions I was allowed to go along to look at the pieces of wood. I suppose this was a bit of a privilege for a boy of ten. I have often wondered since if this is the reason why, when walking through woodland, my eyes roam oak trees looking for likely shapes. My wife has got used to this now, and generally asks, 'How many frames or knees have you found today?' I think that this has as much to do with the fact that I own a wooden yacht and love working proper wood.

Steaming of planks is an event I remember; this meant a warm fire we were allowed to stoke up and feed with wood as needed. Barry Pearce oversaw this or an older gentleman, Cecil Wright or John Pitt, who was the senior shipwright. Barry at the time was the yard's labourer. The oak was steamed for an hour per inch (25mm) of thickness. This process softens the resins and fibres in the wood, which gives the wood pliability, giving it the ability to take up the necessary curvatures. Acute curves can be accommodated by wood when treated in this fashion. It is a time-honoured practice and is an effective method. These were either fitted directly from the kiln, or

The steaming shed. The fire is lit and a plank is being 'cooked' for its requisite period of time. On the left-hand side another plank is in the process of being shaped. In the foreground, various strakes are ready for marking out.

Father with the shipwrights fitting the first of the new side planking, it is being wedged up to the underside of the covering board.

cramped to the outer face of the port rail to obtain the correct shape and fitted cold. John Pitt took a cine film of the inside of the shed during the steaming operation for one of the bow planks.

On these steaming days, billowing steam would be seen drifting from the steaming shed, mingling with the wood smoke. The scent and the feel of the clammy steam is something that has remained with me. As said, we were often, when not at school, supervised by one of the yard workforce and allowed to stoke this fire and keep it burning well to ensure that a good supply of steam was maintained. I'm not sure what the modern workplace Health and Safety system would have made of it, but this was the early 1960s. I assume we also did as we were told – most of the time!

Barry lived aboard a smack, *My Alice*, CK348. He was also part-owner of the *Ida* and *Emily* for a short while, then later the *Kitty* (*My Kitty*). The smack can be seen ahead of the barge in some of the illustrations. Barry used to treat us to tea and cake or biscuits – imagine just how such a generous and sincere deed would be frowned upon in today's society. He made tea with thick, sweet tinned milk, and I can remember creeping aboard one day and having a few spoonfuls. If you read this, Barry, I apologise!

While the barge was at Maldon, Father removed the rudderstock for repairs with the rudder in situ. To do this he made three temporary gudgeon pins out of scaffold tube, drilled through to take a pin. These were dropped through the gudgeons as the stock was withdrawn. The stock was worn in way of the gudgeons and was built up by welding and turned down to correct size. A local engineering firm undertook the work. To drill the holes in the temporary pins, I can remember going aboard the *Gipping*, then owned by June and John Prime, to use a power drill they owned. This was the first time that I was to see hand power tools in use. Some wag commented to my father that it was not a good idea, and that the rudder would probably fall off. Well it didn't. As we were on the blocks, the rudder could not cause the pintle to ride up, as can happen when in a mud berth.

Some work was also done on the steering wheel shaft and big drive nut assemblies. The link bars had their holes built up with weld, which were re-drilled. The result of all this work was a steering system that had minimal backlash in it. The barge had a superb rudder and it can not have been very old when the barge was bought. The fit of the tiller head was tight with no slack. The steering gear was in this same superb condition when I last greased it all up in the spring of 1978, prior to finally moving to a house with my wife after our marriage. The shape of the rudder at its lower end, with Father's mizzen sheet shackle, was still visible when I sailed past her remains at Strood in the summer of 2003, the top having been burnt with the rest of the after end when she was broken up in 1989.

Spiking of the bottom was another job carried out by my parents. This in fact was the completion of a project started a couple of years earlier on the blocks at Whitewall Creek. To do this they had a series of light battens with the floor positions marked off. They used the bilge drain bunghole forward as a reference point. The battens were used to locate the floor positions on the outer bottom and new spikes were driven through. The yard allowed my parents to adjust the moorings to move the barge back and forth

Barry Pearce using an old knee as a pattern: it is being transferred to a thin strip of wood which was used to make a pattern for the new knee.

to ensure all floors could be accessed. I have covered this no mean feat, for a husband and wife team, in no more than a few lines, but it took them many hours to complete.

It was while we were on these blocks that my youngest brother decided to race around the deck on his tricycle. My sister and I had tried to stop this, but to no avail. Eventually, coming from port round the starboard aft main hatch coaming corner, he lost control and hurtled overboard. This may have been funny, but he narrowly missed the block and piled up in the sloshy mud covering the hard under bed of the berth. My eldest brother was home for half-term and he went down and picked the sobbing and bedraggled lad up. Mother had gone to Maldon station to pick up Father who was commuting to London each day to work. I have this visual memory: we got everything cleaned up, but knew that we had to explain the minor cuts, bruises and unstoppable tears. We got into trouble! Barry Pearce remembered this incident and related it to me in a letter, though he thought it was me and not my youngest brother that had gone overboard – he didn't mention how cross my father had been!

During the autumn term school break my eldest brother was invited to sail on the *Edith May* by Jack Spitty. The trip was a sail round to the Thames, then up to the Everard's company wharves at Greenhithe to pick up some spars that had come out of the *Veronica*. This really was quite an honour for my eldest brother and he still carries the memory with him, living in far away Cornerbrook, Newfoundland. Incidentally, it was Jack Spitty who came to my father's defence over an incident that occurred the following year on the River Medway. At the time of writing, *Veronica's* old mast sits ashore at Lower Halstow waiting to be refitted to the *Edith May* when her structural rebuild is completed. The arrangements of the topmast hoops, crosstree structure and forestay position are still as they were on the *Veronica*. As far as I am aware no other barge has this arrangement, which is described in chapter twelve.

When my sister and I were at the primary school in Maldon, we were regularly picked on by a small group of local kids. My sister suffered the most. One day I confronted these girls and boys. One, a girl who was at least two or three years older than I was at the time, was poking and pushing my sister around. I waded in and told her to leave my sister alone. The next I knew of this confrontation was during morning assembly the following day when the Headmaster spoke of an unfortunate incident, and the names of my sister and I were called out. We had to stand up, to be mocked by the whole school.

Our troubles finally ceased when my eldest brother, who had arrived home for the half-term holiday, caught this group having another go at us as we were about to enter the park gates from the road, which was a shortcut to Cook's Yard. He intervened and 'stuck one on' one of the older boys. Hey presto, we suffered from this bullying no longer! Even today, when driving past the school on occasions that I visit Maldon, I am

The *May Flower* alongside the Hythe next to the *Ethel Maud* during a period that the *Remercie* needed to use the blocks for some work. This was the first time the two last Greens Mill barges had berthed together since 1950, and was the last. The *Edith May* and the *Marjorie* are beyond.

reminded of these events. I can laugh to my wife about the incidents now, however at the time it wasn't funny.

At some stage during our time at Maldon, I witnessed a local lad of slightly younger age than I fall into the water from the gangplank to the barge. He obviously could not swim and I leapt in to pull him out. I don't remember how deep the water was, only that the child's mother didn't have the courtesy to call aboard to thank my mother or me. All I got initially for my troubles was a scolding for being wet! I think that some of the local community looked upon us people who lived on barges as a queer bunch. I'm not sure if we were actually looked down upon, but I do remember some interesting moments and I know now that, in many respects, we were discriminated against.

My mother took a view of the *Saltcote Belle* coming into the Hythe Quay one autumn afternoon. She was a beautiful-looking barge. Her hull now lies hulked in a gutway off Woodrolfe Creek, on the way up to Tollesbury Marina off the lower reaches of the River Blackwater. In 2002 her hull was still largely intact, with her stern nearly buried and her bow up high with a shallow layer of mud on her fore cabin top. She rested peacefully and unsullied by the breakers' saws, gradually rotting away to rejoin with the elements from where she came. She has since started to degrade much more rapidly.

The *Saltcote Belle* going alongside the *Ida* during the autumn of 1964. Her topsail has been dropped on the wrong side of the spreet. The barge on the inside is the *Gipping*. The other is the *Ethel Maud*, the last of Green Brothers' barges. Her gear came from the *William Cleverly*. Beyond is the *Edith May* and the *Marjorie*. Beyond and on the inside, against the quay, is the *Olive May*, her wheelhouse can be seen. Some maintenance is being done to the starboard rails of the smack *My Alice CK 348*, at the time owned by Barry Pearce.

We're off! Father, the youngest and I setting out in our Mirror dinghy – this was all part of the diversified sailing we enjoyed. *My Alice CK 348* can be seen coming into her mooring.

While at Maldon, we went to our first public Guy Fawkes Night fireworks display. The display was spectacular; it was set up in the middle of the lake. The area around the yard has changed over the past three decades. Gone is the steaming shed, and other buildings have found fresh uses as museums, recalling the maritime history of the locality and its vessels. A large new shed on the quay adjacent to the blocks now houses an office for a barge charter company, but the major part is still used for maritime work. A half-finished barge restoration project, the *Glenway*, has also joined the centre; she is often berthed at the Hythe. This vessel is, at the time of writing, being used as a static exhibit while the charter trade is slack. How things have changed; in my early days sailing on a barge, such things were not even dreamed of – recently I heard that she was up for sale.

It was not all work. My father and I took part in some local dinghy racing with the club located at the end of the promenade; this was exhilarating to me as a boy of ten.

Now, of course, the sport of dinghy racing is bread and butter to youngsters on the sail learning curve. We also had runs downriver in the barge boat and the Mirror dinghy for picnics. One of these destinations was Northey Island – there were a couple of barges on the other side of the seawall from which we were 'shooed' off.

One of our old crew, George, often turned up in Maldon. He had sailed with a chap out of the river from time to time. They had come in on this occasion with a tale about loosing their dinghy somewhere out towards the Wallet. They hadn't noticed for a time, and had then had to go back to find it! George would have been a little older, or about the same age as my father at the time. George arrived aboard when an amusing find was made by the yard's workforce. The following story was related to me by Barry Pearce, then again in a letter, and on talking to my mother about it she said that she vaguely remembered it too. Barry wrote:

> When the *May Flower* was on Cook's for the port bow work, a friendly old man was aboard, possibly a family friend. We asked him if he had seen the mouse nest in the forecastle. He hadn't, so we pointed it out to him. When the defective inwale (inner wale) was being removed on the port bow, one of the timber heads became exposed that was almost hollow inside but dry. Neatly built at the bottom of the hollow could be seen an empty mouse nest. Placed in it was a perfect, brand new, Green Shield stamp – not a nibble mark on it.'

My mother said that they rarely suffered from mice; certainly from 1966 we didn't, as we had a farm cat as a pet.

The repairs were not actually completed by the yard. There are records of outstanding works that needed to be completed. I cannot find the reason why this was so. Strangely, our long stay here in 1964 and all the work carried out on the barge during her time with Green Brothers is not mentioned in a little booklet *A Barge On The Blocks* by Clifford J. Cook. Perhaps there is more to this than meets the eye! Father had to set up a company, GANTA Enterprises, to enable the job to be completed up to a point that would enable us to take the barge away. In this manner, he became the person directing the work, which must have been in conjunction with Clifford Cook. I believe this all stemmed from the fact that at the outset, the yard initially said that the work could be completed by a certain date. Following the loss of a couple of staff, Mr Cook had written to my father stating that he would still be able to carry out the work required, but could not be held to a date. This was agreed and the barge had duly arrived. I understand from my mother that they needed to be away by Christmas.

Mother said that Father actually acted as the foreman for the duration. There were aspects of the work which did not meet the approval of my parents, and they instructed for certain things to be redone. There is some correspondence relating to the fitting of an outer plank near to the water line, prior to the remaining adjacent inner plank being repaired. Instructions had been given for the damaged inner plank to be pieced out and the section renewed. This was not done and leakage resulted, as my mother had predicted. This had to be put right. It should be borne in mind that my parents had owned the barge for fifteen years, completing some major repairs during this time, and could not in any reasonableness be considered amateurs in this respect. One repair was the renewal of the stem, described in chapter nine, which they had been told could not be done.

We spent a little time moored upriver alongside the mill. This was fifteen years after my parents had originally found the barge in this very same berth. Before leaving Maldon, a new mizzen was ordered from Taylor's; this was the only new sail they purchased. Mother had (as has already been mentioned) stitched the greater part of a mainsail. Over the years she had also renewed large areas of the topsail and carried out repairs to the foresail. Not so many years later, I spent a week of one summer putting in a new cloth in our topsail. All these skills were taught by my mother. My eldest brother also learnt to sew, though his speciality was the rope work that was needed to finish the outer edges, that is, the luff, leach, foot and, on a 'four-sided' sail, the head. His skills also included wire and rope splicing needs.

As Christmas approached, we were moved down to lie alongside another barge at the Hythe; this was the *Marjorie*. The owner (or skipper) of this barge told me that my parents should get rid of their little river barge and get a proper one! At the time, I remember being somewhat hurt by this comment, and it is probably the reason why it is still clear in my mind. However, I must admit that in retrospect, with the passing of the years, had they done something like transferring to one of the younger motor barges coming out of trade and moved the rig, things may have been different at the end of the next decade.

On passage homeward bound, sailing down the River Blackwater. Heybridge and Mill Beach are away behind. (Photograph by R.A. Scurrey)

It was planned that we sail back to Whitewall Creek over the Christmas break. Some members of the Leigh-on-Sea Sailing Club took this opportunity to experience a spot of barge sailing in the winter. These people were Les Proctor, the Oswald twins, Rick Scurrey and our old sailing friend George.

It was extremely cold that Christmas, with hard frosts at night and clear cold days, but no snow. The water was frozen in the area around the barges and on the morning of our departure the ice had to be broken before we could move! We sailed in these delightful winter conditions being blessed with benign gentle winds sufficient enough to sail comfortably. On departure the wind was from the north-west, which was a generally favourable direction for the passage.

The first evening we anchored up under the end of Foulness Point after sailing across the Dengie flats to the River Crouch. It was a tranquil passage. On the second day we made it as far as Stangate Creek for the night, going on up to our berth in Whitewall Creek the following day. My mother has told me that for her, this was an amazing passage, one of the best she could remember. The memory of it is one that she treasures. During this passage I was introduced to tea with a drop of the hard stuff – surreptitiously, I'm sure, as my mother would not have approved! One of the crew had a bottle of rum in the fo'c'sle and kept a pot hot on top of the stove.

An illustration taken during the passage by one of the crew, Richard Scurrey, shows us all dressed up in jerseys, coats and hats – it was extremely cold. Richard, many years later, recounted to me that the sail was superb but it was exceedingly cold outside. The bogey stove up in the fo'c'sle was a favourite spot for warming up. This included, he said, chuckling, 'tea with lots of rum!'

As a postscript to this reminiscence, as a family my wife and I generally purchase Christmas cards from the RNLI. I spotted that the 2003 maritime feature card was from a painting of a barge at Maldon. The picture and some features struck right to the core! It is a stern view of the *May Flower* from the time we spent at Cook's Yard undergoing the repairs described.

The *May Flower* at the time was not fitted with the traditional pair of davits; the aft davit was reinstated much later. Instead a derrick was rigged from a spare mizzen boom. This is clearly seen. The trademark varnished port quarter board is also portrayed, and to port a flash of white for our then white-painted leeboards. Aloft can be seen another length of white which is for the 2m steel extension to the head of the sprit, the dark blue bob fly is also clear. Her transom is depicted with a reddish hue; this was a pretty mid-blue hue, a typical artist's touch to enhance the colour mix.

A very similar photograph has appeared in a recent publication, *Essex Rivers and Creeks* compiled by Robert Simper, and this shows all of the above features. The date depicted is, however, incorrect, the *May Flower* was at Cook's Yard from August to December 1964 and not 1960. The above-mentioned photograph also shows our Mirror dinghy sitting on the main hatch top – they weren't in existence in 1960.

Once back at Whitewall Creek, Father needed to build a steamer to complete the works not finished at Maldon. This was a busy time on the barge. I was by now approaching the end of my junior school life and my parents were seriously considering a move to a new location.

chapter seventeen

Leaving Whitewall Creek for Twinney Dock (1966 to 1968)

In the spring of 1965, after our return from Maldon, my elder brother and I helped to complete the outstanding work on the port bow, not completed at Cook's Yard. This was the final layer of outer wale planking and fitting of the steel plate rubbing bands to the covering board.

Father had to build a steamer box to enable us to steam the timber. The outer planking was treated with linseed oil for about twelve months before a coat of tar was put on. The un-tarred planking can be seen in some illustrations of the period. One is of the barge prior to the start of the 1965 Medway Barge Match in chapter fifteen.

A number of structural renewals were in the planning pipeline, but we still had a summer of sailing to come, including taking part in the inaugural barge match on the River Medway – a new committee having been formed post-1963.

I was by this time considered to be a full-time member of the 'workforce' and I spent many an hour at the bottom of a huge two-handed rip saw, which was 1.5m in length, helping to shape what were, to me, huge pieces of wood.

We helped steam timbers which became new frames for renewals at the aft end. These were cramped to formers set up on a bench. It is amazing to see how far a piece of wood, which has been thoroughly steamed, will bend. So it was no trouble getting the shapes needed for a number of the aft frames. The wood was oak, which behaves well when treated in this manner. These timbers were about 8in wide (180mm) and 1.5in thick (40mm), four or five of these were through-bolted to lock them together. These were basically the shape of a shallow 'S'. The greatest shape was needed for the aftermost frames.

Eventually we replaced a number of frames at the aft end, to starboard with these steamed laminated replacements. A new beam for the aft end in way of the aft end of the aft hatch was put together at this time, but not fitted. The inner wale to starboard and beam knees at both ends, and the aft poop deck, was earmarked for renewal. However, completion of this work had to wait.

Two barge enthusiasts from Leigh-on-Sea visited us at our berth during the summer of 1965. One of these was Dick Durham, who later became the last true trading sailing barge mate on the *Cambria*. They stayed during the week, tarring the sides of the barge. Dick would have been fourteen, only a little older than us older ones, he reappeared from time to time for a number of years – later crewing during a move.

During the later end of 1965, all mooring holders in Whitewall Creek learnt that the whole area was to be redeveloped in the near future. So a new berth had to be found. As it happened, the Young family of the *Henry*, who had been using Whitewall Creek on and off for nearly two years, were also looking for a new berth. They had found Twinney Dock at the head of Twinney Creek, lower down the River Medway in the parish of Upchurch, Kent. Initially Mrs Young and my mother made a detailed visit and this resulted in an agreement to combine forces in a partnership to resurrect the dock.

Twinney Dock was reached from a back road out of Upchurch by a track or narrow lane running down the side of a stand of trees edging a field. At the bottom of the track a little wooded area lay to the left-hand side, falling away to grass and the seawall. To the right was a fenced-off paddock with high ground sloping down towards a bit of scrub woodland with old fruit trees; this last area was also protected by a seawall.

Twinney Dock was a farm dock and was originally built as part of a brickwork manufacturing concern that Wakeleys had here. A lot of small bits of red brick and the typical chunks of burnt or clinkered bricks were scattered around the site. The dock had been disused for a considerable number of years. The dock is 'L' shaped; it was agreed that the *Henry* would have the inner berth, with the *May Flower* using the outer section. The dock was in a pretty poor state of repair, full of debris and old cars! The ground was high enough not to be flooded by normal spring tides, but water did creep up over the wharf areas on exceptional tides.

From the water, the approach was via the middle channel from the top of Stangate Creek. This lead up past an island of marsh separating it from Halstow Creek on the port-hand side going in, and Milford Hope Marsh to starboard with its old strayway curving round to an area of marsh with a footpath which connected it to the land, by Twinney Dock.

The strayway was an old cart track built up with debris, which came down from London by barge, and was the means of access to the marsh when it was used for grazing. After the floods of the 1920s the land was abandoned, as happened to similar areas around our part of the coast at that time. The sea needs somewhere to go; the low marshes that fringe coastal areas protect the land behind, providing a sump for high tides to run into. This naturally alleviates flooding, so it is in our best interest to protect and even increase these areas. Here we found the remains of a vessel under the marsh edge near the landward end of the strayway; these were smaller than a barge, and years later I learnt that the remains were of a small barge some 50ft in length used to ferry livestock to and from the marsh islands for the rich grazing. We still had not left Whitewall Creek, however.

In the meantime, shortly before my time at Wainscott Primary School came to an end, I had a memorable visit to the dentist to have four teeth removed prior to being fitted with a brace and plate. This was a remnant of our time at Maldon; I had jumped off a swing, not moved away quickly enough or something, and got whacked in the face – my sister was involved. This had set a tooth back and now it had to be sorted out. In those days, it was not as common as it is now to see youngsters with braces, and boy did I get teased at my new secondary school when I started later that year.

The *May Flower* at her berth in
Whitewall Creek early in 1966,
before our move to Twinney Dock.

An amusing incident that my younger brother would wish to forget occurred at this
time too. A motor house barge – the *Mayor* – had come into the berth at the head of the
creek. The family had a little girl of the same age as my little brother and they became
great friends for a while, as I myself had with the eldest McCrumb girl. My sister and I
were playing with friends and we saw the pair of them at the bottom of the foreshore
beach, upon which a clinker sailing dinghy was moored. A conversation was taking place
behind the transom, and with much shushing we overheard, 'If you show me yours, I'll
show you mine!' Well, we kept quiet about it and I expect the first my mother will know
anything about it is when she reads these accounts.

We did not sail very often in the spring of 1966. Between about May through to
July, much activity took place at Whitewall Creek to move a plethora of belongings to
Twinney. There was a large shed with a workshop and bench, an outside bench upon
which heavy work was carried out, and the steam box. A fair-sized quantity of timber
was also transported. Prior to the actual move, much of the larger stuff was loaded as
deck cargo. Could this have been construed as a proper cargo voyage? It was certainly
more than a few tons and added some inches to our draught.

As I was moving I would not be going up to a senior school with my childhood
friends. The move terminated relationships built up over a number of years. During
my last year at primary school, I had spent more time up in Frindsbury and Wainscott

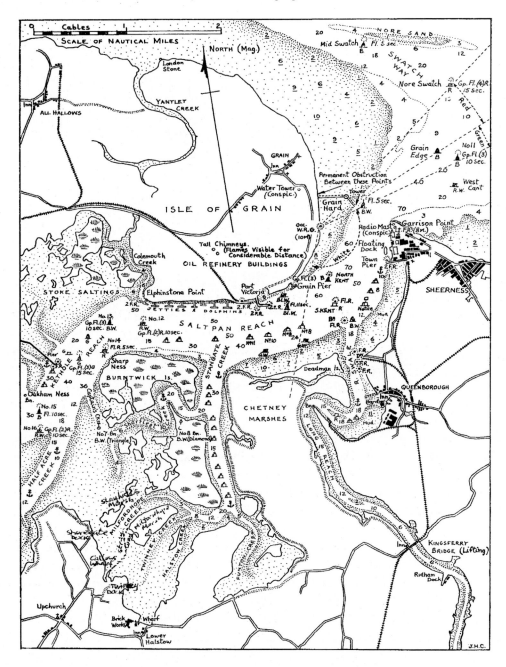

Chart of the lower reaches of the River Medway showing the location of Twinney Dock and Callows Wharf. (Original by Jack H. Coote and reproduced with courtesy of *Yachting Monthly*)

visiting some of my pals. It was with one of these that I watched a Laurel and Hardy film on television. This was one of my first real television experiences, apart from being sat in front of one of my grandparents', probably having to sit through a concert which they enjoyed – it being considered good for us too. I'm sure that it was – I do in fact enjoy listening to various forms of music still.

Eventually the final day at my primary school approached. We had an assembly and party, and then it was time to go. It was sad; most of my class had been together since starting in our first infant class, back in 1960. One of my friends said, 'I'll come and find you', and he did, many years later when we were in our final year at our respective secondary schools. He had changed a lot, as I expect I had also. Some of the others were turning out badly; they were into a drinking and smoking culture, and this was not just ordinary weed either! So I did not pursue his invitation to visit. I often wonder how they all got on, but in life we all generally move on into different circles and expanding worlds. Now, of course, youngsters are always on the move with parents, but when I was at school it was much more unusual.

I will now give a flavour of the efforts that were needed to bring Twinney Dock back into life. As a matter of fact the dock is still in use, some forty years after its rehabilitation by the Young and Ardley families, and this I feel is something to be proud.

During the approach to the school summer break, we were at Twinney most weekends preparing the new berth. All the old car wrecks and other detritus had to be removed. This was accomplished using chains and wires hitched to the back of vehicles and dragging things out; in our case, the trusty old Land Rover was used. Mr Young must be given due credit here as he pulled out the bulk of the larger objects, being able to access the site during the week.

Having cleared the dock bottom and sides of items that could be seen, it became clearer what needed to be done to the structure of the docksides. At the berth we were going to be using, the post structure was in reasonable condition, but a few more posts were added to provide additional shoring for shuttering. Holes were dug for the posts by my elder brother. Once a hole was deemed by Father to be deep enough, a post was dropped in and he knocked the tops with a huge sledgehammer – he had two sizes. These were braced back to the bank. The sides of the dock were disintegrating in places and the shuttering needed to be replaced. The sides had taken up a curved shape through non-use and falls; this meant digging down to replace shuttering before the bottom could be dug out and back-filled behind the shuttering. All this, of course, had to be carried out on weekends when the tide was going to be out.

During this work my mother and I came across an object against the side of the shuttering. Once removed and cleaned up, it was found to be the transom of a barge boat. The carved name of the barge and port of registry was still clear; the boat had belonged to the old Eastwood's barge the *York* of London. The remains of the *York* rest amongst the morass of disintegrated barges at the edge of Chetney Marshes on the eastern side of Stangate Creek. She was hulked sometime during the late 1940s.

During this time we also cleared the track leading round the side of a hillock, believed to have been an abandoned cargo of clay, to where our mooring was being arranged.

A garage was put up in which Father kept the vehicles – the Land Rover and his new car, an Austin 1300. A woodworking bench was also sited within. An area further on was cleared and paved with bricks and fitted out with the steamer, large workbench and timber stowage. Soil from the clearance was used to make raised walls upon which Mother later planted wallflowers and other perennials.

Before we moved, a GPO telephone line was run to the creek; this was now the second time in about four years that the GPO had run a line some considerable distance from a road for our convenience.

A source of fresh water was, of course, of paramount importance for this project to have any sense. My mother arranged for use of a temporary supply of water, courtesy of a local farmer. This source was from a standpipe situated in the corner of one of his orchards; located at a road junction opposite Wetham Green cottages, about a half mile distant. Some while after moving, a pipe with a metering unit was installed, the meter by the water board, the pipe by the two families. The pipe, of some considerable length, was supposed to be buried at the edge of a hedge, but this was never carried out due to events that I recount later. The water, until the pipeline was laid, had to be collected by tanks in the back of the Land Rover. The arrival of piped water at the two berths was a

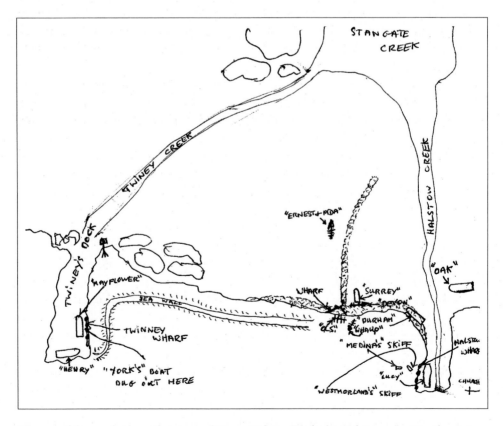

My map of the area between Twinney and Lower Halstow Dock, drawn between 1966 and 1967, strangely enough, I do not show the strayway across to Milfordhope Marsh.

first for both families. As I have said elsewhere, this was 1966 England. It was a huge plus for us, removing one of the major chores that had impinged on our lives for so long. For my mother it must have been a blessing.

Marking of the creek had to be carried out. This was done by walking out over the mud and putting withies on the humps of marsh bordering the channel towards the dock. My eldest brother and parents did this between them. The channel, a shallow 'S' curve, typical of a slow-running gut way, went over towards Lower Halstow then back towards Twinney Dock, in doing so the course was towards the wreck of a barge.

The barge wreckage is now marked by the Lower Halstow Yacht Club, for their extensive moorings now cover these flats. The wreck is of the barge *Ernest & Ada*. She was built at Paglesham in 1865 and hulked about 1940. Local lore has it that this barge was in fact 'dumped' in this spot. Her bilge bungs were left out, allowing her to flood as she picked up on the tide, this would have continued until she failed to do so. She then became a hulk to gradually rot and fall to pieces. She was of course, by then, an old lady, but her remains still linger.

Robert Simper, in his book *River Medway and the Swale*, mentioned that the barge wreck was a hazard for barges entering Lower Halstow. It should be noted that a hard ran out from the vicinity of the wharf near Glass Bottle beach, the remains of which still sit proudly above the mudflats. I believe it is this that would have been the obstacle that barge skippers have had to avoid. The wreckage lies well to the west of the hard. I still have a sketch of this area, drawn when I was a youngster; it shows these features, but it does not show the true course of the creeks.

I helped construct a beacon on the point that ran out from the high ground at the outer end of the dock, where it fell away to marsh at its outer end. The bank opposite the dock was mainly fairly high marsh with a sort of lagoon enclosed by a narrow bank. Further out was flat mud with cord grass humps. These were not considered to be a problem for a barge. Room for manoeuvring under sail would be limited and the use of a kedge for getting out was apparent. We had used the barge boat strapped alongside with a long shaft Seagull Silver Century outboard engine in calm conditions; this would have helped in these manoeuvres.

Moving day finally came around. Several members of the Leigh-on-Sea Sailing Club came on the passage with us. This was not to be a happy day. Before dawn, we had warped away from our old mooring using the kedge to get clear, leaving life as we knew it behind. It dawned clear with early signs of a hot day; there was a very light breeze from the south-west. By the time we had sailed out of Whitewall Creek, the wind had become very fickle; on reaching the turn round St Mary's Island, opposite the Medway Yacht Club, the concerns Father had about the loss of navigable water became a reality.

The breeze was blanketed by the hills above Upnor and we lost steerage way and were at the mercy of the tide. The sails hung in useless folds. Father asked two of the crew members to get the dinghy alongside and start the big Seagull outboard. This gave a little steerage back to the barge, but it was not enough. The look on the faces of all the adults on board was that of the inevitable. Fenders were got out – these were old car tyres – as

The *May Flower* at her berth in Twinney Dock in 1966. Note the dark line just above the barge; this is the strayway across the flats to Milfordhope Marsh. The remains of a small vessel lies near the landward end, this was used to ferry livestock out for grazing, before the sea claimed back the land. The plate also shows the edge of the cleared dock bottom, this was all dug by hand.

the *May Flower*, firmly in the grip of the tidal stream, slowly slid towards the outer line of moored yachts, fetching up alongside a sloop. The sloop's mooring was trapped between *May Flower*'s leeboard and starboard side – we were securely tethered.

A launch from the Yacht Club soon arrived alongside carrying club officials and a policeman. Then fortuitously round the corner came our saviour. This was in the form of John Oliver, a River Medway waterman who had known my parents for years, in his little river tug. He quickly came alongside and offered a tow. John was born without arms and learnt to do everything with his feet; he is an amazing gentleman, and my mother still meets him from time to time. John's tug was called the *Hobbit*; it is one of a class of river tugs called 'Toshers'. At the time of writing the tug is still operating for a different owner on the River Medway.

Eventually, after all the formalities with the MYC had been dealt with, John gave us a tow into the entrance to Stangate Creek. Later that afternoon we were able to sail up Stangate and in towards the entrance to Twinney along our marked channel. We dropped anchor on the flats outside the dock. The *Henry* was already at her new berth, having arrived sometime previously. The next day, John Oliver reappeared to give us a pluck into the dock, where we were berthed stern in. He sat ahead of us for the night. During the afternoon, moorings were run out to anchors that had been placed previously at prepared positions.

While in the dock, John did some maintenance on his engine. One of our crew, Rick Scurrey, who was an Engineer Officer with the Royal Fleet Auxiliary, and I gave John our help. This was the first time that I had worked on an engine. Later, after joining the Royal Fleet Auxiliary on leaving school, I became more than familiar with these noisy and smelly contraptions – many of an enormous size and power.

Once we were at Twinney, we settled into our new environment, finding the area to be both pleasant and friendly. Allotment-style gardens were created from the high ground of the paddock area. Each family had its area and Mother spent a lot of time preparing ground and planting fruit bushes. Eventually she had crops of potatoes, tomatoes, beans and other vegetables growing by the following spring of 1967. I had never seen vegetables growing close at hand before. This was a revelation to us all, although I knew that Mother's parents were great gardeners from our annual visits to Southend to see them. My paternal grandparents were also gardeners, and my grandmother always prided herself on her runner beans. During their annual visits to us each summer, a bag of these would be brought. Grandmother would sit with my mother discussing this and that, while preparing lunch together. She was a grand old lady and I marvelled at the way she got up and down the fo'c'sle ladder!

In time we continued the repairs to the aft end of the barge and some work at the forward end, but this had to be done in conjunction with further repairs to the dock, which took precedence. The work forward included some frames which were renewed and others doubled, on the starboard side. A section of in-wale, from the stem back towards the forward bulkhead, was replaced.

At the first opportunity we made off into the beyond to explore our new terrain. The village of Upchurch has a rambling thirteenth-century flint and brick church that had the very distinguished English seafarer, Francis Drake's father, as vicar during a period from 1562. The church also has an area of medieval wall painting that has survived and a number of brasses. The village had a butcher, post office, Co-Operative general store, general provisions store, paper shop and greengrocers. A pub occupies a prime spot next to the wall of the graveyard. A roadway leading to a car park and the village hall went along the back of the churchyard. The housing was a mix of Victorian, 1930s and early 1960s types. Hop fields and orchards surrounded all of this. The orchards ran all the way to the water's edge in places. Between Upchurch and Lower Halstow strawberry fields abounded, though these had rotational crops, as we were later to notice. In time I found that the village had three public houses and one close by in Lower Halstow. I frequented them all later in my youth.

Otterham Quay is situated within the parish; from here Crescent Shipping's coasters came and went regularly. We found a barge moored here, the *Glenway*. Another was hulked alongside the quay, and this was the *Swiftsure*. Up the eastern side of the creek we found what seemed like a fleet of barges lying sunk up to their decks in the creek bank. The *Glenway* come out of trade in the early 1960s. She was owned by Paul and Cynthia De Bont who, with their family of nine children, lived aboard. She had a mainmast and sprit up during this time, but no sailing gear. One of the children, Catherine, later became very interested in barges and often sails as mate on the *Wyvenhoe*; previous to this she spent a number of years on the *Portlight*.

The De Bont's sold the *Glenway* in December 1973, having had her since September 1964. She went to Maldon, where some restoration work was started, but this project failed and for a time she lay abandoned near the barge graveyard at the eastern end of the promenade. This could have resulted in her demise, however she was rescued and taken to Milton in Kent and her hull was rebuilt at the Dolphin Yard. I sailed up to Milton during the mid-1980s and saw her chine planking out for renewal, the upper works were rebuilt and the tide was being allowed to flow in and out until the final planks were fitted. The *Glenway* is currently owned by Topsail Charters and is being used for exhibition purposes while awaiting re-rigging. During 2005 she was again for sale. The fate of this barge is again under threat. Maybe a keen owner will complete the work needed to restore her to sail, the last of the 'Glen' barges.

From Twinney, a path led southwards across fields to Lower Halstow, which could also be reached round the seawall. The brick works in Lower Halstow were still manufacturing bricks when we first arrived in Upchurch, but closed soon after. Yet another route round the seawall northwards, past low-lying fields with free-range pigs and orchards, came out into an eerie area of high ground with a scattered dump of grubbed-up fruit tree stumps known as Callows, finally reaching Shoregate Dock, which had a collection of vessels moored within, including the little barge yacht *Dione*.

One of the jobs that needed to be done before the onset of wet weather was the laying of roadway tracks along a lengthy section of the lane. We did not get a lot of help from the other people in the creek on this project. When Father said a job needed to be done, it happened; the lack of help should have been a warning of a looming crisis.

During the first autumn at Twinney, the two families got together to put on a fireworks party on Guy Fawkes Night. All the kids, a total of seven of us, spent many weeks collecting driftwood and clearing dead stuff from the scrub woodland around us. A lot of family friends attended this event; I believe it was done to show that we were all settled. We had the usual sausages, onions and rolls with baked potatoes and ginger parkin. The fireworks were good too and I seem to remember being allowed a drink of cider.

During 1967, the *Henry* was readied for a spell of sailing. She had not been fully rigged out for a couple of years. Her sprit was a hollow spar and is said to have been cut down from a boom belonging to one of the big 'J'-class yachts during the time these huge vessels were being converted to Bermudan rig or the Marconi, as it was then known. The *Henry*'s sprit needed some attention along the glue lines. It was still painted blue, as it had been when under the Bennett's ownership.

On the day that the *Henry* was leaving, we had to drop our outer moorings down to facilitate her departure; we also helped to warp her out. This made it quite a communal event. What was really needed was a little launch for plucking us both either in or out! The barge eventually cleared the dock with my father and elder brother assisting aboard. They left the *Henry* when clear of the dock. The *Henry* had an old trading skipper aboard. They had a spot of bother getting clear of the bight and anchored to await the next tide to finally get completely away. Our old friends the Strong family went on this trip with the Youngs. My elder brother was able to reacquaint himself with the daughter, an old flame from Whitewall Creek, however a romance did not blossom!

In the summer of 1967 we did not get out sailing. Instead we went on a camping and touring holiday in Scotland. We were originally supposed to be going to Ireland, in company with an aunt and uncle, but the political situation that was developing stopped this. I vividly remember two things: the breathtaking views and the midges.

Later that summer I was unfortunate enough to meet up with an angry Alsatian. This dog took an instant dislike to me, and I only escaped by climbing one of the gnarled apple trees in the old orchard to the east of the dock. I spent some considerable time in great distress up this tree. Even the police were involved! This memory has remained with me ever since, and sadly I am still very dubious of the intentions and nature of these animals.

Fred Cooper appeared one summer's day. He stayed for the afternoon reminiscing with mother. The tide was in and I was sailing a little model swim head barge that I had made. She was stumpy rigged, in the older fashion, seen from pictures I had come across in one or other of the barge books I had access to. Fred congratulated me, and then went on to point out areas that could be improved. He also said, 'Why don't you give her a topmast like they had, not unlike a modern barge?' The first topsails on spritsail barges were not fitted with a headstick – this was how she was ultimately rigged. Well the upshot of this was the complete dismantling, to my mother's horror, of the rig as it was.

I dug out the hull and put decks and hatches on; it was also given a little dinghy and a set of leeboards modelled on those fitted to the *May Flower*. The topsail did not have a headstick and she only had two shrouds each side. With this model I later won a prize at the Sittingbourne Youth Arts Festival. It sailed in gentle breezes – although it really needed a keel.

The collective children of the two families used to organise model regattas during the warmer weather. For these we generally used knocked-up model boats that we had made. I wouldn't use my barge; instead I used a large 2ft plastic racing yacht. This had been a birthday present some years before, and it was my pride and joy. She had a fibreglass mast some 3ft high. Using this I first learnt about race handicap rules. On other occasions, we used to set it off and chase it in one of the dinghies, either in the Mirror dinghy or *Little Willie*. My elder brother and I had spent many a happy hour doing this during earlier times at Hoo.

As time went by, little effort was being put towards the barge. Cosmetic work was kept up, but the project aft had stalled. During the latter part of 1967 the deck beam, which had been constructed from steamed and laminated timbers, was fitted. Before this the new frames went in; there were four complete and a half frame, coming back from the transom. All this work meant an awful lot of hole drilling with augers, spiking and bolting. The in-wale was replaced to starboard, round the quarter, too.

I settled into my new school and soon made a couple of friends who kept in touch for a long time, later in life. I did suffer from an initial kind of initiation into the village life. The lads of course did not know a lot about me, other than that I was from a family that lived on a barge. One early incident during the first year at school involved being threatened by a local lad with a knife. I told my parents and was severely questioned about it. The next morning my parents took me into school and requested an interview with the Headmaster. I was eventually summoned from my classroom to be interviewed by the Head. The other lad was also outside the office. He told me that the Head believed him and, as I was new, I would not be believed. I stuck to my story. Eventually, after several sessions, the other lad admitted it and apologised. He never troubled me again and from time to time still meets and speaks to my mother.

This behaviour continued, as I was subjected to a certain amount of bullying on the school bus by another group of boys. This revolved around another lad being egged on to give me hassle; I was spat at and my uniform abused. One day my uniform jacket pockets were ripped. That was it. When the bus arrived at the centre of the village, outside the church, I stormed off the bus and dragged the lad into the churchyard and gave him a pasting up against the tree to the right of the gate. This was the first time that in all my school life I had had cause to use violence and it turned out to be the last. The tree still stands in the same spot, though a little bigger; I often wonder what happened to that lad, for it was not really his fault. The upshot of this event was a certain amount of respect from the perpetrators of the trouble towards the quiet lad from the barge.

On returning home from school one day during the spring of 1967, we found our mother in conversation with a young bloke – Dick Durham had come back for more. It was funny how people used to appear – others did as well, such as Richard-Hugh Perks and, later, Fred Cooper again, with Brian Dawson from the Thames Barge Sailing Club. I now realise that they were all basically interested in seeing what was happening to the barge!

Dick dropped in on a number of occasions over the next couple of years. One of these was when he was sailing on the *Cambria*, as mate, with Bob Roberts. They had berthed at one of the Rainham wharves and were waiting to unload a cargo of maize starch. This had probably been loaded at the Royal Docks in London. Dick was the last mate of a spritsail barge trading under sail. This privileged experience lasted from August 1969 to October 1970, when the *Cambria* was sold to the Maritime Trust. My parents obviously knew Bob Roberts, having passed by on the water often enough during the 1950s and 1960s. He was not enamoured with, and was disdainful of, amateur bargeman – but it was amateurs that provided the impetus for the resurgence in the spritsail barge. When Bob Roberts eventually had to call it a day, trying to keep his barge in work, others were re-rigging barges to carry people. His was a grand effort indeed and he rightfully deserves his place in barging and British maritime history – the last of the sailormen. I sometimes feel that we were born into this world a decade or so too late: my elder brother in particular would have been a superb bargeman!

Dinghy sailing was becoming a regular pastime whenever the tide and time allowed. During school holidays, we would take off as soon as the tide had made enough to get afloat. Our limit was the foot of Stangate Creek and round the back of Milfordhope Marsh, across towards Lower Halstow. At Lower Halstow lived the Lowe family. Their two boys had a Cadet dinghy; later they also had the use of a Drascombe lugger, which were then fairly new to the boating world, and we would often meet them. The families had got to know each other during our visit to Lower Halstow Dock in 1963. Our friends' parents took my brother and me to the Medway Yacht Club that autumn to a talk about the Dutch raid on the River Medway in 1667. This was my first visit to these parts since our incident off the clubhouse on the barge, leaving Whitewall Creek. I have been back many times since and nobody remembers the incident.

The vicar of our parish was a huge man with a white beard and had been the incumbent since the early 1950s. He asked my parents to think about bringing us all to church. The result was that we were all confirmed. Neither of my parents had been confirmed as Christians, though we were, as already said, baptised at the church at Frindsbury. We then joined a fledgling Church Youth Group. This later grew and my parents eventually took over as leaders for a number of years. We sang in a concert at the Sittingbourne Youth Arts Festival, the backing provided by Geoff Gransden – the present owner of the *Edith May* – and a friend of his.

My father, after a lapse of a number of years, rejoined the Thames Barge Sailing Club. His reasons for doing this are unknown, but I came across a letter from the then honourable secretary which is reproduced with the good wishes of the present Thames

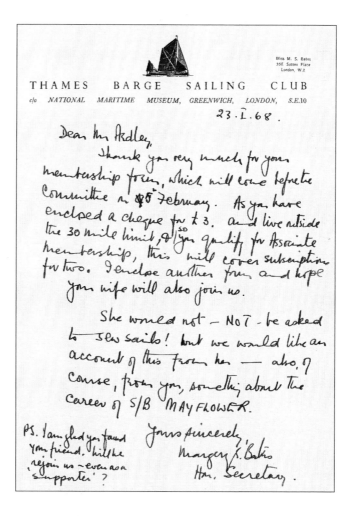

Copy of a note from the Thames Barge Sailing Club secretary in 1968 – they asked for a an account of what had been happening with the *May Flower*.

Sailing Barge Trust. The note makes reference to my mother's sewing of a sail. This of course was the legendary mainsail saga. The secretary asked for an account of what they had been getting up to, but this was not done. I hope my book is recompense indeed! Their membership lapsed again after a number of years. My mother rejoined the organisation during the 1990s. She did a trip or two on the barges and later introduced my son to barge sailing, sailing on the *Centaur* on a club weekend on the River Medway – so barging has remained in the family.

Moving on into 1968, the relationship with the owners of the *Henry* took a serious downturn. It was only recently that I learnt the basis and the truth of this sad occurrence. The two families had set up Twinney Dock as a joint enterprise, however my father, who was usually a stickler for detail, did not get all of this laid out as an official agreement. He relied upon 'my word is my bond'. This was very unfortunate. Mrs Young had, as I understand the matter, bought the plot including the rights to the dock. The first my parents knew about it was when they were presented with a rent bill! My parents were very angry and took the problem to their solicitors, but without an official document there was little that could be done. They were not prepared to continue at Twinney under these terms, especially as the major efforts to resurrect the dock had become, largely, a one-family affair.

Again a new home had to be found. Barge berths, where one could be set up as we had at Whitewall Creek and Twinney, were hard to find, but they fortunately managed it. Round the seawall to the north-west lay Ham Green, where an old wharf had existed at a place known as Callows. No records existed, other than local knowledge. A local farming family owned the land and a legal agreement was drawn up to rent this from them. Early in 1968, we began the process of uprooting the entire barge yard-type arrangements that had been set up. How this affected our schooling I do not know, for I was doing quite well in this department and had joined the orchestra, and eventually became lead second violinist.

The land at Callows needed to be cleared. It had for a number of years been a depository for the stumps of grubbed up fruit trees and these littered the area in large numbers. Our time at Twinney was drawing to a close, and we took no further interest in the upkeep of the dock. It is interesting to note that this dock is still in use, as is the berth at Callows Wharf. Both places now support a wide variety of craft.

In hindsight, this turn of events gave the *May Flower* a new sailing lease of life during the coming years. Twinney Dock was a difficult place to get out of and we had not sailed the barge during our tenure there. Upon moving to Callows, for a number of years, we did at least use the barge for sailing again.

As a postscript, amongst my father's papers I found details about various properties and plots of land locally which were at the time up for sale. They had obviously spent a certain amount of time and thought about the way forward. It would seem that the *May Flower* was nearly sold at this point. However, that event was not going to happen for a few more years yet.

chapter eighteen

Callows Wharf, the Early Years

The wharf at Callows had not been in use for a great number of years. There was nothing to build up on. At the bottom of the beach along the mud line a row of old post stumps was found and these were used as a line for the new wharf. One of these was later dug out and replaced, for the benefit of an archaeologist working for the Port of Rochester. The berth ran north/south and was open to the east, but protected in many respects by the strayway, which ran out to Milfordhope Marsh, from the marsh to the north of Twinney Dock.

Although there was an acceptance that a wharf may have existed on this site, my parents had to apply for various planning permissions and, apart from the Port of Rochester and others, the Oyster Fisheries Association had to give their blessing. Much of this was done retrospectively, after initial verbal permission had been granted.

My father ordered six large telegraph poles from our old friend Mr Day, who still worked a reclamation yard at Whitewall Creek. This gentleman was able to obtain virtually anything! The poles arrived at Callows quite soon and we were then able to set to work constructing the wharf.

Much was being organised at this time as well. This included the clearance of all the tree stumps. We came up with an ingenious use for these; they were stacked to create a fence for what became the garden and barge yard areas. The ground was mixed, with an area protected by a low sea wall and a sluice system and a smaller area of high ground which was not subject to flooding, which was handy. The original sluice for the low ground was located and found to be beyond repair.

The telegraph poles were dropped into holes, which were dug about 6ft deep. The Land Rover was used to get them started, and then by the use of blocks and tackles we got the posts upright. Once all the posts were in, a longitudinal member was bolted to the inner four posts. A jetty was constructed towards the inner end, the aft end of the berth. The posts were supposed to have been fitted with diagonal braces, but for some reason this was not done – the barge didn't actually lie against the posts. At the forward end of the berth was an area which did not have an overgrowth of cord grass. This was hard underneath a thin surface of silt. Old timers living locally told us that this was used to sit farm barges for unloading into wagons.

The area where the barge was to sit had to be levelled. The silt was quite sandy here, further up there was shingle and a sandy beach to the south of where the jetty ran into

The posts are up. Looking down the line of the wharf towards the north, with the Slayhills Marsh in the distance – the River Medway is beyond.

the shore. Some shuttering was arranged to help keep the beach in check. I realise now that the berth should have been a beam width further out. When digging down to put in the shuttering, we came across remnants from the original wharf, which was posts and wattle shuttering. The jetty was constructed of posts dug into the bank. Once through the shingle surface into the clay, it was possible to knock them in further. Father did not brace these at the time; this work was carried out later, the priority being to get it all up.

Anchors were arranged in an 'X' configuration to be picked up at the bow and stern. Springs were arranged to the inboard side, these were all chain. Father still did not believe in the superiority of the newfangled manmade ropes that were then coming onto the market. One of these chains broke many years later, where it had wasted along the wind/water section, which could have caused the loss of the barge.

The general layout ashore was thus: the track from the road came down to the north end of the plot. The plot was oblong and ran north/south. Immediately to the right was a pond, with high ground around. A hedge and trees went away to the south. The high ground also went on from the lane, round onto the area that fronted the wharf. This dropped to a lower grassed level south of where the jetty came into the shore. Log walls were arranged to screen the private areas from the public access that ran along the shoreline. Inside this screen, the higher ground continued inland, falling away to a lower level. The high ground was later transformed into a grassed area and flowerbeds.

Immediately south of the jetty, a flat expansive area was large enough for us to lay out the mainsail and of course the other sails, when necessary, for repairs and tanning. This was kept mown. Stretching southwards, the outer area fell gradually to scrub grass and then marsh. A low seawall ran out from the high ground and protected the inner low pasture from flooding. This was a rare occurrence. To the south, the main seawall ran north towards our plot, and then turned west to meet the high ground at the bottom of the orchards.

A gut-way ran along the side of the main seawall, a drainage ditch from our pasture led into this. To the north of the plot was an area of low grassy marshland, running inland to meet the bottom of an orchard. The marshland was littered with stumps. This would flood on spring tides, but was not part of our plot. Further along, the high ground fell away and this was protected all the way to Shoregate Dock by a sea wall. The *Oak* had moved here about this time from Lower Halstow.

While all the jetty construction work was in progress, which was only when tides permitted, many other tasks were progressed. Much of the equipment from Twinney was dismantled and transported the short distance by road on the Land Rover; this I am sure was grossly overladen on many occasions. The benches and steamer box were put down on a brick-laid bed and all this was screened and largely protected by a 6ft-high wall of tree stumps to one side; beside this was arranged racking for timber storage. On the other was the higher ground, which became a lawn and flowerbeds.

Water was arranged with the local water provider. They put in a new water meter in a box up by the road at the top of the access lane. From this meter we had to run nearly half a mile of hose to the current civil engineering standards and dig this in to a depth of at least 2ft 6in (approximately 75cm). It crossed the access lane just past a row of farm cottages. This was dug in, as was the section near to the meter box immediately.

The rest of the water pipe was dealt with as time permitted, but in a time span agreed with the water provider. An inspector would turn up by arrangement from time to time and inspect a length of dug trench, take measurements and ask for more to be dug out here and there, before allowing us to bury that section of pipe. This went on until we reached 'our ground'. After that he was not interested! My older brother and I largely dug this trench, with help from our sister – our family friend Richard Scurrey also did some of this too.

The General Post Office, as it was then known, yet again ran a telephone line and telegraph poles to our berth from the road. Strangely enough, once these were in, other properties on the lane also acquired telephones too. Apart from the row of cottages, another detached cottage was situated half-way along the lane to the wharf. From this last cottage, the lane was grass. This had to be given a bed of broken bricks to make a suitable roadway. Why we did not at that time arrange for electricity to be run to the berth, I do not know. The present owners of the site did in fact do this some years ago. The difference it would have made to our quality of life and ability to maintain the barge is unquantifiable. The farmer we were renting the wharf grounds from owned the orchards that fringed both sides of the lane.

Before we moved from Twinney, digging out some naturally low areas and creating ponds drained the pasture area inside the low seawall. These were landscaped with footbridges. A ditch ran across the ground towards the boundary at the bottom of the orchards into another ditch running south. These turned east where it met the proper seawall and then out into a gutway. The sluice for the drainage ditch was rebuilt. We also rebuilt a footbridge and steps up the bank to enable the general public better access through, which was a right of way. Previously to this, a path had been forced through a hedge of an adjoining farmer's grounds into the orchard above our plot. The hedge to the south and west of the plot had many types of old trees, including oaks, beech, damson and bullace – a larger, more orange, damson.

July 1968: the *May Flower* rests at her new berth at Callows Wharf. Note that the mizzen tabernacle has been refitted. The *Henry* can be seen in the background to the RHS. The brickworks' furnace chimney is also visible at Lower Halstow.

The beacon that I had helped to put up on the end of the spit running out from the end of Twinney Dock was taken down and placed on the western edge of Milfordhope Marsh. This marked the turn to be made in towards Callows. The owners of the group of vessels using Shoregate Dock appreciated this. No other marking was carried out as the remains of the sea walls on Milfordhope Marsh were well above the highest tides. I do remember though, that my elder brother put a couple of withies on the strayway to the east of our berth. This berth gave us a lot of sailing freedom, and although it was a fairly shallow berth, sufficient water was available during neap tides.

The move was accomplished without fuss; a tow had again been arranged with John Oliver. A number of our old sailing friends came for the trip, and a couple of the younger ones helped to dig in the two anchors which lay out on the flats. On the way round, Father set the topsail to give it an air. The barge was moving again after nearly two years' stagnation – things were looking up!

Shortly after arriving at our new berth, my parents restarted the work at the aft end, which had been jogging along. The frames, which had previously been fitted, had not been fully fastened, apart from the lower planking. By now it was decided to renew the inner wale on both sides. The oak planks were steamed before fitting. A new knee was fitted on the port side at the aft side of the new beam; the others were deemed to be in good condition. Last of all, the deck was renewed across the aft end.

An illustration shows Father being helped by his young apprentices. The decks on the *May Flower* having been doubled over were more complicated to work on. The original deck was of 6in (150mm) width planks; the doubled layer was of thinner section and about 5in (120mm) wide. I have always assumed that this was to ensure that the seams did not line up. The planking seen in the illustration is the lower layer; the doubling had to be spiked down over a layer of felt, in the same fashion when the decks were doubled during the 1940s. The seam to the aft hatch coaming was caulked and paid with bitumen prior to this. When the top layer had been laid, caulking and paying the seams with bitumen had to be done. Finally, the painting etc. had to be dealt with.

I remember drilling the holes for the spikes; the auger can be seen sitting on the cabin top. The drilling of holes had found its way into my hands – my mother said that I had a feel for it, knowing when not to force the auger or bit when a resistance was detected. This resistance found in old wood might be a knot or an old fastening. Hence the care needed. A brace and bit can also be seen further across the cabin top. Something that I will always remember is that amongst the rot found in a piece of timber being removed, would be vast amounts of relatively sound, but useless wood, which when cut produced wonderful yellow sawdust. Power tools for doing all this work were but a dream and remained so!

A bonus for completion of this work was summer sailing. The gear was lowered and refitted. Once the main gear was up the mizzen was stepped and re-rigged, with the new mizzen still not tanned; my mother was very displeased about this. It had, though, been down since early 1966 and stowed in dry conditions, on the port fo'c'sle bunk top. Finally the sides of the barge were tarred. Following all of this, we went out for our first sail for two years!

Left: We are helping our father to spike down the aft deck. I am the one nearest the greasy steering gear with the punch. My sister and younger brother are the other two persons.

Opposite: The *May Flower* at her berth at Callows Wharf, in the spring of 1969. Note the bob fly has yet to be renewed. The rails forward are in the process of being painted. The strayway can be seen in the middle ground.

There followed a period of fairly domestic life. The grounds ashore had been transformed from the ugly sight of dumped tree roots into a delightful spot. We even used to find ourselves attracting visitors, believing that parking was available for them to enjoy a picnic in our gardens overlooking the barge. The casual visitor walking through was no trouble whatsoever. My mother had a fair-sized allotment area for growing vegetables and fruit bushes. We did have a bit of a problem with rabbits that even wire netting failed to alleviate. The ground supported an area large enough for a field big enough for five-a-side football, and a cricket square. My elder brother created the cricket square; he achieved this by continuously mowing the area, wrecking a mower in the process. At least our friends could come for a game.

During the period 1968 to 1970, I was tasked with renewing various things that needed attention around the barge. One of these was a new hatch cover for the forward cabin top. It was constructed from pinewood and I gave it a camber, which tied in with the hatch coamings. The top was varnished plywood and clear Marley perspex sheeting.

The perspex was very tough and suited natural lighting purposes. Many charter barges are now fitted with standard yacht-type hatches let into the cabin top; these are tough and functional – they were not available when the *May Flower* was originally fitted out. My father always believed in the make-do-and-mend mentality.

Another job that I completed with the help and direction of my father was a new cover for the steering gearbox. He had got hold of some pre-curved oak carlines of the right section. The cover was constructed with these with a pinewood top, which was varnished on completion, and very pretty it looked too. Various other areas that I gave attention to were: the forward hatch coaming, the rails forward in way of the thickened section where the sweep crutches were fitted and the making and fitting of some cleats. Some of the 'new' cleats had been removed from the *Gladys* during a raid when we were out in Stangate Creek on one occasion!

During this period, Father had a few of the winches repaired. The two leeboard crab winches had the drive pinion teeth built up by welding and then machined. He also

Digging the *May Flower*'s berth at Callows Wharf in 1970. Note also, that the gear is down for overhaul. The telephone cable can also be seen above the group of people! A raft, which had followed us from Whitewall Creek, is being used for access.

had the drive pinions of the windlass built in way of the bearing in their housings and similarly the drive teeth. He also obtained a spare brail winch – where this came from I am not aware. This was probably meant as a replacement as indicated in the 1949 survey report.

Time was moving on. In 1969, my elder brother, who was now in his sixteenth year, sailed on the *Mirosa* in the Medway Barge Match as a member of her crew, and later went off to a Merchant Navy School at Dover. He joined the Union Castle Co., sailing on their passenger ships, Bowater's and King Line. He also sailed on the *Reina del Mar*, an early purpose-converted cruise ship. All of these groups became part of the Cayzer Irvine Empire. He eventually reached Able Seaman before retiring from the sea.

In this same year a large barge appeared in our locality: she was the *Olive May*. She lay at anchor under the south side of Milfordhope Marsh; a gentleman asked for permission and left the dinghy at Callows. The *Olive May* had just been sold out of trade. She lay in this spot for a number of months. She was a large barge, being 108nrt, built at Sittingbourne in 1920 of composite construction, with steel framing and wood side planking and decks. She had an engine installed from new. We walked out along the strayway to get a closer look, but were told quite firmly not to venture out onto the mudflats as soft holes abounded.

During 1970, the berth was dug out and more shuttering put along the bottom of the posts. A line of shuttering was built along the bottom of the high ground at the top of the beach to protect the base of the bank from the persistent erosion that takes place on any unprotected shoreline. The spoil was used to infill behind this shuttering. A certain amount of seawall stones were placed at the foot of this; these were left over from some seawall work and Father negotiated our use of them. To dig the berth, the barge was moved out past its normal position and the central area was skimmed to remove the hump that tended to build up. This was hard and messy work, but we did have a bit of fun. I remember doing this once more before I left some years later. This was not an occupation that I remember being carried out at our Whitewall Creek berth.

The barge was by now comfortably settled at these moorings. Although we were not sailing as much as we used to in earlier days, it was an easy berth to leave and get back into, however sailing was increasingly being limited to my parents' holiday periods – for the first time since they had owned her.

During the course of our barging life, family would visit for the day or, as happened on odd occasions, they camped ashore for a night or two. Often visits coincided with a stopover while driving to, or from, Europe during the summer holidays. Some of my cousins have quite vivid memories of the barge, but alas none of sailing on her, as my uncles did in their earlier lives.

The grounds of our patch had been significantly improved, enough to attract increasing numbers of visitors stopping for picnics when out walking. Mother's vegetable patch was a success and her fruit bushes did well. Father even managed to get a patch of rhubarb going – he had a thing about this edible leaf stalk: he always maintained that it was good for the bowels, which of course it is! As a family we were probably more settled now and had become firmly immersed in rural village life, albeit living on the marshland fringes.

chapter nineteen

Our Last Sailing Years

By the summer of 1968, shortly after we were at our new berth at Callows Wharf, the renewal of the poop deck planking was finally completed and the barge was returned to a condition fit for sailing. The barge was given its usual cosmetic refit, and then we were ready to go.

We again made a trip across to Leigh for a long weekend visit during the holiday. Our new mizzen was still not tanned. I can remember my mother telling my father that it was about time that it had a coat of tanning. I'm not sure what my father was playing at, but he should have known better. I believe it was a vanity thing, it being the first all new sail that they had fitted to the barge. Mother was quite cross about this, but it was done by the following summer. In mitigation it had been in dry storage for two years or so.

Mother often took photographs when underway, and one in particular, from 1968, epitomised family sailing on the barge. The Mirror dinghy was now always taken with us and could be seen stowed on the main cabin top. A little dinghy that my younger brother had been given was carried in the davit aft. The barge boat trailed obediently in our wake. Dinghy sailing was something that we all enjoyed. During periods at anchor the dinghies were put in the water and we had the opportunity to be masters of our own. We all ultimately learnt to sail well, and all have had, from time to time, our own dinghies, and in my case now, a Finesse 24, wood-built clinker sloop.

It was upon leaving for the first time after our move to Callows Wharf that the vicar of Upchurch, a wizened old gentleman of great age, arrived at our berth on a parochial mission. He walked to the end of the jetty and was aghast at not finding the barge. He apparently made his way back up to the village on his bicycle and muttered to some bystanders that, 'They have gone, completely gone, except for the cat.' The bystanders later related the story to us. This had been the first occasion that the barge had been taken for a sail while we were living in this parish, so the local populace were not fully aware that we did in fact live on a vessel that could drop her moorings and disappear into the far yonder! The cat, sensing that a strange occurrence was happening, jumped ship just prior to our departure and bolted; strangely enough it did not stay behind the next time. He was from a farm litter and came to no harm – being very partial to rabbit.

The refit of 1969 was a little different to those that had occurred time and time again during our years growing up. Father had entered us for the Medway Barge Match

A general view looking aft, with all the crew gathered around the wheel, except Mother, while sailing in 1968.

and we hoped to be able to sail in this event. Father had moved from an architects partnership in Greenwich to become a senior architect with the Borough of Gillingham (Kent). My mother was at this time studying to be a schoolteacher at the College of Further Education in Sittingbourne. My eldest brother was in his last year of school and about to join a sea training college to train as an Able Seaman. I was just fourteen.

My elder brother and I led the other two in all that needed to be done. That is, to keep the rig, sails and preservation up to the fairly high standard that was maintained through most of the years we had the barge. Father would give instructions to us before departing off to work in the mornings. We went through the procedure for getting the gear ready for lowering without the assistance or watchful eyes of our parents. The chain was removed from the windlass and lowering wire hauled out from below and three turns were put on the windlass ready. The stoppers were not touched. The mast case bolt was removed and we rigged the topmast for lowering, this being lowered in the evening upon Father's return home. The chocks and rollers, on which the sprit sat when lowered, and the mast post were brought aboard from their designated stowage ashore ready for the big moment. On this occasion the gear was lowered in the evening after Father's return from work – ready for us to get stuck in the next day!

Masts and sprit were sanded and given a coat of varnish, all white work washed and freshly painted. The top of the topmast would have been given a fresh coat of white paint, and the yellow for the cap and bob top. Mother always made up the new fly to the Ardley house bob; this was always fitted immediately prior to hauling up again. The rigging wires were wire brushed and oiled, along with any other repairs.

The hull below the waterline would be thoroughly scrubbed off on a falling tide ready for a coat of heated tar. Scrubbing of the bottom was actually a regular feature of our early years and teens. It was a task carried out monthly to prevent the build up of mud and weed. My elder brother was the mainstay of this exercise; at least up until he went away, then the task fell to me. After I left to go off to college in London, the job lapsed. My elder brother upon arriving home on leave would set to and scrub off possibly months of detritus – often muttering about it all.

As for tarring, this tended to be a messy job, both in relation to the tar and mud. Amazingly I was able to nearly always keep myself reasonably clean – I still do, when doing similarly messy work, such as antifouling the bottom of our boat. My wife has never understood how I do it – it is an in-built self-preservation instinct carried over from my barging childhood! My youngest brother escaped this job, except towards the very end of my parents' ownership.

Mr Simpkins, the barge cat, on an occasion he deigned to come with us!

A lot of painting preparation, if not already done, was completed at this time. Final coats to the deck was completed after the gear had been raised; gear work causes a certain amount of unavoidable mess.

The barge having been got ready for the Medway Barge Match, we were saddened when we found that we were not going to take part, due to the previously mentioned professional skipper saga. However, during Whitsun of 1969 we took one of my school pals for a long weekend away. He was a Boy Scout and his father, a Senior Scout Leader, wanted his son to have the experience. My pal did too! Interestingly, the lad's grandparents were Captain George 'Doggy' Fletcher and Mrs Ada Fletcher. I had the honour of meeting Mrs Ada Fletcher not long before her death; she was extremely pleased that her grandson had had the opportunity of this experience, which he had greatly enjoyed. Sailing was becoming more limited in duration and geographically.

During 1970 we sailed mainly at weekends; we did have a week out in and around the River Medway, but by this time my eldest brother had departed off to a sea training college, to train as a deck boy. It was not often now that we went very far; an anchorage in Stangate Creek was often as far as we went. For my parents, this was the gathering dusk – the twilight of their barge sailing. A trip to Leigh was the longest passage taken.

We had got to know a local family, the Gransdens. They had a yacht kept at Shoregate Dock. The youngest son, years later, purchased the *Edith May*, berthing her in Lower Halstow Dock where extensive restoration work could be carried out. They were sometimes met out in Stangate. On one occasion, we anchored over the shell banks at the western foot of the creek to scrub off and tar the sides. We did all this while our parents visited their friends' yacht. By the time that they got back, we had scrubbed down both sides and one side had been given a coat of tar. The other side was done the next day. We also collected mussels and mother produced a lovely supper from them. We had done the self same thing some years earlier in the Swale.

It was very busy during the summer of 1970; I had an awful lot of schoolwork to catch up on. I had been moved up from a CSE to a GCE class. This meant reading up on poems by Wordsworth and Tennyson and the reading of Dickens' *Hard Times*, which I thoroughly enjoyed, and a few years later even bought my own copy, and a Shakespeare play. Later in life I realised that I would have been better off staying on in the CSE class – where I would have gained a greater level of passes.

During the summer holiday, my sister had a girl from France to stay on a school exchange. She hailed from a farm: I don't suppose the conditions on the barge were that much different from late 1960s French rural life! The girl had two weeks with us. She was of good sturdy stock and not a bit like the mental picture I had of French girls. During her stay my mother and sister took her to London, Canterbury and other places, plus just meeting friends locally – but she wouldn't go out in a dinghy.

Over one weekend we took the lass out for a sail on the barge. At the end of this trip, we were running late to get back to the home berth. Father had to be back at work on a particular day and the wind was rather lacking in strength. We got the barge to a position some distance from the moorings and anchored on the mudflats. Our parents went off ashore in the barge boat with my sister to bring it back. I was left in charge to bring the

Looking up the mainmast, past the hounds, to the topmast head to check that, 'All is well aloft!'

barge into her berth on the afternoon tide; we did this by using the kedge and dolly winch. By the time my father came home from work, the barge was safely moored up. My mother was not with us, so I can only assume that she had to be somewhere also – probably school. My sister remembers this occasion too – making a comment about our ages. The girl enjoyed her time with us and her sail immensely.

On one of our sailing trips, my mother went ashore in the boat with my elder brother, who was home on leave, to collect some shopping. Why? It was probably to fetch fresh food, we having been out for a while – I do not recall, but we could have sailed round to Queenborough. We were at anchor in Stangate, near the entrance. The breeze was a fairly light 3-4 from the west. My father thought it would be a good idea to prove the 'Man and Boy' statement that is often said about the ease of barge sailing. I had just turned fifteen. The youngest two were back aft on the cabin top and were instructed to keep out of the way.

I climbed the ratlines and loosed the topsail from its gasket, then sheeted it out. Some slack was taken up on the anchor chain. While doing this, Father had carried the mainsheet block back aft and hooked it onto the traveller and moused the hook. He also dropped the mizzen down. The foresail was hoisted up to its almost set position and the gasket removed to the last few turns. I then heaved more of the cable in until it was near the up and down position. The topsail was then fully set and the main let out to the sprit, with the upper and lower brails slack. The foresail was dropped by throwing off the last gasket turns and heaved up; it having already been secured to the windward side with its bowline reeved – it was then ready to take the barge off on the desired tack. The down haul tackle was then hooked on. On this occasion we were not surrounded by the inevitable yachts, though a few were in the anchorage.

With the barge trying to forge away on the tack, I continued to heave until the anchor needed to be broken out; my father came forward to help me with this. Father had also let down some leeboard on both sides. Once sure that the barge was ready to go off on the desired tack, the hard part of breaking out the anchor commenced as quickly as possible. The cable of course needed to be cleared away from the windlass and fleeted back over the barrel to starboard regularly, due to its propensity to 'walk' to port. Depending upon the situation, a short fleet was used when needed and the cable was not slacked off onto the dog (a special claw shackled to a strong point for doing this job). After wetting the barrel and pressing down on the port coils, the starboard coil was flicked over with some slack. By pressing down on the last turn, the middle coil could be flicked over, some cable runs out, but the turns are further to starboard. Then winding is recommenced. It goes without saying that this is actually quite a dangerous operation to perform, and great care is needed to preserve fingers!

Once the anchor was broken out, I wound away quickly to get the anchor to the surface. I remember that Father let the foresail go over as he went aft. I then moved back to the mainmast to let out the rest of the mainsail. I had to let the main brail winch run out, while back aft Father sheeted in the mainsheet. We were sailing. As soon as this was done, it was back to the windlass to complete bringing the anchor up to the stem head, tidy up the chain stowage and wash down. Whilst dealing with all this, the foresail tack was tensioned and I would undoubtedly have had other things to deal with too. Finally the area at the bottom of the mainmast needed to be tidied up, hanging ropes back on their cleats and carefully coiling the topsail hoist out in a figure of eight configuration, ready for a free run, when dropping the sail. This is important on a barge, because by the quick action of dropping the hoist and leaving the sail sheeted out greatly reduces the sail area in a squall and helps prevent the loss of the topmast!

We then spent a couple of hours sailing about, before going back to anchor. My mother apparently watched our departure with my older brother from ashore – aghast at what we were doing! I think that we proved that we could get our barge away from anchor and get sailing manned in this manner. My parents, however, had in their early years often sailed the barge alone, so what this exercise actually proved, to this day I do not know – perhaps my father was putting me through a test. It has, though, remained a vivid picture in my mind.

On another of our trips out, Father rigged the barge boat with the Mirror dinghy rig and we sailed into Queenborough for stores. Father did things like this – the reasons even now are not obvious.

The refit in 1971 followed the usual pattern. Once the gear was lowered, the topsail was removed ashore for some repairs. The topsail needed a whole length let into the leach. Talking about this with my mother, she said that it was virtually a repeat of a repair carried out only a few years earlier – possibly a fault with the sail cloth used at the time – or being left un-tanned far too long! As Mother was now a 'college girl', this

*May Flower, c.*1971. Note the sail repair to the topsail, this virtually mirrors that completed some years earlier. Also note the recent patch and a new section in the hoist of the foresail. (Original by Bowler Family – Nick Ardley collection)

job fell to one of us. As I have said earlier, I discovered a gift for this work, which was strange considering it was my elder brother who became a seaman and was again home on leave. I removed the offending panel and spent the good part of a week stitching in a new section. The receipt for this sail cloth and stitching twine has, incidentally, survived with the barge records.

The mainsail, only needing a few minor areas to be dealt with, was left on. The foresail had a small repair carried out – I believe that Mother did this, as I do not remember doing it. Running rigging was removed, new rope was reeved and the ends whipped. All the wire standing rigging was wire brushed and oiled; seizing was coated with the famous Stockholm Tar. It was now my youngest brother who often did these tasks. On completion of all the jobs, the gear was winched back up after putting the stayfall wire back onto the windlass in the correct manner for this operation.

This 1971 season was my last sail for a couple of years. I was due to go off to a college in London to begin a four-year training programme as an Engineer Officer Cadet with the Royal Fleet Auxiliary. My mother had by now completed her training and became a full-time schoolteacher. Father moved from being a parish councillor to being elected onto the Swale Borough Council. This and other duties within the local community curtailed the level of time that they gave to the barge. This meant that much of the later maintenance fell to me when home on college breaks. My sister and mother did the necessary as and when it was needed, assisted by my youngest brother, who was still a comparative youngster and still learning things that we had known for years and grown up with – bless him.

An abiding memory during that year was a joust we had with the *Mirosa*. She was berthed at a wharf in Lower Halstow while owned by the Walker family, but had recently changed hands, being owned by a lady, Carrie Spender, with Jim Didhams sailing as skipper. We had seen the *Mirosa* leaving Lower Halstow on the morning tide, and she was reaching up Stangate Creek as we were setting sail from our anchorage. She came up alongside and the pair of us turned out into the River Medway together. The wind was a lovely westerly, we ran out side by side, and, believe it or not, we pulled away from the *Mirosa* and cleared the entrance at Garrison Point ahead of her. This for me has always been one of those magical moments on the water. As we overhauled the *Mirosa*, the skipper hailed my father, calling 'Well sailed skipper' – what a compliment! I have on occasions recounted this story of our joust with the *Mirosa* to barging folk, and it has generally been met with incredulous disbelief – well it happened! She was not rigged with a bowsprit in those days.

On this trip we went on across to Leigh-on-Sea for a brief visit. This was the last occasion the barge was sailed this far. The daughter of my father's cousin took a photograph of the barge from her sailing dinghy during this period. Years later, the cousin, Brian Bowler, gave me the photograph during a visit I made to him. The photograph of the *May Flower* coming across the River Thames was taken in the vicinity of the West Leigh Middle Ground, with us heading in towards the Ray, sailing towards Leigh. A motor coaster can be seen on the extreme right-hand edge of the picture; she was one of Priors' vessels, these coasters, or their newer sisters, still traverse this course up

For this plank I have two helpers! I am using a wooden jack plane to put a bevel on. Note the barge is rigged and ready to go.

and down the London river today. Coasters of this type are a direct evolution from the spritsail barge, being small enough to access many of the little wharves previously used by their sailing forebears. Cargoes are mainly ballast and other similar bulk cargoes.

Sadly, in 1972 the barge was only sailed for the odd weekend. I was away for part of the summer on an extra curricular college course, pulling lumps of engineering hardware to pieces and trying to remember how they went back together. This in fact I had a knack for; I believe in part this had a lot to do with my upbringing. I also went on a hiking holiday with a friend in the West Country, where we camped near Cheddar Gorge and drank copious quantities of scrumpy! The rest of the family were away on a camping car tour to Sweden and Denmark. As far as I can remember, the sailing gear was left on and the barge was ready to go. When this was done my father always aired the sails on a regular basis – it kept the sparrows away, if nothing else. Our sailing days were by now numbered and had definitely moved into a twilight period.

In 1973, prior to going away to sea, it had been agreed that I would help with a large project to renew a lengthy section of the starboard wale. I started this job on completion of the college term and my first batch of marine engineering exams. However, when I finished at college I had to spend three weeks at Chatham Dockyard finding out about its workings and other interesting things. I spent one of the weeks attached to the nuclear submarine refit group; this was fascinating stuff and light years in difference to my project on the barge, which was now over eighty-five years old.

During the early part of July, my father developed problems with his eyesight. He gradually lost the sight in his one good eye and was now virtually blind, seeing only white light. This was caused by a detached retina. The enormous responsibility to complete the work which had been started now fell heavily onto my shoulders. I spent most of the evenings, after working at the Dockyard, completing this, with his and Mother's guidance. I did not have a lot of time, as I was due to go off to sea as part of my Engineer Officer Cadet training. This for me was an exciting period of my life: new horizons and opportunities lay in wait.

The work was continued with the help of my sister and younger brother, who did the bulk of the much-needed holding, heaving and help with offering up and 'gophering'. In this way we got cracking with the replacement work. Our raft had been put alongside as a working platform. Once we had completed the removal of the sections of old planking, I doubled the tops of quite a number of the frames, forward of those that had been replaced a few years earlier. A section of the covering board was also cut back to sound timber, for replacement. The planking was taken back some 30ft from the transom towards the leeboard.

The wood was duly ordered and soon delivered from a timber firm in Chatham that Father had used for many years. The frame lines and other marks had been completed sometime previously by Mother. Planking shapes were lifted by using a dummy plank and taking measurements. When shaping the planks, for once I was the person at the top end of the double-handed saw. I cannot remember whom it was that was beneath, but it would have been either my sister or youngest brother. It was not too long before I had reached the stage for the fitting of the outer run of planking. Of course each layer, and there were three of them, was fastened with galvanised spikes as planking progressed. I remember marking the locations of the spikes on the edge of the covering board to try and avoid putting one on top of another – probably after a prompt from my mother.

I had to make sure that the butts of the planking were well staggered; this I did with my mother's help and in discussion with Father. He would at times come and have a look at the progress. The 'looking' of course was a discourse on what had been achieved that day, what was to be done next and any problems encountered or likely to be encountered! The major part of the cutting and shaping of the planks was carried out in the working area ashore. The shaping required to the planks was not great, as the curve given to the plank virtually ran it along the sheer line.

Due to the curvature of the planks along the wale in both the longitudinal and lateral directions not being extreme, steaming was not required. The timber having a natural flexibility was pulled into the side using a Spanish Windlass at the aft end; we also used vertical timbers wedged against the raft at the bottom and a tackle at the top. Once the final plank was fitted and spiked, bolts were replaced where they had been removed when stripping out the old woodwork. These were fitted into the many knees that tied the sides of the hull to the beams and a fabricated steel angle knee, inside the transom.

Once the planking work was completed I replaced the outer edge of covering board. Had the decks not been doubled, I would have liked to have removed the whole area completely and renewed this section; however, it was sound enough. Finally the steel rubbing band was fitted. The wood was coated liberally with creosote until it stopped soaking in, then tarred. The rest of the side planking was then given a coat of tar.

When doing this work, I am sure that I drew upon knowledge and experience of seeing the way things were done when we were at Maldon in 1964. We had, of course, carried out a fair amount of plank renewals over the years, specifically the inner wale to the starboard side forward and both sides under the aft quarterdecks. Many of these jobs would have required the wood to be steamed.

The receipt for the timber to complete this project has survived. Recently my mother was sitting on the seawall sketching Lower Halstow Dock, where the *Edith May* is presently being re-constructed, when a lorry turned up to unload a quantity of timber. One of the men approached mother and asked if she was 'Mrs Ardley of the *May Flower*?' He had been a young man in 1973 and, amazingly, had remembered delivering oak planks to us at Callows.

It should be appreciated that all structural maintenance carried out to the *May Flower* during the Ardley ownership, from 1950 to 1981, was completed using hand tools only. These included a huge double-handed saw, with which large timbers and planking was cut. A sturdy bench with a central slot was used to support timber for cutting. From the age of nine, from time to time, I spent many an hour being the pitman, at the lower end of this saw with my father above. It was the lower person's job to push the saw back up to the upper person whose job it was to guide the saw along the cut line during the downward cutting stroke, the saw's weight doing most of the work; it is incidentally the hardest part of the two-man process.

As previously mentioned, when I carried the work out to the starboard quarter, I was in charge and either my youngest brother or sister helped with the sawing and did what was needed under. All holes were drilled laboriously with a brace and bit or an auger; my mother tells me that these were all specially lengthened by a blacksmith after purchase. Augers were turned, half a turn at a time every now and then, having to back out with a pulling turn to ensure cuttings were removed, and the entry screw remained clean. From time to time these needed to be sharpened using tiny Swiss files. I used chisels with up to 60mm (2.5in) blades down to the smallest size; rounded chisels were used where required. When shaping, removal of wood was first carried out using large wooden jack planes, then moving down to standard steel planes. The sweet and sometimes peppery scent of fresh shavings, depending upon the wood being worked, is an abiding memory and is still something that I appreciate.

On the day I was due to go off to join my first ship with the Royal Fleet Auxiliary, I aired all of the sails. I can remember stowing the topsail carefully, and especially making sure that the gasket was correctly fitted to the upper section of the sail, this was something we were always taught to do. Now, I often cringe on a windy day when I see the upper part of a barge's topsail flogging around because this little bit of effort has not been put in! This was only a few hours before a taxi took me to the station.

I just had enough time to get my breath back, pack my bags and head off to an airport run by the RAF, to catch a flight to Cyprus, where I was due to join the RFA Replenishment Tanker *Grey Rover*. I remember joining that ship, out in the summer heat of Cyprus, with signs of tanning still on my hands! Another year had gone by, and the barge had not been sailed.

During the year of 1973, I did not see my elder brother much, as his voyage leaves did not coincide with the summer school and college breaks, though we did have a few sessions supping beer at a pub or two in Greenwich where I was lodged while at college. On another occasion I met him in Rochester as he was about to head off to sea again. We met up the following year, towards the end of another project, after which we were together as a family to once more sail the barge.

My older brother (in the foreground) and I, doing a running repair to the foresail, at anchor in Stangate Creek in 1974.

At the end of July 1974, on completion of my year at sea, I had nearly two months' leave before being due back at college for another year of study. My father's sight problems had not changed during the intervening period. I remember speaking to my parents about the sense in keeping the barge. I wanted them to sell up and purchase a bungalow in the village. I think that at the time they still held some romantic notion that perhaps I would eventually take on the *May Flower*!

It was agreed that I would replace the starboard aft quarter rail and quarter board, thus completing the original scope of the project of the previous year. The timber for this had been in storage for some time. It was a relatively simple job and progressed well. I carried the renewal of the main section of rail forward some distance from the main horse.

The lower section was pre-drilled ready for fastening and then steamed. When the steaming exercise was completed, I had the help of the rest of the family. The rail was fastened along the straight section forward first, and then moving aft, as it was pulled in against formers laid on the deck against the aft cabin sides. The doubled deck edge also helped to maintain the line of the curve given to the timber. Pulling in of the timber was achieved by the use of a large 'G' clamp on a strop attached to the rudder pin. The fastenings, or dumps as they are known, which I had made from steel rod, were driven in as the rail came into position. The aft end of the rail where it met the stern chock was fitted with a fabricated steel angle bracket; this was bolted up. The aft end was finally trimmed and finished off.

While dealing with the quarter board, my elder brother arrived home on leave. He assisted in fitting this. It was fitted in a similar manner to that carried out for the lower rail. On completion, the cleats were refitted and the whole prepared for painting. The quarter board was varnished to match the port side, which had been completed during the early 1960s. I also fitted the aft davit shoe and shipped the davit; this being the first time that it had been fitted since about 1953.

Once we had achieved this, the gear was lowered for a refit. Even though my father could only see white light, it was decided that we would take the barge out sailing. He entrusted the barge to us, my elder brother sailing as skipper, with myself as mate.

My elder brother carried out lowering of the gear, with Father now tailing the stayfall wire. This was a reverse to all that had gone on before. The rest of us watched for snags and readied the mast props etc. The spars were sanded and varnished; the topsail and foresail were removed ashore for tanning. The mainsail was not in need of attention, so was left on. Much of the running rigging was renewed. New ropes can be seen in the accompanying plates. The bob fly was renewed, but this time the four white dots were omitted; my mother always regretted this! Once all the jobs were completed, the gear was raised and everything proved operative and correctly rigged.

At some stage towards the end of August we were ready to go; it was close to the bank holiday weekend. The weather picture was settled and fine, with gentle winds. Our departure from the berth was watched by a group of ramblers, which must have been an enjoyment for them as they rested their feet. We sailed out round Milfordhope Creek, into Stangate. We anchored here for a day. The next day some sailing was had out into the Thames, returning to Stangate for the night. It was now no longer possible to anchor

My elder brother is aloft carrying out a, long splice to the topsail sheet. The spars still sparkled and glistened with their gorgeous colours under the varnish.

in the entrance of the West Swale abreast of the entrance to Shepherds Creek due to the expansion of yacht moorings and buoys for larger vessels. I have seen sailing barges moor here, but they always arrive under power.

On one of the days we carried out some running repairs to the foresail. This sail was by now exceedingly old and, like all the others, really needed to be renewed. In the 1949 survey of the barge, this sail was stated to be nine years old, so it had now served the barge for nearly thirty-four years. It had, of course, been well looked after and obviously had not had constant use. I did the stitching of the new cloths and my brother attacked the rope work. Mother was very proud of our natural progression – the expertise was of course all taught by her.

My mother and sister spent some time doing some cosmetic work together, repainting the coamings. My youngest brother was pretty well occupied keeping Father amused;

they used to go off in the barge boat to walk the cat – my brother giving directions. The barge cat by now was a ginger and white, called Sisal, after the colour of the rope. Little did we all know it at the time, but this was to be the last time we were to be on the barge doing these things together, things that had been part of our lives from my earliest memories.

Another job that came to light was a snag in the topsail sheet which caused a strand to run. My elder brother repaired this with a long splice. We did not have a roll of this size rope aboard, though plenty spare of the size for vangs and brails. The mainsail brails, vangs, mainmast and topmast backstay tackles had all been reeved with new rope during the refit.

We were accompanied in Stangate one evening by two other barges, one of these was the *Ethel Maud*. This was the first time that these two had been in the same anchorage as rigged barges for over two decades, other than when we were at Maldon in 1964 when the *Ethel Maud* was being re-rigged. This was also to be the last. Incidentally, for a number of years the *Ethel Maud* was managed by Clement Parker, while the *May Flower* was a Parker barge, on behalf of her owner, his brother John Parker, before being sold to James W. Keeble of Maldon, then to Green Brothers, where the two barges once again traded under the same bob.

The following morning, one of the barges was seen to prepare for departure. Some trouble occurred when she picked up some old mooring gear with her anchor. After what seemed a considerable time, they managed to free themselves by eventually heaving up the anchor sufficiently to get a slip rope round the debris to clear their anchor. Later on it started to blow quite hard from the west-north-west and the forecast predicted it to become more southerly. The wind increased through the night to a phenomenal level and we had most of the cable out. This stretched out bar taught. I expect the barge that had left had VHF radio – this, of course, we did not have.

The forecast the following morning was for the weather over the next few days to worsen. We seemed to be enjoying a lull from the winds of the previous day and it was decided that we should head back to the moorings. By now the other barge had gone and the yachts had all disappeared. Getting the anchor up was very hard work, requiring two people on each windlass handle to break it out. This was a potent display of the power of a barge anchor when well dug in. We set off under plain sail, with a few cloths picked up in the main.

On rounding Slaughterhouse Point at the foot of Stangate, we came more on the wind and would probably have had to put a tack in to clear the eastern end of Milfordhope Island. Shortly after this the starboard vang tackle rope parted with a sound like a pistol retort. When this happened, the sprit took up onto the slack port vang tackle with a violent snatch, taking the full force – the whole rig vibrated with the shock. This needed to be dealt with before we could go any further. A quick decision was made to anchor as we did not have sufficient room and time to go onto the other tack, to reeve a new rope. As the barge was brought up into the wind to drop anchor, looking aloft my brother spotted something amiss at the top of the topsail on the headstick. The topsail was immediately 'rucked', that is dropped to mainmast cap and left sheeted out.

The *May Flower* at anchor in Milfordhope Creek. Note the taught ness and angle of the anchor chain. Look also how clean the bottom is forward. The dot in the name on the rail can be seen.

As soon as we were safely at anchor the sails were brailed and clewed in. I went aloft to look at the headstick, where I found a few of the lashings coming adrift. The two outer ones were seized with wire and these were fortunately sound. The inner ones were of cod line, and were starting to come apart. I replaced all these lashings while the others dealt with the broken vang tackle. The rope, which had been new, had parted almost as if it had been cut.

Once all of these repairs were completed, we set off again. The barge went up past Milfordhope Marsh like an express train. As we came up towards the turn southward to reach our berth at Callows, the wind gusted violently and backed. This caused the barge to momentarily stall. Father, rightly or wrongly, called for the anchor to be dropped. My mother, drawing on years of experience, was throwing loops of chain over the windlass barrel as rapidly as possible, as she has since said to me, 'The anchor did not want to bite. I feared for the worst. Suddenly it caught and we brought up with a violent snatch on the windlass.' My elder brother felt that the situation did not warrant this. Later, when talking about it all privately in our local, over a beer, we put it down to the fact that Father acted on an impulse because he could not visualise completely the whole picture – we had a huge expanse of water, although relatively shallow, in which to manoeuvre. We did not have sufficient experience to do anything differently, or to ignore the owner's command.

It seemed to take an interminable age before the anchor bit and the barge stopped. Sails were stowed. The ferocity of that wind was something I have only ever experienced out in the deep, wild ocean. The stern of the barge was dangerously near to the edge of Slayhills Marsh, just down from Shoregate Dock. At times the rudder was over the marsh, brushing the sea lavender and sea pursalane. My sister was posted to keep an eye on the situation. We were very fortunate that the tides were springs.

Any attempt to winch in at the windlass was quite impossible. The cable was bar taught, and we could not turn the handles. On the turn of the tide, the barge, with a few nudges of the rudder at the edge of the marsh, miraculously swung clear, knocking off the edge of the marsh in doing so. Mother then went ashore with my father and youngest brother in the barge boat into Shoregate Dock, where they found a group of onlookers who had witnessed our earlier troubles. Their objective was to see if they could get hold of an old boy in the village, who they knew had an old cockle boat which could be used for a tow. Later another rope broke; this was one of the two barge boat painters, the other fortunately held. The broken painter had come from the same reel of rope that the vang tackle had been renewed from. I don't know if my parents ever spoke to the suppliers about this – the first failure was bad enough and could have been the cause of a catastrophe.

Mother and Father returned later with news that a tow was arranged for the next tide, which was not due until around midnight. When the tide went out, the *May Flower* was sitting in the middle of the creek on a firm flat bottom, with only a thin coating of sloppy mud over hard clay. The anchor chain was like a rod of steel and led out to the anchor, from which a long furrow could be seen stretching away towards the point it had first touched the bottom. The underwater areas up forward had been cleaned utterly of dried mud, due to the action of the ferocious seas that had been running – even in these protected environs. The topmast was lowered during the late afternoon to reduce the windage aloft; the bob streamed out, audibly crackling like pistol shots in the gusts. It was a long wait.

The tow duly arrived in the pitch-black. Over towards our berth, we could see a light being flashed. My elder brother quickly realised it was Morse, and rapidly decoded the flashes, which was 'light at mooring'. Knowing how to use Morse code by lamp, he signalled back that we were aware of their presence on the wharf at Callows. These persons duly kept a light on the wharf to lead the way in, which was virtually south of our position. We berthed with the assistance of these people, who we found were the group who had recently purchased the *Henry*. They leapt aboard at the first opportunity to help get the moorings aboard. I was very thankful to all of the people that helped that night. Later when all was tidied up, we broke out the medicinal bottle!

The next day, listening to the news on the radio, we were all deeply thankful when we discovered that the end to our sail, although a little traumatic, was not the disaster that overtook many others the previous day and evening. Many vessels had been overcome by a typical late summer gale. The rescue services had had a very busy period indeed and it was not far from our minds that we ourselves very nearly became a statistic! I recollect that Edward Heath's yacht was lost in the channel, while on passage from Burnham to the Isle of Wight during this storm, with a sad loss of lives.

As I wrote the last few words to this chapter, I felt a tingling sensation run through me and I shook involuntarily. It was as if a ghost had been laid – the past was becoming the very words that were appearing. Although we didn't know it, this was going to be the last time that we sailed the *May Flower*, never to see or feel her underway again. It is strange indeed and rather ironic, but the first sail the *May Flower* made under the ownership of my parents was in similarly appalling conditions, a quarter of a century earlier.

chapter twenty

Callows – Our Last Berth

After the rather traumatic return from our short cruise of 1974, my parents came to realise that this was the last time that it was likely that they would be sailing the barge. They were truly into the dusk of their ownership. The *May Flower* needed to be sold.

The high winds that punctuated the return from our last sail continued for a further few days, often with much strength and violence. The bob which had a long fly was at times shaking the top of the topmast and eventually it had come adrift. As planned, the gear was lowered and all the sails and associated running rigging removed. The sails were later carefully folded and stowed on top of the main hatch, under a tented cover. The running rigging, much of it new and little used, was removed and stowed in the fo'c'sle. The topmast was removed ashore, it not being a lot of use in its present condition. Upon surveying the damage, which consisted of some rot in the upper section, running down the heart of the pole, causing part of one side to split away, the gear was raised bereft of the topmast. The topmast stays were coiled and hung up on hooks down in the fo'c'sle.

At this point my elder brother was due back at sea and I had to return to college. This was a potent reason for my parents to call it a day – they were completely reliant upon us. My final year at college was very important for my future and I needed to study hard to keep abreast of the work (apart from chasing girls and drinking beer!) to ensure that I attained my qualifications.

On completion of my college life in June 1975, while waiting for my first sea appointment, I renewed the runners to the aft cabin sliding hatch. The grooves had to be cut with the use of hand chisels alone, a piece of mahogany was used and the finished results were good. When doing the work, I found that the outer plank on the port side of the aft cabin top needed replacement too. The forward coaming had been repaired some years earlier by scarfing in a major section. This whole area of the barge now looked good.

At the beginning of July, I had a week's holiday in Devon with my girlfriend. We were beginning to form a relationship that has stood the test of time. In late July, I was summoned to my first ship as a Junior Engineer Officer. I was away for nearly seven months. My employers now dictated my life; my absences were for anything up to nine months of each year for a short period, then later for periods of six months, when voyage

Left: Shaping up the topmast with an adze, this was then continued with a large wood jack plane.

Below: Shaping of the spar is completed, with just the bottom to trim off.

lengths were cut in an attempt to stem the flow of highly trained personnel away from seafaring.

During the early part of 1976, I came home on leave. This partly coincided with that of my elder brother. We agreed to look at the topmast and investigate the options. The rot in the mast was extensive, deep in the heart of the spar, and it was deemed redundant. The age of this spar was not known, but was in all probability in excess of fifty years. We tracked down a supplier of Douglas fir, which our father said was the correct wood to use. The firm was near Erith, Kent; we travelled up by train and selected a complete log. The receipt is long gone, but I seem to remember that it cost around £50, with delivery.

Once the log was delivered, we assessed it against the old mast and decided which was to be the forward side. The log had a very slight curve, our old spar had had a nice forward bend to it and this dictated the way the log would be worked. The bulk of the shaping was carried out with an adze, leaving an eight-sided shape. Once this was completed and checked, we took off the corners and started final shaping with wooden jackplanes. One of these actually came from my great-grandfather, who had been a house builder in Westcliff-on-Sea and Southend in Essex. This sort of work is quite satisfying as the result reflects the care and effort put in.

Once the corners were removed and the spar was becoming rounded, the shaping was carried out with standard smoothing planes until the correct sections were achieved. We finished the spar with marginally more volume, allowing for years of sanding that will have taken place to the old mast. The various fittings at the foot of the spar and the hole for the support pin were dealt with next. A groove was cut on the aft face in which the heel wire is fitted. The top of the spar was shaped and reduced in diameter to suit the crane iron for the topsail hoist. This can be seen fitted upon completion of all work when re-housing onto the lowered mainmast in an accompanying illustration.

I had a long think about the bobstay; it was traditional for it to be inserted into a hole drilled down the centre of the spar. This, in many respects, is not good practice, being a way for moisture to travel into the top of the spar. I decided to break with tradition and fit the bobstay to the side of the head. It was fitted in a groove and secured by clamp bolts – of course this may not have worked. The top of the spar was painted with several coats of red lead, primer and topcoats. The main body of the spar was treated with linseed oil for a few weeks. I made new top pieces for the bobstay. Recently, walking along the Hythe at Maldon, I noted the bobstay on a barge with her gear down, this was wobbling around in the top of the mast – in a fresh water trap, with all that that means.

Once the spar was ready for fitting, the gear was lowered and the topmast put back in its rightful place. The perfectionist in me even required that I touched up some damage that occurred to the top white work. My elder brother had by now gone back to sea, so it fell to me to organise the lowering and heaving up of the gear. This was the last occasion that this function was carried out by the Ardley family.

During this period, I became better acquainted with the group of young men who had purchased the *Henry*. I'm not sure if they had at that time comprehended fully the scope of the work needed to renovate a barge. I am sure, though, that their efforts

My youngest brother has just handed me the paint pot, to touch up the top of the topmast, prior to raising the gear in 1976. Note that the bobstay is not fitted into a drilled hole in the top of the spar.

eventually helped to keep the *Henry* going long enough for a concentrated major rebuild later. At the time she was still a relatively young barge, compared with the *May Flower*.

With a friend from the village and this group, I would have fairly regular sessions at the Three Tuns in Lower Halstow. Often we would adjourn back on board the *Henry*. My friend and I would stagger back round the seawall to Callows, he then going back to the village, and I to try and tiptoe back aboard the *May Flower* in a sober manner. Sometimes, my elder brother joined us; our efforts, if seen by a bystander, would have been hilarious. My mother has recently said to me that she always used to listen out!

My mother was by now a full-time schoolteacher, Father was still doing some advisory work on a huge project he had been the leading light for – a new school in Gillingham – but was in affect, retired. The next task that I had agreed or had been asked to deal with was the renewal of a section of planking on the starboard bow. A short length of wale

Shaping the aft end of the plank to suit the staggered butt joint, the youngest of us is doing the holding.

needed to be cut out and renewed. This was about 15ft long, but right on the curve. My youngest brother helped with this job – as my apprentice. My friend in the village also gave me some of his time. He was at this time living a dream, investigating the feasibility of purchasing the *Sirdar*. I did all I could to persuade him otherwise, however as it turned out, apart from the fact that she was virtually derelict, Crescent Shipping would not even entertain the idea. Then he talked about taking on the *May Flower*!

The aft join was not a straightforward vertical butt and it was a difficult plank to fit due to its relative shortness. It would have been wiser to have taken more out and fitted a longer section. You live and learn. This was the last time that I did anything like this on the barge. My father helped me with the bolts as the rest of the family were at their respective schools. He fitted nuts to the bolts after I had knocked them through. He was exceedingly good at this, even though he could not see. The mental picture of what was being done was clear in his mind, drawing on years of previous experience and knowledge.

During the following year, 1977, my elder brother was away at sea and planning a permanent move to Canada to marry his sweetheart. I had another little job on the books; this involved renewing a section of decking, including some sections of the original under deck. Mother had complained of an annoying leak, which had ruined one of her best frocks! On investigation, some rot was found in the upper planking around the port leeboard crab winch. Dealing with deck planking on the *May Flower* was complicated by the 30mm doubling completed during the 1940s.

While fashioning a half joint to a lower plank, I came across a tie rod. These run transversely through the deck, tying together the covering board, deck planks and the inner king plank upon which the hatch longitudinal coamings sat. The wood in this area was in exceedingly good condition. This can be seen in an accompanying illustration. The colour of the old wood is not a lot different to that of the new, the old, I expect, was probably of far greater quality.

Once the lower planking was fitted and spiked, the seams were caulked, sealed with bitumen and finished flush. The upper planking was laid on a layer of tarred felt, spiked, caulked, and the seams payed with bitumen. The last job was to treat all new wood with red lead paint, primer, and undercoats, then finish off with the traditional deck coating. From memory, I believe that this was the last structural job that I completed on the barge, apart from routine preservation maintenance. The illustration of this work shows the position of the main horse chock. Father had moved these inboard when fitting a new beam beneath the waist deck, years earlier. This alteration prevented the main sheet block pin coming into contact with the quarter board.

This last renewal yarn, typified a greater proportion of all the work that we carried out to the *May Flower*, which was on the whole, piecing out old decaying timber and making good. I have not detailed many of these tasks as they were numerous and were what I would term, general up-keep requirements, these were needed in order to maintain this old vessel in a reasonable condition.

The barge received various fairly heavy renewals over the thirty-one years that my parents owned her, but it must be said that during those last few years, age was catching up. At the time, much more needed to be done if she had any chance of sailing on into her centenary. Some were obvious and other less so, but still in need of attention. Both main hold hatch beams needed to be replaced and, in my opinion, this would have included decks, covering board and rails. Areas of the sides were showing signs of age and deterioration due to drying out and damage from her trading days.

From time to time, work needed to be carried out to the barge boat. The boat that originally came with the barge had been set aside in favour of a boat dug out of the mud at Strood in about 1963. Father towed this down to Hoo one weekend while we were anchored on the flats during the school holidays – this became another project.

I clearly remember helping my elder brother to clean out the mud. Structurally this boat was in good condition, except for a few cracked ribs and one damaged plank. These were repaired on the beach, just east of the old brick fort. This boat, though more stable,

Removal of the lower planking is in progress. Note the deck tie rod that was found. See also the yellow colour of wood that had probably been in the structure of the barge for all but ninety years. Note the crab winch set to one side.

Drilling holes with a brace and bit, ready to spike down the lower deck planks. I had pre-drilled this plank, prior to fitting – but still had to go into the beam beneath – I could have used an auger.

The barge boat turned upside down on trestles for repairs and painting – this work always required two persons. I learnt by helping my mother!

was not as handy as the old boat that came with the barge. She was much broader in the beam with flat sections, unlike her predecessor, which had rather fine lines, a sweet sheer, was much lighter and 'a delight to scull or row' said my mother.

In about 1969, I helped Mother to renew a section of the garboard on the port side; we also repaired another bottom plank by letting in and doubling. The fitting of planks or doublers needed two persons working together, one to punch through the new copper nails, the other to fit the ferules, snip the nails to length and rivet the ends – at this point, the other person had to hold a dolly firmly to prevent the nail from being knocked back out. Finally, during 1977, we did some more work on the boat, letting in two short lengths of planking to the port bilge. An illustration shows the boat upside down on trestles, with painting of the sides also in progress. Much of the work described can be seen.

A little job that I completed at some stage in my early teens was the renewal of one of the mainmast case winch barrels; this was shaped up by hand tools. I had to heat the steel bands to shrink them onto the barrel ends. Another was replaced a spare my father had obtained. This did not look as if it had ever been used – where it came from I am not aware.

While staying aboard for a weekend, my future wife helped me refurbish the paintwork on the transom and bow badges. My wife comes from Middle England, from the town of Royal Leamington Spa – about as far from the sea as it is possible to be in England. She was training to be a schoolteacher when we met and our relationship blossomed, even though I was away at sea and lived on a barge, which also needed some of my time too! The results of her work were recorded and sit in our family albums! During September 1977, my sister, youngest brother and I gave the barge her last coat of tar in our care.

The very last job that I completed was making a new mizzenmast for the barge. I had found a large area of rot in the foot in way of the steel shoe. Making this was a simple task compared with the topmast previously crafted. This was perhaps my parting gift.

All of us children were growing up and moving rapidly into our own circles of life and respective careers. My eldest brother departed to a life in Canada and marriage. I was working hard with the Royal Fleet Auxiliary and progressing with my Certificates of Competency as an engineer. My sister was by now away at a teacher training college and my youngest brother was working studiously towards his A-Levels. The time that we all had available to give to the barge (for my parents) was diminishing rapidly. The *May Flower* had reached the end of her journey with the Ardley family. She would have needed a major input of money, time and energy, apart from the inclination. My mother told me many years later that my father had held a romantic notion that one of us, me in particular latterly, would wish to take the barge on. This, unfortunately, was not going to happen. I'd had enough!

Fred Cooper wrote to my mother in October 1976, having heard that a move ashore was in the offing. He wished them both well; he mentioned various barges up for sale and prices. He also said that they were 'the last of the old crowd', and had achieved something not previously done – that is maintained a barge in a sailing condition, as a home, for a great number of years. He went on to say that this 'Would be a record not likely to be bettered.' During a trip on the *Pudge*, over the weekend of 25 September, 1976 visiting Lower Halstow, he had tried to pick the barge out, but said that he couldn't. He commented that our berth was probably the best of any that were available to barges.

The *May Flower* had been placed on the market during 1977. Initially she attracted a fair amount of interest. One group that appeared were looking for a vessel to get onto the charter market fairly quickly. I remember discussions taking place about slipping her at the Acorn Yard in Rochester, for a survey. This would have proved interesting.

A house was being looked at during this time and was eventually purchased. Just before my elder brother went off to Canada, he and I helped to strip the property of numerous layers of linoleum and wallpaper. Outwardly the house looked like a typical late seventeenth-century town house, but in fact originated from around 1500. As they

The *May flower* at her moorings in 1977 – ready for a suit of sails. She sits peacefully amongst her reflections in the twilight of her life.

were moving from a barge which was ninety years old, I did not at the time consider that this was a good idea. My youngest brother made an architectural model of the roof to allow my father to feel and picture it in his mind. He had studied timber-framed buildings during the 1940s when studying to be an architect, so his mind was familiar with the general construction principles. The reconstruction of the house took several years to complete before the move ashore could be made.

I found amongst my father's papers several documents relating to his placing the *May Flower* back on the ships register. The particulars are exactly as the document of 1950 (apart from the fact that it is written on a 1962 standard form.) The re-registration fee amounted to £15.20, and is dated 23 February 1977. Other papers relate to a mortgage placed upon the barge during the purchase of the house. This was ultimately transferred to the house on completion of certain essential building requirements, the house having been derelict and stripped out. All of these papers had been returned to my mother during the mid-1990s, following their discovery by a bank official carrying out a routine clearout.

Just before I left my childhood home to embark on a new life divorced from barges, I took various photographs of the barge and of a sunrise and sunset over the mudflats and fields that surrounded this enchanting environment fringing the land, a wild marsh environment in the true sense, which at the time I was only just beginning to appreciate. Nowadays, whenever I am out on the water on my own yacht, anchored up a secluded creek, I listen to the sounds of gulls, oyster catchers, curlews and other estuary wading birds. A breeze might be wafting across the marshes after a spring tide, carrying with it the strong tangy taste of brine and wild scents; it all reminds me of the carefree times that I enjoyed during my childhood: sailing and messing about in boats remains very much in the blood – a lasting endowment.

In the spring of 1978 I was back at college studying for my Marine Engineers Second Class Certificate of Competency. Following this, I in turn left home to marry my sweetheart. We set up our home in Essex, where my wife had obtained a teaching position. From that time I had no further input with the maintenance of the *May Flower*. I had new responsibilities, my own home, family and career. The responsibility now rested with the youngest, who himself was about to go off to university.

We did not always sail great distances, often only in our own locale, but sail we did, regularly through to our final sail in 1974. The barge was then in her eighty-seventh year and, at the time, the oldest Thames Sailing Barge still sailing. The experiences of this unusual upbringing have left their indelible mark upon us all. We all have many memories of our life afloat, a great number lay fondly, others do not, and for me, apart from sailing, some of the most prominent memories revolve around the ever present maintenance needs: all through my childhood and formative years, the needs of the barge had been paramount.

The *May Flower*, I'm sure, far outlived the expectations of her builder, George H. Curel, and subsequent owners. Her builder, especially, would have been rightly proud of the longevity of his yard's product of 1888. When talking with Bernard Lewis, the manager of Green Brothers, Maldon operations at the time my father purchased the barge in 1950, he expressed absolute amazement that the *May Flower* had been maintained in sail for a quarter of a century after completing her trading life with them.

You will have seen that this was achieved through the efforts expended upon her, by all the family, in carrying out structural renewals, the regular piecing out of parts that needed replacement, the ever present preservation needs, the prompt attention to decks, in the old customary fashion of caulking and paying the seams with bitumen to keep leaks at bay, and, of course, the attention demanded of the spars, sails and rigging – that enabled us to sail her. These are but a few of the needs of a barge and with the myriad of skills that we were either taught, developed or found out by trial and error, enabled the family to keep the *May Flower* active as a family barge, without financial help from chartering or sail sponsorships.

The sun had truly set on my barging childhood.

The May Flower's Final Berth

During 1981, after nearly thirty-two years of ownership, the *May Flower* was sold to a local couple, Barry and Sue Barnes, who had both held a long desire to live on a barge! They kept her for about six years before selling the barge to a hospital nurse, who had a dream of re-rigging her, but only for use as a static home. A steel lighter replaced her, it being converted for living aboard and is still in use. Some small craft moorings now exist here also, but the mudflats are now largely covered by spreading cord grass.

Before her move from Callows, the *May Flower* had to be surveyed and assigned fit for towage by the Medway Ports Authority. Following this, the barge was towed upriver to Strood. When I was shown some prints of the *May Flower* on her last passage, I said to the couple that I could clearly visualise her sailing away under sail, as we ourselves had many times during the late '60s and early '70s. The tow took her to a berth next to the Strood Boat Yard. This yard is on the site of Curels Upper Barge Yard, where the *May Flower* was originally built. It is overlooked by the grave of her builder, George Curel, who is buried in the churchyard of Frindsbury parish church. He would, I'm sure, have been proud to have known that one of his barges had survived to such an age, but saddened with the outcome of her homecoming.

Unfortunately the berth was hard, causing the hull to strain fatally, it being too much for her tired chine fastenings. The *May Flower* failed to float or to be kept from flooding and she rapidly became a hulk. Eventually the owners of the waterfront required the barge to be removed. Colin Frake of Faversham obtained permission to remove and retrieve useful gear and fittings. The windlass carriages, trunions and pawls, brail and crab winches and other gear were removed. He was to have had the windlass barrel, but this was not to be. He also had the rigging dead eyes and went on to say that the barge had a lot of good ironwork built into her. During the time of her build, a foundry was an integral part of the barge yard run by Curels. The *May Flower* was then partially broken up by the waterfront owner. Her keelson was removed and towed upriver to Bramble Tree Wharf for use in the rebuild of the *Violet* (of Maldon).

Her spreet also went upriver to the *Violet* where it lay alongside for a few years. During the 1990s the owners of the *Marjorie* acquired this spar and fashioned it into a new topmast, she having suffered a broken topmast in Gravesend Reach at the start of a passage match. At present the spar continues to serve her well. Incidentally,

The *May Flower* out in the River Medway for the first time in fourteen years, unfortunately this was her last passage. (Photograph Mrs S. Barnes)

Marjorie's bowsprit was previously the topmast on the *Orinoco*; this spar also started life as a spreet. The mainmast was bought (for £50) by Neil Pemble, presently rebuilding the *Seagull II* at Gillingham, Kent, he had undertaken the task to rebuild a Rochester bawley, *Katie RR9*, this unfortunately proved too great a challenge and he built a replica, *Minion*, this vessel had her mast fashioned from our old spar. The *Minion* later went to new owners in Brittany, France. Talking to the owner of the *Orinoco*, I was told the davit shoes, the bases of which were shaped for the deck camber, were reused, but by which vessel he was unsure. What happened to all her other gear – numerous blocks, sufficient to rig a barge, the stayfall tackle blocks and steering gear – I was not able to ascertain.

I had first come across the *May Flower* again while sailing on the River Medway with my family during the late summer of 1988. We had pottered up into Bridge Reach, because I'd wanted to photograph another hulked barge. On the shore, west of Strood Dock, I saw a barge whose shape made my heart leap. Although I had not seen the *May Flower* since the summer of 1979, when I berthed alongside her in a friend's yacht while enjoying some sailing in old home waters, her features are imprinted on my mind. I remember saying to my wife that my gut feelings said to me, 'That is the *May Flower*.' She lay just downstream of a little boatyard and adjacent to a car scrap business; her spars were down and were lashed alongside. She looked a forlorn and hopeless sight: I sailed away, feeling saddened – the moment is recorded in a sailing logbook. Later I found out that she lay on the site of Curels Upper or Strood Yard.

The remains of the *May Flower* as found in August 1989 at Strood, on the site of George Curels Upper Barge Yard.

The following year the pull of 'let's see what's happening to her now' seemed to let the boat take us up to these waters again. As we closed the shore, I saw a barge, but things did not seem to be as they should. A barge was being broken up. I initially thought perhaps it was another; these thoughts were immediately dispelled when I recognised the line of the rudder laying at an angle and the faded colour and shape of her windlass bitt-heads, which are for ever etched into my soul. I knew then that it must be, and had to investigate. We anchored up along the shallows and rowed over in the dinghy to take a look. As we got closer, it was for me a chilling moment and gave me a tight, fluctuating hot and cold feeling, a sense of unreality. This had been my home, this had been my life; this was once a living, sailing entity. I called to a chap who assured me that it would be alright to have a look. I went 'on board' with more than a little trepidation.

I took a photograph looking forward, but it was unfortunately an end of film print. It clearly showed the gap where her pine keelson had been removed. I looked at the ceiling coated in dried mud and thought of the hours that I and all my brothers and sister had spent polishing them during our childhood! The whole of the after end had been removed, and it was obvious that this section had been burnt. The rudder was burnt down to the top of the blade. Father's mizzen sheet shackle of 1951 was still in place. I picked up an iron dump sitting atop the charred remains of the stern post. I still have this dump; it has been rust proofed, treated with metal paint and is preserved for posterity!

While at the aft end I spotted a familiar object sitting on the mud near the starboard side. It was the bobstay from the topmast. The yellow of the paint on the top and ring

Looking towards the after end (from the fore deck), my son was about six at the time of his first and only visit. Note: on the LHS of the plate, the bobstay can be seen lying in the mud. Note also the barge beyond; this is the *Viking* which I had initially come up river to see.

was coloured by immersion by the tides. I retrieved it before leaving. This was cleaned up and given to my mother. The bob was unfortunately left in the cellar of their first house, after the barge, when my mother later moved to a bungalow in Lower Halstow during the 1990s following the death of my father. The bobstay now stands in her garden as a reminder.

Moving forward, I saw the remains of the aft sailing beam, under the forward end of the main hatch. Part of the registration information was still discernable. The level of degradation in the ten years since I had last seen her was quite astonishing. This is a beam that should have been replaced when the centre beam was renewed. Moving forward under the deck, I entered the area of the workshop to starboard and my old cabin to port. In the fore hold area, the hull was still intact and some of the paint colours were recognisable. Some of the linings were stripped out to reveal frames that were in pretty good shape.

Moving up towards the position of the fore hold forward bulkhead, which was removed to starboard, I came across the spare brail winch that my father had obtained some twenty years previously. This had been refurbished and had been ready for use.

The spare brail winch! The bitumen box is still in its old home!

To starboard, still sitting on the higher area of the fo'c'sle ceiling, was the box, discussed earlier, containing bitumen for deck seam repairs, and a box that contained a few rusting tins of spikes. The area was littered with the remains of ropes; these from the sizes would have been brails for the mainsail. The bottoms of frames that had been fitted by us many years earlier could be seen; these were made of oak laminations.

I stood and looked around me; an inner voice was coldly running through my mind, and it struck me that perhaps I should not have had this encounter. Memories flooded back, these were mixed and a little emotional. We had so many memorable times as children on the *May Flower*, not all were good and it was hard work. This was a sad sight.

Looking to port were the remains of the fo'c'sle fire, a place of warmth and comfort on a cold autumn or winter's sail. It lay on its side with various coils of wire lying on top. These wires were the stays for the topmast and must have fallen and been cast aside in a pile for removal. These wires would have been stowed up against the port side, forward of the windlass bitts. They were hung on hooks under the deck. The serving on the stays was still in a good condition.

The extent aft of the frame renewals and those doubled when the barge was at Maldon for repairs in 1964 was clearly seen. The planking in this area to both sides was intact. Moving back up onto what remained of the deck, it was obvious that very little had been done to her. The condition of paintwork was old and in all probability had not seen much attention for some time. It all looked sad and desolate.

I found a pile of rigging wires. These were the topmast stays. Note the new and doubled frames to port.

Some twelve years later, in the autumn of 2001, I made another visit to the site, this time by road, gaining access through the boatyard workshop. The workforce, numbering about a half dozen persons, was surprised to learn that the remains of the old barge, beyond, had been built on this site over a century before. I had seen from time to time, from the river, that the remains were being used as a hard stand for boat work – the *May Flower* even during her slow lingering death, in this her final berth, was still serving a useful purpose.

My intention was to record her remains and look at certain aspects of the barge, as I had had for some time considered writing this book, chronicling what I could find of her history and specifically about my experiences of being brought up on an active sailing barge during the 1950s, '60s and '70s: it crossed the boundaries of the old ways – of cargo carrying, most of it, well before the advent of the new era of charter barge sailing.

I looked at the starboard side, the stem and the attachment of the planking to it; I noticed that none of the planks had pulled away. It spoke volumes for the work that my parents carried out some forty-four years earlier. The plank that I had replaced to the starboard wale was seen to be coming adrift at its after end, probably due to the loss of a fastening bolt during breaking up.

Following the initial removal of her stern in 1989, the hull was gradually cut back towards the bow, above her chines. The upper edges of the planking and structure where

The port bow in 2001, note the castle shape to the tops of the bitt-heads – most barges have flat tops. Note also the tops of the 'new frames, side planking and inwale' – which have been cut through.

it had been cut back showed that an immense level 'goodness' was left in her bottom sections. Like many old vessels, reframing and a top rebuild is all that is needed to give far greater longevity – this is especially true for the ubiquitous Thames Sailing Barge.

To port, the planking renewed at Maldon in 1964 was still completely intact; one could almost imagine it awaiting a coat of tar! The edge of the doubled decks, overlapping the covering board where the rails had been removed, could be seen. Under sheets of steel littering the remains of her foredeck, the beam that was renewed at Cook's Yard was visible, but the decks were in a state of total decay. The stem was in excellent condition, as was the stayfall tackle iron stem band. The big steel stem-head knee, still firmly attached to its wood deck pad – a thick piece of oak – jutted out from the stem. Aft of the knee was the dog for the anchor chain, still shackled on. The windlass had been removed some years earlier and during that visit only one of the two windlass bitts remained standing.

At the time of writing, this area of Strood was undergoing redevelopment. The riverbank was in the process of being reclaimed, slowly creeping out towards the remains of the *May Flower*, it is probable that soon she will be but a memory.

Next to the boatyard, just upriver to the west of a public house, against the riverbank, her windlass barrel sat in the mud. I walked slowly away, not looking back, remembering...

I have not returned: I believe now, that I have at last cleansed my soul.

Bibliography

Ardley, J.G., Private Papers. (Ardley Family Collection)

Barnard, D., *Merrily to Frendsbury. A History of the Parish of Frindsbury.* (A City of Rochester Society publication, 1996)

Bennett, A.S., *June of Rochester* (Edward Arnold & Co. London, 1949 ed.)

Bennett, A.S., *Tide Time.* (George Allen and Unwin Ltd, 1949)

Bennett, A.S., *Us Bargemen.* (Meresborough Books, Rainham, Kent, 1980)

Benham, H., *Last Stronghold of Sail.* (Harrap Ltd, London, 1981)

Carr, F.G.G., *Sailing Barges.* (Terence Dalton Ltd, Lavenham, 1989)

Carr, M., *Call of the Running Tide.* (Sail Trust Ltd, Maldon, 1983)

Cook, C., *A Barge on the Blocks.* (Published privately, Maldon, 1984)

Cooper, F.S., and Chancellor, J.A., *A Handbook of Sailing Barges.* (Adlard Coles, 1955)

Cooper, F.S., *Racing Sailormen.* (Percival Marshall & Co., London, 1963)

Coote, J.H., *East Coast Rivers.* (*Yachting Monthly*, London, third edition (revised) 1961)

Childs, B., *Rochester Sailing Barges of the Victorian Era.* (Rochester Sailing Barges Publication, Rochester, Kent, 1993)

Davis, D.F., *The Thames Sailing Barge (Her Gear & Rigging).* (International Marine Publishing, USA, (David & Charles), 1970)

Farnham, A., *A Conversation with Dick, the Dagger.* (Chaffcutter Books, Ware Hertfordshire, 2003 edition)

Hazelton, I., *Time Before the Mast.* (Chaffcutter Books, Ware, Hertfordshire, 2003)

Kemp, J., *A Fair Wind for London.* (Sailtrust Ltd, Maldon, 1983)

The May Flower: A Barging Childhood

Leather, J., *The Salty Shore*. (Terence Dalton, Lavenham, 1979)

Leather, J., *Barges*. (Adlard Coles Ltd, 1984)

March, Edgar J., *Spritsail Barges of the Thames and Medway*. (Percival Marshall, 1948 and David & Charles 1970 & 1981)

Marriage, J., *Maldon and the Blackwater Estuary*. (Phillimore & Co. Ltd, 1985)

Perks, R.H., O'Driscoll, P. and Cordell, A., *Spritsail (A portrait of sailing barges and sailormen)*. (Conway Maritime Press, 1975)

Platt, S., *My Three Grey Mistresses*. (Atlantic Nautical Press, Penryn, Cornwall, 2002)

Rippingdale, J., Records of James Rippingdale, Barge Master. (Mrs Bird)

Simper, R., *Essex Rivers and Creeks*. (Creekside Publishing, Lavenham, 1995)

Simper, R., *River Medway and the Swale*. (Creekside Publishing, Lavenham, 1998)

Stevens, P., *The Story of Lower Halstow*. (Published by Pauline Stevens, Lower Halstow, 1999)

Taylor, F., *A History of Faversham Creek and the Faversham Navigation*. (Chaffcutter Books, Ware, Hertfordshire, 2002)

Winter, C.W.R., *The Run of the Tide*. (Patrick Stevens (Collins) Publishing, 1990)

Yearsley, I., *Islands of Essex*. (Ian Henry Publications, 2000)

Glossary

Adze – An implement with a very shallow 'S'-shaped handle with a blade in an 'L' attitude, similar to a mattock (farm implement). The blade is curved and has a very sharp edge.

Apron – Vertical timber fastened to the stem, to which the side planks are attached.

Bitts – The vertical timbers to which the anchor windlass is attached. These are anchored to the floors and lodged against a deck beam. The tops are usually referred to as the bitt-heads.

Bob – Owner's flag, flown from the topmast truck (top).

Bobstay – The steel pole at the top of the topmast to which the bob is fitted. Also, a stay that is tensioned to hold a bowsprit down.

Bonnet – An additional area added to the foot of a sail.

Brails – The ropes which are used to clew or furl the mainsail and mizzen.

Bushel – Unit of dry or liquid measure equal to 8 imperial gallons. 1 imperial bushel is equal to 0.03637cu.m.

Carline – Beams for a cabin top or underside of a deck.

Ceiling – The floor of a hold or accommodation deck.

Clew – Aft bottom corner of a sail.

Clew Line – Line used to mouse the topsail when it is lowered, pulling the topsail head stick and sprit sheet end of sail, down the starboard side of the mainmast.

Chine – The corner of the side and bottom planking. Sometimes known as Chime.

Collar – Steel bands at throat or nock of the mainsail and around mast for attaching the sprit, in this case it is called a Muzzle.

Covering Board – Outer deck plank that sits above and covers the top of the side planking, frame tops and outer part of the deck carlines.

Crab Winch – Winches located aft, outboard of the steering position to port and starboard. Used for lowering and raising the leeboards.

Cringle – A loop of rope which is worked round a steel concaved ring along the bolt (edge) rope of a sail, for attaching sheet blocks, lines, shackles or for running brails through.

Crosstrees – Port and starboard spreaders for the topmast side stays, on a barge, these are called standing backstays.

Dog – Iron bar with two claws secured by a short length of chain to a strong point, between the windlass barrel and the stem. Placed onto the anchor chain to allow slacken of turns on windlass, to move chain across barrel – fleeting the cable.

Dolly Winch – Barrel winch, housed on the forward face of the windlass bitts. Has a light dolly wire used for kedging and manoeuvring operations.

Doubling – A sheaving or additional skin of planking added to the original planking. This can be to the hull sides and deck.

Fid – 1. A specially shaped tool for making or forcing holes in sail material for the fitting of cringles and rope work. 2. A steel pin inserted in foot of topmast to sit on lower hoop, to support the weight of the spar.

Fleet (the cable) – To move the anchor cable across the windlass barrel. When heaving up, the chain has a peculiar tendency to walk from starboard to port on the windlass barrel during the winding operation.

Forestay – Wire stay from stem head to mainmast top.

Gudgeon – Fittings which are fixed to rudder and stern, through which the pintle (or gudgeon pin) is passed, providing a hinged joint.

Gybe – To take the stern of a vessel through the wind, moving sails to other side. To cause or bring over the sails from one side to the other unintentionally.

Halyards – Ropes used for hauling up or hoisting sails.

Headstick – Short spar laced to the head of the topsail. (Allows for an increased area of a sail, within the dimensions or height of the topmast.)

Horse – A transverse bar of wood or steel, curved to the camber of the deck, for attaching the main sheet traveller and foresail sheet strop.

Hounds – Area of mast (shoulder) where the shrouds (side stays) are lodged, at the crosstrees.

Inwale – Inner Wale, a thick strake of timber fastened to the frames, under the deck, upon which the beams are lodged.

Ironpot – Term for a sailing barge built of iron and later of steel.

Jack Plane – A large plane for removing wood in thick cuts, the body of which is usually made of wood.

Glossary

Keelson – Longitudinal strength member bolted to the inside of the hull above the bottom frames (floors). Can be of Pine or a steel 'I' girder. Fitted in place of an external keel.

Knee – Traditionally a shaped timber that lodges to a vessel's side and deck beams. These were often specially grown and cut from the point where a branch leaves the trunk of a tree. Can also be an 'L' shaped iron forging, or fabricated steel.

Leeboard – Wing-shaped board pivoted by the mainmast shrouds. Lowered when tacking or reaching to provide bite in the water and reduce leeway (sideways movement).

Leeway – Sideways movement of a vessel from her heading.

Middlings – Second of three grades. In specific sense to cereals – flour of medium fineness.

Mizzen – A relatively small sail at the aft end of a barge.

Mousing – Several turns of light line round an open hook to prevent it from unhooking when not under tension.

Nrt – Net registered tonnage, a measure of internal capacity, where 100cu.ft represented 1 ton. Sailing barges were always sized by this tonnage. Grt, gross registered tonnage is a similar measuring system,

Palm – Leather bracelet that fits across the palm of the hand with a thumb hole and held by wrist strap. A steel disc with indents is held in a hard gut piece. Designed to protect hand and force needles through canvas and rope.

Port – Left-hand side of a vessel looking forward.

Quarter – 1. Part of a vessel - at the aft end. 2. Unit of capacity of grain etc., usually equal to 8 imperial bushels.

Quarter board – Fitted to the top of the rail at the aft end. These were traditionally white, although other shades have been seen over the years, temporarily painted blue if an owner died. (The *May Flower* eventually had hers varnished.)

Ratlines – Light lines attached to the shrouds, to enable crew to climb up the rigging. On a barge, these are usually to starboard only.

Serve – (Serving) Covering of a rope at the ends to prevent it from unlaying, and to a wire at the ends or round an eye splice (i.e. shroud looped end) – in this case a layer of canvass is usually first laid on. Wire serving is treated with Stockholm Tar to protect and preserve it.

Sheer – The curve of the deck running from forward to the aft end.

Spider band – Iron or steel ring band with lugs sited to accept rigging shackles or fittings as may be required. (One is fitted to the foot or heel of the sprit).

Sprit – Originally pine, but more usually of steel. The spar is up to 60ft (18m) in length, supported at the mast by collars and a wire stay, supporting the peak of the mainsail. Is permanently rigged and gives the characteristic look of a 'spritsail barge'.

Stayfall – Tackle and blocks. Wire for lowering and heaving up the gear. (Masts, sprit, sails etc.)

Stanlift – (Standing Lift) Wire stay for taking the downward weight of the sprit. It is rigged from the foot or heel of the sprit up to the mainmast hounds.

Starboard – The right-hand side of a vessel looking forward.

Stopper – A rope used to bind two or more lines or wires together. Stopper knot on the stayfall wire to keep the tackle captive, often supplemented with an additional u-clamp.

Tackle – A purchase comprised of blocks and a line or wire, used to gain a mechanical advantage. These have many uses on a barge.

Throat – Upper corner to the mast, usually at the hounds, of a four sided sail. On a barge this is called the Nock.

Transom – Flat lateral part at stern, bolted to the sternpost, to which side planks and deck are fastened.

Unreeve – To pull out a rope, or wire from a sheave or block.

Vangs – Wires with associated tackle to port and starboard for controlling the sprit. Sometimes called or pronounced Wangs.

Wale – Upper planking on a barge (Sheer strake). This section or strake is of thicker section than the lower planking.

Ways – 'On the Ways' – Slip or more usually blocks, or even a hard stand at a barge yard.